I0814487

For King and Country

For King and Country

The Role of Patriotism in Mobilisation in the First World War

Richard Batten

First published in Great Britain in 2025 by
Pen & Sword History
An imprint of Pen & Sword Books Limited
Yorkshire – Philadelphia

ISBN 978 1 39906 002 8

A CIP catalogue record for this book is
available from the British Library

Typeset by Mac Style
Printed in the UK by CPI Group (UK) Ltd, Croydon, CR0 4YY.

Pen & Sword Books Limited incorporates the imprints of After
the Battle, Atlas, Archaeology, Aviation, Discovery, Family History,
Fiction, History, Maritime, Military, Military Classics, Politics,
Select, Transport, True Crime, Air World, Frontline Publishing, Leo
Cooper, Remember When, Seaforth Publishing, The Praetorian Press,
Wharncliffe Local History, Wharncliffe Transport, Wharncliffe True
Crime and White Owl.

For a complete list of Pen & Sword titles please contact

PEN & SWORD BOOKS LIMITED
47 Church Street, Barnsley, South Yorkshire, S70 2AS, England
E-mail: enquiries@pen-and-sword.co.uk
Website: www.pen-and-sword.co.uk
or
PEN AND SWORD BOOKS
1950 Lawrence Rd, Havertown, PA 19083, USA
E-mail: uspen-and-sword@casematepublishers.com
Website: www.penandswordbooks.com

Contents

Abbreviations

APL	American Protective League
BWG	*Brixham Western Guardian*
CO	Conscientious Objector
CCNDG	*Crediton Chronicle and North Devon Gazette*
DCC	Devon County Council
DCLI	Duke of Cornwall Light Infantry
DEG	*Devon and Exeter Gazette*
DFU	Devon Farmers Union
DPF	Devon Patriotic Fund
DWWSC	Devon Women's War Service Committee
JHC	John Heathcoat & Company
JP	Justice of the Peace
LGB	Local Government Board
MARO	Munition Area Recruiting Officer
MSA	Military Service Act
NDH	*North Devon Herald*
NDJ	*North Devon Journal*
NECW	National Egg Collection for the Wounded
NMRO	Navy and Marines Recruiting Office
NWAC	National War Aims Committee
PC	Police Constable
PoW	Prisoner of War
PRC	Parliamentary Recruiting Committee
RDC	Rural District Council
SDWE	*South Devon Weekly Express*
UDC	Urban District Council
UGAPCE	*Union des Grandes Associations contre la Propagande Ennemie*
TPG	*Teignmouth Post and Gazette*
VTC	Volunteer Training Corps
WEH	*Western Evening Herald*

WLA	Women's Land Army
WMN	*Western Morning News*
WO	War Office
WSA	War Savings Association
WT	*Western Times*

Acknowledgements

This book has been a long time in the making. It is a revised and evolved version of my doctoral thesis that I originally started in 2008. While studying for my PhD at the University of Exeter, I was fortunate to have two great supervisors: Professor Richard Toye and Dr Tim Rees. They were confident about the validity of my research into Devon during the First World War and encouraged my efforts to get it published as a book. I am grateful for their unwavering support and their constructive feedback. My doctoral thesis also benefitted from the feedback from Dr Pierre Purseigle, Professor Catriona Pennell, and Professor Andrew Thorpe. I would like to express my gratitude to them as well.

I want to thank and express my deep appreciation to the following people: Dr Lester Crook of Pen and Sword Books for his confidence and support in this project. The Devon Heritage Centre, Plymouth Archives/The Box, the Dorset History Centre, and the National Archives for allowing me to quote from materials held in their respective repositories. Lady Arran for granting me permission to cite and quote from the private papers of her great-great Grandfather, Hugh Fortescue, the fourth Earl Fortescue. Stephen Pugsley from Halsgrove Publishing for allowing me to quote from Christopher Scoble's book *A Fisherman's Friend*. I am also grateful to all the scholars who granted permission for me to quote from their research.

The book contains pictures from my private collection and images from collections located in repositories, including the Library of Congress in the United States of America. I am very grateful to the individuals and organisations that granted permission for these images to be used in this book. These include Sidmouth Museum, Devon County Council, Exeter City Council, the Trustees of the Devon and Exeter Institute and the British Newspaper Archive.

Throughout this long project, my friends, fellow PhD students, and family have been a great source of continual reassurance, during both good and difficult times. In particular, my mother, Valerie Batten, has always encouraged my education and supported me throughout this journey. Therefore, I would like to dedicate this book to her in appreciation of her kindness and faith in me.

West Dorset, 2024

Introduction

Superintending Patriotism on the Home Front

In the summer of 1914, Stephen Reynolds, social thinker and contemporary man of letters, was appointed the District Inspector of Fisheries for the South West.[1] As District Inspector, he endeavoured to protect the interests of fishermen in Devon and Cornwall as a special interest group and mediated with the Royal Navy in Plymouth during the First World War.[2] However, the unending process of recruiting fishermen into the Navy had provided Reynolds with a 'continuing source of anxiety and criticism.'[3] In fact, due to his status as the most significant figure in the fisheries of the South West of England, Reynolds was placed in the 'firing line of the inevitable resentment as if he had been the recruiting master himself.'[4] Reynolds alluded to the criticism he had endured locally in a letter to Henry Maurice, a civil servant and fisheries' secretary at the Board of Agriculture and Fisheries, on 8 December 1917. As a result of implementing the government's instructions 'only too effectively', Reynolds claimed that he had earned the enmity of local notables whom he labelled as the 'provincial patriots.'[5] He subsequently expanded upon this label and described the patriotic behaviour of these eminent provincial figures in the context of military recruitment. Reynolds proposed that these individuals' patriotism, 'while they are on the safe side of military age, consists in superintending the patriotism of those who aren't [exempt from military service].'[6]

This book uses Reynolds' definition of the 'provincial patriots' to explore the wartime experiences of members of Devon's land-owning, political, social and economic elite as these 'superintendents of patriotism'. These figures from Devon's local elite attempted to superintend or police the patriotism of men in the county who were eligible for military service. Through the process of weighing the patriotism of eligible men against the strength of their own patriotism, Devon's 'provincial patriots' acted as the self-appointed arbiters of patriotism. Based on the evidence from Devon, men and women from the county's elite undertook this superintendence of patriotism and functioned as the policemen and women of patriotism. However, the superintending remit of these 'provincial patriots' went beyond the patriotism of Devon's eligible men as they sought to regulate the wartime behaviour of the county's population. In late 1914, contemporary anxieties about how young women would behave when they encountered soldiers in their khaki military uniform led to a movement that sought to regulate the sexual behaviour of young women. Prominent figures in this movement to address this moral panic of 'khaki fever' included notable individuals from civil society, such as bishops, politicians and social reformers.[7] In the English county of Devon, Hugh Fortescue, the fourth Earl Fortescue and Lord Lieutenant of Devonshire was a civic figure deeply concerned about women's behaviour following the declaration of war. On 28 October 1914, Fortescue relayed his moral consternation to Sir William Acland, a Deputy Lieutenant of Devon, about the conduct of some women in the county who were 'often thrusting their wares on men who have little wish to traffic with them.'[8] Since 'every loose woman' was 'placing herself gratis at the disposal of any man in uniform', Fortescue claimed that the High Street of Exeter resembled Piccadilly Circus.[9] Although the City's police force informed Fortescue that they would exercise their powers to help resolve the situation, Devon's Lord Lieutenant had a plan to rectify these instances of 'indecent' behaviour. He proposed that aid rescue workers and other good women from Devon's civil society could intervene to 'get among the girls and their parents and bring home to them the results likely to follow from their behaviour'.[10] Through the war years, Devon's 'provincial patriots' used their own standards of patriotism as the basis for prescriptions and pronouncements for how the county's residents should behave during the conflict. Simultaneously, they used these same standards to reprimand some Devonians who engaged in activities or expressed attitudes deemed to be instances of unpatriotic behaviour.

Reynolds' satirical description of Devon's local elite and their patriotism is worthy of further analysis since it is an intriguing observation that evokes the notion of a negative 'Home Front'. During the Great War, the involvement of civilians in various war-related activities in the home societies constituted a 'front (albeit a secondary one) that supported or complemented the [military] front.'[11] This secondary front in Britain and the belligerent nations has become identified as the 'Home Front'. Alongside the civilians on the Home Front who selflessly demonstrated their commitment to support the war effort, a negative Home Front had also emerged in the minds of contemporaries. This negative Home Front was populated by unheroic male figures such as 'shirkers', 'profiteers,' and 'armchair patriots' who remained at home whilst other courageous men undertook their duty by serving in the military.[12] Reynolds' description of figures from Devon's civil society and their patriotic conduct in wartime suggests that some people in the county viewed these notable figures as 'armchair patriots'. The reason for this was that since the 'provincial patriots' were men above the age requirements for military service (between 18 and 41), they resided on the 'safe side of military age.'[13] However, notable figures outside the conditions of military service, whether due to age or gender, participated in voluntary recruitment efforts on the British Home Front. John Morton Osborne proposes that many older men and women viewed their involvement in such endeavours as a 'patriotic and visible substitute' to military service.[14] Since they could not serve in the military, Devon's 'provincial patriots' believed it was their patriotic duty to direct eligible men to join the Army. Indeed, Trevor Wilson suggests that older men and women were 'often eager to impose military service on youthful men.'[15]

One man who could be characterised as a 'provincial patriot' was John Loosemore, a farmer from the north Devon village of Bishops Nympton. As a man in his sixties, Loosemore could not enlist because of his age. Although he was ineligible for military service, Loosemore was anxious that the country should be defended. Consequently, he had taken an active role in trying to get eligible men to enlist by supplementing official recruitment efforts. However, his concerns about the nation's defence meant that Loosemore held 'rather strong views with regard to the duty of eligible men to take some part in military service' and believed that every military-age man who refused to defend his country was a coward.[16] Driven by these strong views, Loosemore never missed 'an opportunity of pointing out to others what he thought was their duty.'[17] In the district surrounding the north Devon town of South Molton, Loosemore met and confronted many military-age men and farmers who were still at home, telling them they were cowards for not going off to fight. Loosemore attempted to embarrass one eligible man by asking him whether he should be fishing 'while men were fighting' and called him a damned coward.[18] However, Loosemore's endeavours of challenging and shaming eligible men not yet in khaki led to a violent confrontation with local farmer Robert Passmore Junior on 22 March 1916.

The altercation between the two men led to a court case at the Guildhall in South Molton on 18 April 1916. Under cross-examination by Passmore's solicitor, Michael John McGahey, Loosemore revealed that when he met

Passmore's father at the local cattle market in November 1915, he had pointed out the duties of his sons. However, since Passmore's sons had decided to remain at home rather than enlist, Loosemore had called them 'contemptible cowards' several times.[19] McGahey declared that based on Loosemore's abusive behaviour towards every local farmer and single man he came across, it was a surprise that no one had punched him before. Nevertheless, Loosemore told McGahey that he felt justified in challenging eligible men because it was his duty as an Englishman. However, McGahey responded that he was unconvinced that that was the frame of mind in which Loosemore had reproached many respectable farmers in the district. In his reply, Loosemore argued that these agriculturalists were 'wanting in patriotism.'[20] After hearing Loosemore's answer, McGahey retorted: 'Oh yes – you have got it all, and they have none. Because they choose to stay at home, exempted [from military service] by Tribunals even, and work the land to produce food, they are "cowards". Is that your state of mind?'[21] Loosemore answered that yes it was in most cases including this one.[22]

With this line of questioning, McGahey characterised Loosemore as a self-appointed arbiter of patriotism, judging upon the patriotism of eligible local men because he knew what was patriotic and what was not. For every farmer and single man Loosemore encountered who decided to stay at home, he saw fit to call them cowards and contemptible cowards because he was appalled by their lack of patriotism.[23] Yet, by his actions towards men of fighting age, Loosemore could also be characterised as a self-important, prying busybody who, like many others during the war, was 'ready to tell fellow citizens how to run their lives.'[24] In the context of recruiting, an article in the *Devon and Exeter Gazette* suggested that the lady who thrust white feathers upon military-age men still in civilian clothes to shame them into volunteering could be regarded as 'another kind of do-nothing busybody' who, despite her well-meaning intentions, may have unintentionally 'driven more people to suicide than into the Army.'[25] Indeed, many eligible men probably felt aggrieved that figures outside the requirements of military service imposed their views on them to pressure them to volunteer for the forces. Since these figures were detached from military service, these prescriptions were more difficult for some fighting-age men to accept. Reynolds' definition of the patriotism of the 'provincial patriots' touched upon this sense of detachment since they remained on the 'safe side of military age.'[26] However, it was similar to how Reynolds had previously defined the word inspection as 'the judgement of one class by the standards of another; the teaching of people how to live under circumstances of which the teachers have had no personal experience'.[27] Just as these teachers had no personal experience living under the circumstances of the people they taught, Devon's local elite had the same sense of separation since they would never experience frontline combat and sought to superintend the patriotism of men who would have to face military service. Through the enthusiasm of ineligible figures encouraging eligible men to serve rather than volunteer themselves, they could be negatively characterised as hypocritical, judgmental, inexperienced armchair patriots. The negative characterisation of these figures who merely paid lip service to the war was even more acute when they broadcast these prescriptions from a location of relative comfort and detached safety (i.e. their armchairs). An anonymous letter submitted to the *Western Evening Herald* in May 1915 summarised these sentiments:

> 'What busybodies some of these "ineligibles" are. I always view their shouting with suspicion. Whenever I hear an "out and out" conscriptionist or one advocating that it is everyone's duty to enlist, I am sure for some reason it is [uttered by] an "ineligible." ... This class of person should "lie low" because they would be the last to come forward until they were forced, even if they were eligible.'[28]

Studies of the British Home Front during the First World War have previously concentrated their analytical focus on the administrative framework of the nation-state.[29] However, the analytical approach of contemporary studies has shifted away from the nation-state to scrutinise the experiences of local communities during the war years. Jay Winter has advocated that studying local communities in wartime is the best method to apply greater scrutiny to the illusionary veil of a supposed unitary 'national' experience of the First World War.[30] By breaking away from the traditional national focus, these local studies have enabled an 'appraisal of the true scope of the mechanisms at work within the belligerent societies.'[31] The histories of specific localities such as counties, cities, towns or villages during the First World War have shown that the wartime experiences of civilians did vary considerably across the United Kingdom.[32] Keith Grieves suggests that these histories constitute a 'new' cultural history of the Great War since they emphasise 'the effects of war on local communities in their distinctive settings.'[33] Finally, since these studies are informed from below, they have also reinforced the importance of locality and local identities for civilians in Britain during the conflict.[34]

Simultaneously, through comparative analysis of the experiences of civilians from across the combatant countries, the wartime experiences of British civilians have been placed within a transnational context.[35] The ambition to assess the war across national borders has also led to a motivation to look beyond and below the nations by cross-examining specific local communities across the belligerent nations. One example of this is the research of Pierre Purseigle, where he compares two medium-sized towns in England and France during the Great War: Northampton (situated in the East Midlands region of England) and Béziers (located in the Occitanie region in the south of France) respectively. Purseigle emphasises that the local elite functioned as the critical group during the war years since they reflected and shaped the mediation of the war experience on a local level. Since they held such a significant status in wartime, the history of the local elite is an enquiry into the 'war experience through a cross-section of the local societies, an intermediary of that experience.'[36] In the case of Devon, notable figures from the county's local elite, such as Earl Fortescue, were also intermediaries who shaped and mediated the war experience. As intermediaries of the war experience on a local level, the contribution that the local elite could make to gain and marshal the support of their respective local communities behind the war effort was crucial. The landed gentry of Ireland also supported the war effort through involvement in various war-related initiatives like recruitment efforts and charities.[37] In particular, Irish noblewomen were pivotal figures in organising and promoting philanthropic activities to support the war effort.[38] By contrast, notable figures of Russia's rural elite were ineffectual and unreliable intermediaries of the war experience, undermining the efficacy of the Tsarist war effort in the Russian countryside.[39] Therefore, across the belligerent nations, the effectiveness of the local elite was a crucial factor in mobilising their local communities for war.

John Horne has defined mobilisation during the Great War as the involvement of the belligerent nations in their respective war efforts, both organisationally through the activities of the state and civil society, and 'imaginatively, through collective representations and the belief and value systems giving rise to these.'[40] Examining mobilisation as a 'process' or a 'totalising logic' gives the historian the benefit of scrutinising its form and development alongside considering its limitations through the war.[41] During the first two years of the conflict, civil society in Britain, France, and Germany played a crucial role in mobilising their respective nations through self-mobilisation.[42] In Britain, the strength of civil society's self-mobilisation manifested itself in recruitment efforts, charitable work and other projects to support the national war effort. As the demands of industrialised warfare increased with the continuation of the conflict, the meaning of wartime mobilisation changed from its 'original military definition to encompass the contribution of civil society, whose human, financial, and cultural resources were also expected to directly support the armed forces in the field.'[43] The effects of this prolonged war had taken their toll upon Home Front morale in Britain and France by 1917.[44] To safeguard the possibility of victory, the nature of wartime mobilisation shifted in both nations from self-mobilisation to a second mobilisation or remobilisation of their respective war efforts. During 1917 and 1918, this remobilisation of the British and French war efforts necessitated an acceptance on the part of civilians to make sacrifices previously deemed intolerable to overturn the prospect of defeat.[45]

Although the powers of the state grew during the conflict, local civil society in Britain and France still played a central role on the Home Front at a local level as intermediaries of the war experience.[46] Like the local elites of Northampton and Béziers, Devon's local elite were critical campaigners for the war effort because they functioned as the local transmitters of national organisations rallied to the war effort.[47] Accordingly, the local elite disseminated the cultures of war to their respective local communities. These multifaceted wartime frameworks of meaning, with their distinct representations of patriotism, duty, and sacrifice, provided civilians with a means to understand and participate in the war.[48] As a result, the vision of the war that the local elites broadcast to their local communities conformed with the national mobilisation whose 'totalising logic' enlisted each nation's 'cultural, moral, and ideological commitment ... to fight an uncivilised enemy to its capitulation.'[49] In particular, local identities ran at the core of the mobilisation process on a local level. The materials produced by civic authorities, newspapers and voluntary organisations reveal how local elites in towns and cities employed the 'main symbols of local identity to stress that victory would belong to the urban community as well as to the nation.'[50] Figures from Devon's civil society also utilised symbols of local identity to support and root the campaigns for wartime mobilisation in a specific

Devonian context. The local cultural codes linked to Devon that these figures used included the county's unique landscapes (Dartmoor), the county's folklore (Drake's Drum), the county's local food products (Devonshire cream) and notable figures from the county's past, like the Elizabethan privateer Sir Francis Drake. Accordingly, Devon's local elite hoped these overtures to local identity would resonate among Devonian audiences and inspire them to participate in various forms of wartime mobilisation in the county. Due to the significance of the local elite during the Great War, Purseigle advocates that examining these figures allows the historian to address methodically the dedication of local communities to the national mobilisation 'and the mental imagery which allowed the transcendence of the war experience.'[51]

Yet, members of local civil society were more than intermediaries of the war experience and sought to undertake other activities on the Home Front. In fact, across the belligerent nations, local civil society contributed through various activities to the 'monitoring and censoring of public opinion.'[52] As the policemen and women of patriotism, prominent figures from Devon's civil society attempted to monitor and superintend the discourses of patriotism across the county. Through various formal and informal channels, i.e. local newspapers, speeches and meetings, Devon's 'provincial patriots' endeavoured to control how the county's population understood the notion of patriotism. In the context of voluntary recruitment efforts, Catriona Pennell has defined patriotism as a 'considered, reflective sense of obligation.'[53] Devon's local elite proclaimed that the men of the county who had enlisted had displayed 'true' patriotism since they had fulfilled their 'obvious' obligation as men to defend their country in a time of war. By contrast, the county's eligible men reluctant to volunteer faced admonishment from Devon's notable figures, who criticised them as unpatriotic shirkers who had failed to undertake their duty to serve in the military.

Based on Reynolds' definition of the county's local elite, Devon's 'provincial patriots' were similar to the men of the formal vigilance organisation known as the American Protective League (APL). Christopher Capozzola suggests that the volunteers of the APL were 'professional men, typically above draft age or otherwise exempt … [who joined] … out of patriotism and a sense of duty, to feel important in their communities, or just something to do.'[54] On the American Home Front, the men of the APL took an active role by upholding the draft of eligible men into the military. Unlike Devon's 'provincial patriots', the APL's members employed coercion to superintend the patriotism of military-age men in the United States of America.[55] Although the APL had 'an ambiguous legal status', the League's volunteers claimed to possess wartime authority and behaved similarly to a police force.[56] Motivated by an intense sense of patriotism and wearing APL identification badges, the League's members challenged and interrogated eligible men they suspected were evading the draft. When confronted by the men of the APL, military-age men needed to present their draft registration or classification cards as required under the Selective Service Act of 1917 or face the prospect of arrest.[57] In Devon, figures from the county's local elite challenged Devonian men of military age who were still at home to explain why they had not yet enlisted. If these men had refused to enlist and tried to justify their decision against joining up, these figures judged upon the rationalisations these men used.

Devon's local elite possessed an explicitly exhortative role since they acted as autonomous social agents of the war effort with distinct agency. Through their engagement with activities related to the war effort, they advocated measures deemed necessary for the national interest. They also endeavoured to educate Devonians in the codes of ideal conduct in wartime. Like the attempts made by the men of the APL to regulate the wartime behaviour of citizens in America, Devon's 'provincial patriots' tried to police the behaviour of Devon's population during the war years. Notable figures in the county who sat as members of various war-related organisations used the proceedings of such bodies to commend individuals whose behaviour was considered an example of patriotism worthy of praise and broader recognition. Conversely, Devon's local elite also used these proceedings to reprimand individuals whose conduct was deemed, in their view, to be unpatriotic. Accordingly, these wartime organisations allowed Devon's notable figures to exert their influence on the Home Front in the county and reinforce their authority as the 'superintendents of patriotism'. These attempts by members of Devon's local elite to police the wartime behaviour of the county's population also dovetailed into the notion of upholding law and order on a local level and tied into the social morality that the war generated. Horne has defined this wartime social morality as a 'set of reciprocal moral judgements on the contribution of different groups to the national effort.'[58] Accordingly, the language and meaning of this wartime social morality (what was perceived as 'reasonable' or 'unreasonable', acceptable or unacceptable) served as the framework for negotiating the relationships between social actors.[59] A sense of equality of sacrifice also informed this framework of meaning. This wartime social morality tapped into the immoral characteristics of greed and selfishness, which 'directly contravened the equality of sacrifice, and thus the uniform moral yardstick of civilian action in relation to the war.'[60] Throughout the war years, Devon's elite attempted to police this moral yardstick on a local level. However, the ability of Devon's 'provincial patriots' to police wartime behaviour and superintend patriotism was dependent on the efforts of individual members of the county's civil society since it would be wrong to envisage that they were a cohesive group.

The evidence from Devon reveals that the attempts of the county's local elite to superintend the nature of patriotism across the county achieved varying degrees of success. During the war, industrial conflict revealed that patriotism was a contested term with different meanings.[61] In December 1914, Earl Fortescue acknowledged in a speech on patriotism that the term was not easy to define. Nonetheless, he advocated that the nearest and shortest definition of patriotism was a 'Readiness to make [a] sacrifice of self on behalf of one's country and of the greater interests which it involves.'[62] However, as Derek Rutherford Young has emphasised, it is evident that a contemporary 'working class man with little or no higher education could not have the same concept of "patriotism" as the educated, landed or moneyed classes.'[63] Male patriotism was not limited to a single discourse centred on notions of military service as prescribed by figures from Devon's local elite. Patriotism manifested itself in many discourses since there were other ways that eligible men claimed to be able to demonstrate their patriotism than just enlisting. In the county's agricultural sector, Devon's farmers asserted that for every man on the farm to drop their tools and take up arms against the Germans in France or Belgium was not the 'only way in which they could show their patriotism.'[64] Many of the county's agriculturalists believed it was their patriotic duty to stay at home to produce food for the nation. McGahey touched upon this during Loosemore's court case when he stressed to the Bench that there may be 'justifiable reasons why a man is not in khaki ... [since] ... some people thought it just as important that a proper number of men should be kept at home to work the soil and produce food.'[65] As a result, some people in Devon disagreed with the argument, as advanced by others in the county, that 'patriotism was confined to the khaki suit.'[66] Although the volunteering ethos did not inspire some men in Devon to join the Army, it did motivate many of the county's residents to support charities related to the war effort and present their patriotism through philanthropic endeavours. Based on how the population of Cornwall responded to the war beyond voluntary recruitment efforts, Stuart Dalley contends that 'Cornwall's patriotism was arguably of a more humanitarian variety.'[67] In many instances, the patriotism of Devonians was also more humanitarian than militaristic. One such demonstration of this was on 7 December 1915. When reporting on the sale of priceless heirlooms and goods in Exeter to raise funds for the British Red Cross Society and the Order of the Hospital of St John of Jerusalem in England, a correspondent for *The Queen* suggested that such selfless sacrifice had shown that 'the patriotic heart of Devonshire beats true.'[68]

Winter has pointed out that when 'common sense on the popular level diverged from state propaganda, the official message [either] turned hollow or simply vanished.'[69] Some notable figures in Devon struggled to convince all of the county's population about the importance of the war, and the mixed fortunes of the voluntary recruitment campaign reveal that there were limits to the self-mobilisation of Devon's men. The evidence from the county during the war years questions the effectiveness of some language used to encourage national mobilisation. Horne suggests that class and nation could, unintentionally, provide the basis for expressions of counter-mobilisation against the conflict.[70] When faced with prescriptions and interrogations from Devon's local elite and army recruiters, some Devonians vocalised their objection to what they regarded as the war's 'meddling' interference with their affairs. Many of the county's residents often developed their own rationalisations for abstaining from wartime actions, such as the eligible men of Devon should enlist, that the 'provincial patriots' and other authorities prescribed for them. Many Devonians did not necessarily accept and adopt measures deemed necessary for the war effort since they opposed being ordered or 'dictated to' by local wartime committees. Throughout the war years, the county's population criticised the efforts of Devon's local elite to mobilise them for war. Thus, wartime mobilisation had distinct limitations in Devon since many people in the county were partially resistant to the logic of modern industrial war.

Alongside the tension between voluntarism and state-driven totalisation, there was another tension between individual and national survival. The reluctance of some men in the county towards military service reinforced the challenges that Devon's 'provincial patriots' faced in their attempts to reconcile the tension between individual priorities and national ones. At

Barnstaple's Congregational Church on 2 January 1916, Reverend Robert James Edmund Boggis tried to convince his parishioners in his sermon that self-interest must 'give way to loyalty and patriotism' since Britain was fighting a war for its very existence.[71] However, it is challenging to gauge the blurring line between them as the nature of where public and private interest merged or diverged is a topic for historical debate.[72] Paul Rusiecki suggests that many civilians in Essex were 'prepared to place their own self-interest above the cause of patriotism in order to enjoy a more comfortable war.'[73] Studies have also demonstrated that tensions existed between urban and rural communities in Germany as the latter had different priorities in wartime and were primarily concerned with their own needs.[74] For example, in a village outside Freiburg in December 1915, one dairy farmer's wife flatly refused to sell milk to the city's residents. Even if she had an ample supply of milk, she was adamant that the needs of her calves and pigs came first.[75] During the war years in Devon, individual priorities remained more powerful impulses than national priorities. The prevalence of individual concerns in the responses from Devonians towards the calls for sacrifice strengthens the idea that the war effort was not a unifying principle for many in the county.

Based on the testimonies from some commentators, some in Devon were oblivious to the war and its importance.[76] Many Devonians regarded the conflict as a distant phenomenon since they were further away from the war's proximity due to Devon's peripheral location within the United Kingdom and its distance from mainland Europe.[77] Women's Land Army (WLA) member and writer Olive Hockin claimed in June 1917 that Dartmoor's farmers were hardly aware of Britain's participation in the war due to the distant and isolated nature of communities in that part of Devon. Indeed, she asserts that these agriculturalists only became conscious of the war after discovering the ban on selling wool in 1916.[78] Contemporaries also viewed Devon as a predominately rural county that lagged behind changing trends and modernisation.[79] In addition, Devon's well-established image as an idyllic and remote holiday destination led many people to consider the county as a location where they could escape the war's influence.[80]

With a few exceptions, the historiography of the Home Fronts has yet to consider the variation between urban and rural localities on a local level.[81] Instead, there has been a focus on the wartime experiences of urban communities and their responses to mobilisation efforts.[82] In light of the unique perspectives offered by evidence from the countryside, examinations of the rural Home Front act as a valuable counterpoint to urban studies of the Home Front.[83] Microhistories of counties are part of this shift towards a balanced critical analysis of civilian experiences in rural and urban communities during the First World War.[84] Previously, the wartime experiences of Devon's population were the subject of historical inquiry in works by Bonnie White and David Parker.[85] The recent centenary of the conflict (2014 to 2018) also provided the impetus for new research by historians, local history groups, and academically led heritage projects into various aspects of Devon during the Great War.[86] The histories that have emerged during the centenary have added significantly to our knowledge of the county during the conflict.[87] However, more remains to be said about how Devon's local elite functioned in the war years. In particular, the occasionally frictional relationship between these notable figures and the county's populace. Accordingly, this book contributes towards a greater understanding of communities 'where locally-defined attitudes proved remarkably resilient in war.'[88]

Through a critical exploration of Devon's local elite as the 'superintendents of patriotism', this book imparts a more detailed enquiry into the efficacy of their efforts to superintend patriotism and police the wartime behaviour of the county's population. The ambiguous responses of Devonians towards the appeals for mobilisation further underline the limitations of wartime mobilisation in the county. These responses also reveal how local populations engaged with the demands of the war effort as urged by the county's notable figures and how Devon's residents rationalised these demands. The attempts of Devon's local elite to negotiate through the ambiguous responses from Devonians towards the appeals for mobilisation and the competing interests of individual priorities and national ones is an important theme that transcends the chapters of this book. By using the local elite of Devon as a case study, this book imparts a deeper understanding of the wartime role of the local elite. Hence, this is a new interpretation of domestic patriotism and dissent on the British Home Front of the First World War on a local level as it emphasises the complexity of the war years for the county's local elite and the agency of Devon's population.

This study utilises a wide variety of sources from Devon's archives, including the Devon Heritage Centre, Plymouth Archives, The Box (formerly the Plymouth and West Devon Record Office), alongside material from other archive repositories in the United Kingdom. The memoranda from figures of Devon's civil society shed light upon their wartime experiences and those of the county's population. A tremendously valuable collection of materials employed in this study is from the private papers of the fourth Earl Fortescue. As Devon's Lord Lieutenant during the Great War, Fortescue was a central figure in mobilisation efforts across the county. Due to his prodigious involvement with numerous aspects of the war effort in Devon, Fortescue kept a vast and diverse array of documents related to his wartime experiences. These documents offer significant insights into the great challenges that Fortescue and other members of Devon's local elite faced in their attempts to mobilise the county's populace during the war years.[89]

Another important primary source of great merit to this study is the *Letters of Stephen Reynolds*, posthumously published in 1923 and edited by his literary executor Harold Wright. Rather than record his experiences and impressions of events in a private diary, Wright revealed that Reynolds was a voluminous letter writer who 'felt an irresistible impulse to share his thoughts with a friend.'[90] The letters that Wright selected and edited for publication from Reynolds' wartime correspondence reveal that Reynolds was a unique commentator with a distinctive journalistic sensibility. These letters contain remarkable and thought-provoking observations about the war years in Devon and chronicle his involvement with fisheries in the South West during the conflict. Moreover, the content of these letters reinforces Christopher Scoble's assertion that Reynolds was a unique social explorer because 'motives of class guilt or the desire for quick journalistic copy, academic reputation, or political solutions' were not his primary motivations for his work.[91] Instead, since Reynolds had 'made his whole life with the poor and wrote from the inside looking out', he viewed himself as an outsider to Devon's civil society.[92] The book of Reynolds' letters conveys this unique perspective. It allowed the 'authentic Reynolds voice – from the intellectual and lyrical at one end to the humorous, quirky and obsessive at the other – to breathe and sing just as Reynolds himself had wanted.'[93]

The pages of Devon's local newspapers also possess significant historical merit for a study of the county during the war years. A prominent example of this is evident in the reporting of the meetings of wartime bodies in the county, such as the Military Service Tribunals, whose records generally have not survived to the present day. Fortunately, local correspondents who attended these events recorded what happened during these proceedings. Although there may be factual inaccuracies present in these accounts, these newspaper reports are still important sources that shed valuable light upon the wartime role of Devon's local elite as the 'superintendents of patriotism'. Furthermore, the value judgments and prescriptions about the nature of patriotism as expressed by Devon's 'provincial patriots' reached a wider audience across the county through their publication in Devon's newspapers. Consequently, the coverage of the county's Tribunals, together with other wartime committees, in Devon's local press impart significant insights into how the county's elite attempted to superintend patriotism and wartime behaviour in the county.

At the same time, it is vital to emphasize that newspapers are not simply 'neutral conduits of information, but rather [they are] gatekeepers and filterers of ideas.'[94] Like their counterparts on national tabloids, provincial newspaper editors and correspondents fix the 'premises of discourse and interpretation' for the stories they had selected for publication.[95] Thus, local newspaper commentaries and editorials are edifying sources in their own right since their reporting directly contributed to the discourses of patriotism in the county, whereby they would praise or condemn 'patriotic' or 'unpatriotic' responses to military service. An example of this was in the *Devon and Exeter Gazette* when the paper argued on 2 January 1915 that no man was a 'true patriot if he points to thousands of men in khaki around him, remarking: "There seems to be enough for the time being – I shall leave it until I am wanted".'[96] Devon's newspapers are also essential for understanding individual voices, not just those from above but also those from below. The newspaper commentaries of wartime events reveal how the county's population responded and, in some cases, objected to the appeals and prescriptions from Devon's local elite. Unique perspectives on the war years in the county can also be found in local poems by Devonian writers and poets published in the local press. These local poems are, in fact, mostly overlooked sources in studies of the county during the First World War despite the insights they can provide into the Devonian experience of the conflict. Ultimately, Devon's newspapers are a historically rich and indispensable record of community life in the county during the Great War.

This book employs a chronological structure that allows for greater scrutiny of how changes on the Home Front shaped the campaign of the county's local elite to superintend patriotism in Devon as the war progressed. Simultaneously, the structure of this book reveals the strengths and limitations of different forms of wartime mobilisation across the county's rural and urban localities. Chapter 1 imparts a survey of Devon by 1914, establishing a valuable context for understanding the county through the war years. With the notable exceptions of the urban centres of Plymouth and Exeter, Devon had a predominately rural population scattered across the county. Although Devon was a maritime county with strong ties to the Royal Navy, it also had a distinct agricultural culture. Furthermore, due to Devon's outlying location in the South West of England, many contemporaries claimed that Devonians possessed a clannish nature and that politics in the county were still predominately local by 1910. Similarly, local identity still strongly influenced the county's residents, and Devon had a high patriotic reputation due to its revered sea-faring past. Devon's distinctive social, economic, religious and political composition reveals a tremendous amount of diversity within the county's borders. Alongside the religious and political figures from the county, notable figures within Devon's civil society also significantly influenced the socio-cultural fabric of county life by 1914.

Chapter 2 centres on the emergence of the Home Front in Devon and the engagement of Devon's local elite with the war effort in 1914. Following the declaration of war, the county's notable figures sought to occupy a central role in Devon's preparations for war and mediate how the county's population should respond to the transition from peace to war. In addition, the county's local elite had high hopes that Devon would set a fine patriotic example for other counties in England regarding the number of Army recruits. However, the county's 'provincial patriots' were dismayed by the indifferent responses and objections from eligible Devonian men reluctant to serve in the Army. As a result, the low recruitment rates from Devon were a cause of great concern for the county's local elite. Yet, the county's residents presented their patriotism and commitment to the war effort through their involvement with war-related charities. Chapter 3 focuses on 1915 when Devon's local elite intensified 'self-mobilisation' efforts in the county. The county's notable figures attempted to revive the fortunes of voluntary recruitment in Devon and increase the number of Army recruits from the county. Nevertheless, these efforts to restore the county's patriotic reputation and convince Devon's reluctant men to enlist achieved mixed success. In the autumn of 1915, the Derby Scheme experienced similar varied fortunes in Devon. At the same time, Devonians continued to demonstrate their patriotism and support for the war effort with humanitarian endeavours.

Chapter 4 evaluates how the introduction of conscription in 1916 was a precursor of the state-driven totalisation of the British war effort and acted as the transition between 'self-mobilisation' and 'remobilisation' in Britain. On the Home Front, conscription had ramifications for wartime citizenship and the superintendence of patriotism in Devon. The arbitration of the appeals against conscription allowed the county's 'provincial patriots' to extend their campaigns to superintend patriotism and judge upon the wartime behaviour of Devon's population. At the same time, suspicions that men had avoided military service or registration led the police and military authorities in the county to conduct searches, otherwise known as "round-up" raids, to find them. Although conscription provided greater urgency for Devon's farmers to take on women workers, the county's agriculturalists were averse to accepting the introduction of inexperienced female labour. Meanwhile, some notable figures in the county raised concerns about the loyalty of the German and Austrian monks of Buckfast Abbey, which led to calls for the Home Office to remove them from the Abbey and send them to an internment camp.

Chapter 5 covers the final two years of the conflict, 1917 and 1918, to examine how Devon's elites attempted to undertake the 'remobilisation' of the British war effort on a local level. Despite incentives and new methods to convince Devon's farmers to grow more cereals, the county's agriculturalists were reluctant to change their farming practices. The new measures introduced in the name of remobilisation such as restrictions on food prices also gave the county's 'provincial patriots' new avenues to attempt to superintend patriotism and wartime behaviour in Devon. The dire situation concerning domestic food supplies led to allegations of profiteering and contributed to feelings of war-weariness amongst Devon's residents. The county's local elite played their part to remobilise civilian morale in Devon, acting as speakers at local meetings of the National War Aims Committee. Remobilisation was very successful in economic terms in Devon as the county's population supported the war through subscribing to war loans, war bonds and war savings certificates. Alongside superintending patriotism on Devon's tribunals, the county's tribunalists experienced more significant pressures and increased criticism during 1917 and 1918. Following the emergency created by the German Spring Offensive on the Western Front in 1918, Devon's War Agricultural Executive Committee faced the strenuous process of finding additional manpower for the Army from the county's agricultural sector. In addition, the anxiety surrounding the German and Austrian monks at Buckfast Abbey continued to linger.

Chapter 1

Devon by 1914

Located in the South West peninsula of England, Devon is an outlying and predominately rural county that borders the counties of Dorset and Somerset to the east and is flanked by the county of Cornwall to the west. Like Cornwall, Devon is a maritime county since it has two distinctive coastlines containing harbours, bays, cliffs and estuaries. The north Devon shoreline meets the Bristol Channel, whilst the south Devon seashore faces the English Channel respectively.[1] As the third largest county in England, Devon possesses large stretches of beautiful countryside surrounding the two distinctive moorlands of Dartmoor and Exmoor in the middle and north-east of the county, respectively. These areas of countryside contained fertile valleys, rolling hills, apple orchards, hedgerows, trickling streams, old country lanes, spectacular coasts, and quaint villages.[2] This idyllic landscape loomed large in how contemporaries thought of Devon as a county by 1914.[3] Early twentieth-century travellers' guides reinforced the county's picturesque qualities through their narratives and iconography that advertised Devon as a charming holiday destination.[4] The county's beautiful landscape was a source of immense gratification for many of Devon's residents.[5] For instance, they took pride in the distinct geographical features of specific local areas, such as the fertile red soil of some Devon localities, that seemed to make Devon quintessentially unique as a county in England.[6]

Despite the forces of modernisation and centralisation during the nineteenth century, local identities continued to have a pertinent significance amongst contemporaries in England and France by 1914.[7] For rural and urban communities in England and Wales, local identity rested on an attachment to a distinct sense of place.[8] This connection to specific local settings was a crucial part of how the county's population saw themselves as natives of Devon. Indeed, they identified themselves as 'Devonians' from the Latin name for the county: 'Devonia'.[9] Like the counties of Cornwall and Yorkshire, Devon was renowned by contemporaries for the 'clannishness of its inhabitants.'[10] The strength of this sense of belonging and distinct clannish character amongst the county's population was partly due to Devon's peripheral location within England.[11]

Alongside the county's landscape, many Devonians took pride in Devon's local agricultural produce or the unique food items that originated from the county.[12] A quintessentially Devonian foodstuff created using milk produced on the county's dairy farms was the famous 'Devonshire' clotted cream. To the county's residents, this thick dairy product, alongside cider made from apples grown in Devon's orchards or the Devonshire dumpling, represented both the quality of authentic Devonian food produce and what the county meant to them.[13] During the Edwardian era, Devonians also expressed the delight that they felt about the county through music.[14] One famous song extolling the county by composer Sir Edward German was 'Glorious Devon'. Utilising the poem by Sir Harold Boulton, the lyrics of 'Glorious Devon' evoked the great sense of prestige that many felt about various aspects of the county, including its geographical features, food products, and history. Accordingly, the melody was a rousing celebration of Devon.[15] A ballad that also functioned as a distinct evocation of Devon in the minds of contemporaries was the folk song 'Widecombe Fair'. Otherwise called 'Uncle Tom Cobley' or 'Uncle Tom Cobleigh and All', the tune focuses on a group of twelve men who borrow the old grey mare of a local man, Tom Pearce, to travel to the annual fair at the Dartmoor village of Widecombe-in-the-Moor. However, the excursion ends in disaster after Pearce discovers his mare has died on the return journey from the fair. Nevertheless, the charming melody of the song, along with its locally rooted lyrics, resonated amongst many Devonians. This evocation of Devonian solidarity was evident when the soldiers of the Devonshire Regiment sang the song as they marched off to fight in the South African War (1899 to 1902).[16] The folk song functioned as an expression of local belonging amongst Devon's men, taking pride in their identity as Devonians. Due to the song's significance, Todd Gray suggests it was a part of the 'rich diversity of the county's identity' alongside other local cultural codes of Devon.[17]

Nicholas Mansfield has labelled the pride of place contemporaries felt towards their distinctive local landscapes during the early twentieth century as local patriotism.[18] Yet local patriotism could be more than solely an attachment to the county's landscapes. For Devonians, the county's history was another source of local patriotism.[19] Indeed, when talking about Devon, they praised the county under its older, grander name of Devonshire. Although contemporaries expressed the words Devon and Devonshire interchangeably, the latter title was historically significant and poignant to Devonians. For the residents of Devon, the title of Devonshire was a basis of great distinction and a term loaded with various connotations. They used the term to evoke the county's heritage, its reputation for steadfast loyalty, and its prestigious status as one of the historic 'shire' counties of the Anglo-Saxon Kingdom of England. Accordingly, many Devonians were proud of Devonshire's noteworthy status in English history.[20]

A time period that contemporaries used to emphasize the outstanding role that Devonshire had played in England's past was the 'Golden Age' of the Tudor monarch, Queen Elizabeth I.[21] In the summer of 1588, Elizabeth faced a great danger that threatened the very survival of her reign. King Philip II of Spain dispatched a mighty naval fleet known as the Spanish Armada to invade England, depose Elizabeth and destroy the Protestant state. Once the flotilla of Spanish ships was sighted off the coast of England, the English Navy stationed in Plymouth set sail to face the Armada. The Vice Admiral of the English Navy was the Devonian naval captain, explorer, and privateer Sir Francis Drake.[22] After the two fleets clashed off the coast of Plymouth, the English Navy fought and pursued the Armada along the English Channel. However, as the Spanish Armada continued its journey to rendezvous with the Duke of Parma's Army in the Spanish Netherlands, the flotilla of ships experienced significant setbacks. Problems of mismanagement, poor communication, and unfavourable weather conditions had worsened the Spanish fleet's fortunes. On 7 August 1588, the English fleet used fireships to strike against the Armada. This strategy of these drifting fireships caused disorientation amongst the Spanish fleet, and many ships became scattered from the Armada formation. The following day, the English Navy attacked the Armada sinking several Spanish vessels in what became known as the Battle of Gravelines. In the battle's aftermath, the Spanish Armada's Commander, the seventh Duke of Medina Sidonia, ordered the remaining Spanish ships to sail around the British Isles and return to Spain.[23] For Elizabethan England, the fact that the nation had prevailed against such overwhelming odds was interpreted as an act of divine providence and a cause for thanksgiving.[24]

When the event's tercentenary occurred in 1888, civic authorities in Victorian Britain commemorated and celebrated the Spanish Armada's defeat.[25] The London Devonian Association honoured the rout of Phillip

II's naval fleet by organising a special Armada Day on 20 July 1912 at the Earl's Court Exhibition. In attendance was the Right Honourable Winston Churchill, First Lord of the Admiralty and the Liberal Member of Parliament (MP) for Dundee. On the deck of a replica of Drake's ship *The Revenge*, Churchill gave an address that touched upon Devon's importance in Britain's naval past.[26] However, the eminent figures from Devon's civil society who also spoke that day, like the Mayor of Plymouth, Alderman H. Hurrell, went to greater lengths in their speeches to accentuate the unique contribution that Devon's men had made in defending Elizabethan England and, more significantly, Drake's role in British history.[27] Civic figures in Hampshire shared this ambition to promote their own county's unique place in English history, especially the city of Winchester's connection to King Alfred. Like the spectacle to honour Drake and the Armada's defeat during the Armada Day of 1912, the commemorative activities in Winchester for the millenary anniversary of King Alfred's death in 1901 was an equivalent demonstration of locally rooted English patriotism.[28]

The Armada Day of 1912 also reflected how popular culture had glorified Drake to such a high degree after the Armada's tercentenary that he emerged as the chief architect of the Armada's defeat.[29] For Devonians during the late Victorian and Edwardian periods, Drake represented the spirit of action and heroism innate in the character of Devon's men. Moreover, since the county was the birthplace of Elizabethan seafaring men like Drake, Sir Richard Grenville, and Sir Walter Raleigh, Devon was known as the 'Shire of the Sea Kings' to reflect the county's distinct maritime tradition.[30] A more recent figure evoked as an example of the extraordinary character of Devon's men was the British Army General Sir Redvers Buller. During the mid to late nineteenth century, Buller had a distinguished military career in campaigns across the British Empire.[31] Despite the criticisms directed against Buller later in his military career, he was still highly revered in his native county, where many Devonians regarded him as an imperial hero.[32] However, many Devonians also felt similar admiration towards the county's Regiment within the British Army.

Established in 1685 to help put down the Monmouth Rebellion, the Devonshire Regiment was previously known as the Eleventh Foot. The unit was engaged in conflicts that involved Britain since the eighteenth century, such as the Napoleonic Wars. However, in the late nineteenth century, the Eleventh Foot became the Devonshire Regiment, colloquially known as the

'Devons'. Through their involvement in the skirmishes and battles of these past wars, the Devonshire Regiment gained a reputation for fighting prowess and steadfast loyalty. During the South African War, the Regiment's actions in defending 'Waggon Hill' against the military forces of the Boers reinforced this high reputation.[33] Indeed, contemporaries believed that the defence of Waggon Hill had demonstrated that the soldiers of the Regiment upheld the noble traditions of Devon's men.[34] Accordingly, many contemporary Devonians invested tremendous pride in the Devonshire Regiment to the extent that it became an emblem of county identity.[35]

The veneration of Devon's past and recent military figures reflected the tendency in late Victorian and Edwardian culture to promote the role of illustrious local men in English history.[36] Texts written about figures from Devon's history before 1914 followed this pattern since they honoured the men from the county, like Drake and Buller, as 'worthies' who made valiant contributions to England's past.[37] These heroic narratives about Devon's figures enthused the county's past with a 'strong patriotic charge' and reflected a distinctly localised 'sense of Englishness.'[38] Through this presentation of their history in the classroom, many contemporaries learned how the men of Devonshire had broken the 'power of the Spanish Armada.'[39] Indeed, as was demonstrated during the Armada Day of 1912, the defeat of the Spanish Armada was a unique but integral feature in a narrative of Devonian exceptionalism.[40] The accolades of Devon's great men of action, whether these were Drake, Buller or the Devonshire Regiment's soldiers, were used by contemporary Devonians as evidence that confirmed the existence of this exceptional Devonian character. The *Devon and Exeter Gazette* summarised these sentiments of Devonian exceptionalism on 3 March 1911: 'Devonshire has a glorious past. No county in England has produced a finer set of patriots.'[41] At the same time, this Devonian exceptionalism was incorporated into the broader history of British Imperial expansion. Historical accounts of Devon's past published during the late nineteenth and early twentieth centuries stressed how the contributions of the county's men helped to lay the foundations of the British Empire.[42]

Alongside classroom patriotism, Devon's local elite sought to promote the county's past and its role in English history more widely in Devon and further afield. In Germany, the local elites or *Honoratioren* (local notables) sought to educate others in their local communities about who they were.[43] Notable figures from Devon's civil society shared a similar educational ambition to inform Devonians about their heritage. They sought to teach the county's population about who they were by promoting Devon's history, folklore and local customs to stimulate a distinct sense of local consciousness amongst its residents. In the case of the county's historical figures like Drake and Raleigh, civic figures went to great lengths to enlighten Devonian men that they had a justifiable right to be proud of their county for raising such courageous men.[44] Likewise, local elites in France and Germany attempted to foster a sense of belonging in specific localities through the exaltation of local history, rituals and customs.[45] One example in Devon of the exaltation of the county's folklore was the legend of Drake's Drum. The fable suggested that if England were ever in grave danger, the spirit of Sir Francis Drake would return to defend the nation upon hearing the beat of his drum at Drake's home at Buckland Abbey.[46] The legend also gained popularity outside the county when Sir Henry Newbolt wrote a poem about it in 1896. Later in 1904, Sir Charles Villiers Stanford composed a song about the legend and utilised the poem for the tune's lyrics.[47] Civic organisations such as the Devonshire Association and the London Devonian Association also played an important role in stimulating local pride within the county and further afield. These entities attempted to foster a 'spirit of local patriotism' amongst Devon's population through civic activities and events.[48] The great mission to educate the county's population about their history was evident with the civic movement to immortalise Devon's notable figureheads with statues in public spaces. For example, in Plymouth and Tavistock, two statues of Drake were erected in the late nineteenth century to commemorate his achievements, whilst Buller had a statue of him riding a horse unveiled in Exeter in 1905 to honour his military career.[49]

The Composition and Demography of Devon

By 1911, Devon had a total population of 699,703 inhabitants.[50] Most of Devon's populace was situated within the three towns of Plymouth, East Stonehouse and Devonport, located in the south-west of the county. The amalgamation of these three localities in 1914 created the single borough of Plymouth, with a population of nearly 200,000. By contrast, the cathedral city of Exeter was Devon's capital and had a populace of 57,925.[51] Apart from Plymouth and Exeter, most of the county's population was thinly and widely spread in the towns and villages across Devon's sizeable geographical expanse. As a result, some areas of Devon were more inhabited than others.[52] For example, the beautiful untamed landscape that formed the moorland of Dartmoor, along with the boroughs that constituted the hilly but remote district of North Devon, were the county's least populated areas.[53] With a population of 14,485 people, the market town of Barnstaple was the largest town in North Devon. At the same time, the largest town in West Devon, located on the western edge of Dartmoor, was Tavistock and had 4,392 residents.[54] On both the north and south Devon coasts, seaside towns such as Ilfracombe and Seaton possessed large retired populations.[55] Within Devon's geographical borders, the county contained a significant amount of internal local variation to the extent that the county had five districts. These were north Devon, east Devon, west Devon, mid-Devon, and south Devon (also known as the South Hams), which possessed their own distinctive characteristics. The populations in the north and west of the county were typically politically Liberal, religiously Nonconformist, radical, not very affluent and more likely to attend religious services in Chapels. Bruce Coleman has observed that since the areas forming the district of West Devon were on the border with Cornwall, these localities shared similar characteristics to their neighbouring parts of Cornwall.[56] By contrast, the people of south and east Devon were politically Conservative, religiously High Church Anglicans or Roman Catholic and would most probably be present at services in Churches. As a result, south and east Devon shared more attributes with southern England than the areas of north and west Devon.

When the novelist and agriculturalist Henry Rider Haggard visited Devon at the turn of the twentieth century, he observed that the agricultural depression of the nineteenth century had less of an impact on farming in Devon compared to other counties across England.[57] Indeed, agriculture was still one of Devon's primary industries by 1900.[58] Listed in the 1911 census were 10,865 farmers/graziers and 9,537 people who were sons, daughters or other relatives of agriculturalists who assisted in the work on the farm.[59] Most of the county's farms were family-managed smallholdings with less than 100 acres. In some areas, the same family had rented the farm for three to four generations.[60] Devon's agricultural workforce also included 7,242 agricultural labourers, skilled with either horses or cattle, and 14,259 unskilled farm labourers. Agriculture, in total, provided a living for 42,609 men and 5,055 women in the county. Devon's rural economy also included occupations which included 2,484 Blacksmiths and 738 Wheelwrights.[61]

Although dairy farming was strong in the county and most of Devon's 1,671,364 acres were pasture land used for grazing cattle, there were local variations in the types of farming practices within the county.[62] For example, farmers around the Mid-Devon town of Crediton mainly used the land for growing arable crops due to the fertility and productivity of the red soil of the locality.[63] By contrast, agriculturalists utilised the hilly landscape of the uplands of north Devon for grazing cattle and sheep, including native breeds of livestock such as the 'Devon' breed of cattle and Exmoor horn sheep.[64] Due to the strength of agriculture in Devon, the county possessed a distinct rural culture.[65] However, despite organisations that championed farming interests in the county, such as the Devon Farmers Union (DFU) founded in 1908, Devon's farmers were not a cohesive block.[66]

By the Edwardian period, the holiday industry was another of the county's most prominent sectors since it employed a domestic labour force of 55,000 people.[67] In Devon's seaside resorts, tourism-related activities accounted for around a quarter to a third of commercial businesses by 1910. Ilfracombe was one exception to this rule since holiday-related activities accounted for nearly 70 per cent of companies in the north Devon coastal town.[68] The origins of Devon's holiday industry lay in the eighteenth century. Sea-bathing amongst the higher classes had transformed fishing villages and seaside towns on the county's two coastlines into 'exclusive' holiday resorts for wealthy patrons who could afford to travel to Devon.[69] The county's peripheral location within the United Kingdom meant that Devon's seaside resorts were at a disadvantage compared to holiday resorts, like Brighton and Blackpool, that were closer to urban centres such as London and Manchester. However, during the nineteenth century, the railways' expansion to Exeter and Plymouth significantly improved access to the county from London and other parts of England. The enhanced transport links also encouraged the proliferation of railway networks across the county from the railway stations in Devon's two major urban centres.[70] As a result, the railways contributed to the improved fortunes of the holiday industry in the towns and villages along both of Devon's coastlines. South Devon seaside towns such as Torquay, Paignton and Dawlish had increased in size and popularity since these locations benefited from their proximity to the railway line along the South Devon coast to Plymouth.[71] The same could not be said for the seaside towns of North Devon since the less developed transport infrastructure of the district had rendered these resorts more remote and inaccessible for holidaymakers.[72] Indeed, communication by train between the north and south of the county was still both 'slow and inconvenient' by 1914.[73] The growth of the railways and other modes of transportation also meant that transport employed 23,000 people in Devon and was the county's third-largest employment sector.[74] The residents of the South Devon town of Newton Abbot benefitted greatly from the employment opportunities that the railways provided. Although the South Devon Railway established the railway works at Newton Abbot in the mid-nineteenth century, the Great Western Railway absorbed the works in 1876 to repair and maintain their locomotives.[75] The latter company was highly regarded as an employer in the county to the extent that the Great Western Railway was colloquially known as 'God's Wonderful Railway'.[76]

Another industry on the south Devon coastline was the sea fishing sector. Although the county had 1,725 fishermen in the 1911 census, 1,600 of them harboured their fishing boats in the south Devon town of Brixham, an important fishing port in the South West of England.[77] However, by the early twentieth century, Devon's fishing industry was in decline because the county's fishing vessels struggled to gather their catches. Accordingly, the total value of the catch landed by Devon's fishermen dwarfed in significance compared to that landed by fishermen at other British fisheries such as Grimsby.[78] A significant figure who sought to improve the fortunes of Devon's fishermen was Stephen Reynolds. From 1907 until just before his death in 1919, Reynolds lived in the east Devon seaside town of Sidmouth with working-class fisherman Robert (Bob) Wooley and his family.[79] Inspired by his personal experiences of living and working with the Wooleys, Reynolds used the writing skills he had gained earlier in his career to document his insights into working-class life in his book, *A Poor Man's House*, published in 1908. Although he went on to write other books such as *Seems So!: A Working Class View of Politics* and *Alongshore, where Man and Sea face one another*, Reynolds dedicated his time and energies to fishery politics and administration. As a result, he became a passionate advocate for the fishing communities of Devon and Cornwall.[80] Reynolds' involvement with fishermen in the South West and his articles in *The Times* brought him to the attention of Walter Runciman, the President of the Board of Agriculture and Fisheries.

Following a request from the Devon and Cornwall Sea Fisheries Committee, Runciman established a committee in November 1912 to consider whether to provide the fishermen of the two counties with government funds to install motor power in their fishing vessels.[81] Reynolds was an active member of this Committee, chaired by Cecil Harmsworth, Runciman's Parliamentary Private Secretary and the Liberal MP for South Bedfordshire.[82] After a tour of the Devon and Cornwall coastlines, the Committee produced a report with proposals to improve the conditions of fishing communities in both counties.[83] However, on 27 January 1913, Runciman established a new Inshore Fisheries Committee that continued the work of the original Devon and Cornwall Inquiry but operated with a broader remit to consider the fishing communities of England and Wales. Under the Chairmanship of Sir Stafford Howard, the former Liberal MP for Cumberland East, the new Committee also included Harmsworth and Reynolds. When the Committee published its report in May 1914, it proposed establishing a Fisheries Organisation Society alongside recommendations for cooperation in marketing, utilising motor power for fishing vessels and new insurance systems for fishermen.[84] Through his membership of these two Committees, Reynolds implemented these reforms in the fisheries in the South-West when he became fisheries advisor to the Development Commission.[85]

At the same time, Devon had a manufacturing sector mainly associated with the textile industry.[86] As well as the presence of traders of lace in the county, there were two large factories in mid and North Devon which manufactured lace: the Derby Lace factory in Barnstaple and the John Heathcoat & Company factory in the mid-Devon town of Tiverton.[87] By 1911, these lace manufacturers employed 375 men and 1,343 women.[88] Devon also possessed a shipbuilding industry based in locations on the county's coastlines, such as Dartmouth in the South and Appledore in the North. Yet these commercial shipwrights were dwarfed in size compared to the Royal Dockyards at Devonport, which provided shipbuilding and maintenance services for the Royal Navy. By 1914, 12,290 men worked as highly skilled workers in the Navy base.[89] As a result, the city of Plymouth was a key port for the Royal Navy. Like Cornwall, Devon was a traditional recruiting ground for the Navy.[90] Indeed, the 1912 official return for the Royal Navy recorded that the two counties had contributed more men to the Navy than the whole of Wales and Scotland.[91]

Religion and Politics in Devon

In Devon, the religious affairs of the Anglican Church were administered by the Diocese of Exeter. As a clerical body of the Church of England, the Bishop of Exeter managed the affairs of the Diocese. From 1903 to 1916, Archibald Robinson held the office of the Bishop of Exeter. In 1916, Lord William Cecil took over as the Bishop of Exeter and held the office until 1936. Across the county's geographical area, the Diocese retained 588 parish churches and chapels, along with 127 other places of worship. On a local level, 66 full-time parish clergy represented the Diocese.[92] Coleman has suggested that the religious picture of the county remained relatively unchanged through the mid-nineteenth century into the early twentieth century.[93] In both south and east Devon, most of the population attended Churches administered by the Diocese of Exeter.[94] Across these two districts, the Church of England held a strong influence. The notable exception was the city of Plymouth, where religious support was divided into one-third Anglican to two-thirds nonconformist.[95] One prominent nonconformist group from Plymouth was the sect of the Plymouth Brethren. During the nineteenth century, the Brethren had established themselves in the city and had grown in influence across Devon.[96] Simultaneously, there was a solid nonconformist presence in North and West Devon, where denominations such as Methodists and the Bible Christians were well-supported in these areas.[97] Nonconformity had gained a foothold in these districts because the Diocese of Exeter had left a religious vacuum.[98] John Wesley and his successors filled the absence of the Church of England in these areas in the late eighteenth and early nineteenth centuries.[99] Chapel-goers rather than church attendants were the majority in the north and west of Devon because nonconformity had gained an appeal amongst the rural working class.

At the same time, the Roman Catholic Church had a modest presence in the county. In 1901, the Catholic Church established a Diocese in Plymouth that covered the counties of Cornwall, Devon and Dorset.[100] Alongside this Diocese of Plymouth, the Catholic Church in Devon also included the expatriate community of Benedictine monks at Buckfast Abbey, located near Buckfastleigh in South Devon. Although the original Buckfast Abbey was disbanded as part of the dissolution of the monasteries, a group of French monks established a new religious order in 1882 on the land where the monastery once stood. The small community of French monks dedicated to the monk Benedict's peaceful principles expanded in the subsequent years when monks from Germany and Austria joined the fraternity.[101] Following the growth of the Benedictine community, the Second Abbot of the new Buckfast Abbey, Anscar Vonier, directed that the monks rebuild the Abbey on the original monastery's twelfth-century foundations. Local noble and practising Catholic Lord Clifford of Chudleigh also provided financial assistance towards rebuilding the Abbey. The work on the reconstruction of the Abbey commenced in 1907 when Anscar Vonier laid the foundation stone for the new structure.[102] The monks continued constructing the new Abbey through the war years, and the building's construction was completed in 1938.[103] Devon also possessed a Jewish population primarily based in Plymouth and Exeter, with synagogues in both cities.[104]

In the realm of politics, Devon was divided into eleven Parliamentary constituencies. Nine of these were Parliamentary Divisions which returned one MP. These were Ashburton, Barnstaple, Exeter, Honiton, South Molton, Tavistock, Tiverton, Torquay, and Totnes. Devon also had two double-member boroughs: Plymouth and Devonport. For residents in these two constituencies, each voter had two votes and returned two MPs.[105] In total, Devon had thirteen MPs in the House of Commons in the period before 1914. Generally, the county's political constituencies had a somewhat mixed composition that was neither predominately middle class nor working class.[106] However, there were exceptions to this varied configuration as Exeter and Torquay had high proportions of middle-class residents, typical of cathedral cities and seaside resorts.[107] Yet there were significant local variations in the political sympathies of the county's population. For example, support for the Liberal Party was solid in north and west Devon, where constituencies such as Ashburton and South Molton were deemed bastions for the Liberals.[108]

The Liberal Party received great political support in the north and west districts of the county due to the strength of nonconformity and the importance of the nonconformist vote. A politician who personified this nonconformist sensibility was George Lambert, the Liberal MP for South Molton. As a nonconformist yeoman farmer, Lambert represented Liberalism's influence amongst nonconformist and tenant farming families in the locality.[109] During his campaign in the 1891 South Molton by-election, Lambert described himself as the candidate of the tenant farmer. As a result of his popularity in the constituency, he became known as the 'Farmers Friend'.[110] Lambert's commitment to advocating for the interests of agriculturalists was a characteristic shared by other Liberal parliamentarians in Devon, including Ernest J. Soares, Hugh Luttrell, and Charles Seale-Hayne.[111] By contrast, the Conservative Party held a strong position in the south and east districts of the county, where wards like Exeter, Tiverton and the East Devon borough of Honiton were viewed by contemporaries as strongholds for the Conservatives.[112] The Conservatives had great support in these areas due to a deep presence from the established church, the weakness of nonconformity and the structure of rural society being more akin to other parts of the South of England.[113] Devon's remaining constituencies were largely marginal seats.[114]

Competing for electoral support in Devon against the Conservatives and Liberals was the Liberal Unionist party. This political party was formed in 1886 after a group of Liberal MPs broke away from the Liberals since they opposed the plans of Liberal Prime Minister, William Gladstone, to introduce Home Rule for Ireland. From its formation to the early twentieth century, the Liberal Unionists gained support in areas of Devon where the 'Free Church movement was strongest.'[115] The noticeable success that the Liberal Unionists achieved in Devon electorally also indicated the perseverance of a school of thought that, although conservative on Imperial concerns, was radical on domestic issues.[116] Even during the early twentieth century, the residents of some Devon constituencies continued to support the Liberal Unionists at the ballot box. At the general election of 1900, Devon returned two Liberal Unionist MPs, six Liberal MPs, and five Conservative MPs.[117] Although the Conservatives enjoyed significant electoral success in 1900 across the country, the results of this election indicate there was virtually no change in Devon.[118] The 1900 election has also been described as the 'Khaki election' due to the suggestion that the South African War overshadowed domestic political issues.[119] However, the conflict was not a prominent feature in the electoral campaigns in the three constituencies of Devonport, Tavistock and Ashburton. Whilst the South African War was touched upon by both Unionist and Liberal candidates in Devonport, the 1900 election for these constituencies centred mainly on local issues relevant to each constituency.[120] Indeed, Michael Dawson contends that politics in Devon were not 'nationalised' even by 1910 since politics in the county was still primarily fixated on local matters.[121] However, this is not to say that Devonians were oblivious about national political issues. Margherita Rendel has shown that whilst the campaigns for women's suffrage in the county experienced peaks and troughs in interest, a women's suffrage movement existed in the county from 1866 to 1908.[122]

At the 1906 general election, the political fortunes of the Conservative Party and the Liberal Unionists worsened in Devon. Whilst the Conservatives lost three seats, the Liberal Unionists retained only one MP. As a result, two Conservative MPs remained in Devon: Sir Edward Kennaway for Honiton and William Walrond for Tiverton, respectively. By contrast, the 1906 election gave the Liberals a strong position in the county as they gained ten seats that included both the two-seat constituencies of Plymouth and Devonport.[123] However, between the two general elections of 1910, there was a swing in support in Devon from the Liberal Party towards the Conservatives in several key seats. In the January general election, the Liberals lost three seats (Exeter and the double-member constituency of Devonport) to the Unionists. With the returns of the December general election, the Liberal party experienced further defeats in the county since the Conservatives gained Ashburton and the double-member borough of Plymouth. Meanwhile, the Liberal Unionist party won Torquay and Tavistock. As a result, the Liberal Party's representation in Devon went down from seven to three MPs.[124] In the spring of 1911, the Liberals lost their newly gained seat of Exeter after the original December 1910 election result was overturned. Accordingly, Henry Duke, the Conservative MP for Exeter from January to December 1910, regained his parliamentary seat but with a majority of only one vote.[125] After Duke had taken back his seat, the Liberals had two MPs in the county by the summer of 1914.

A factor in explaining why the Conservatives increased their political representation in Devon in the two general elections of 1910 was due to the constitutional crisis created after the House of Lords had blocked the 'People's Budget' of Liberal Chancellor David Lloyd George in 1909. The fact that the House of Lords had vetoed Lloyd George's budget prompted the Liberal Prime Minister, Herbert Henry Asquith, to attack the upper house of Parliament. However, Asquith's condemnation of the Lords deeply offended the county's residents, who held the county's gentry and landed aristocracy in high esteem. Across Devon, it was an issue that transcended political and religious differences. The county's chapel-goers were so incensed by Asquith's stance that they set aside their own nonconformist traditions to support the House of Lords by voting for the Conservatives.[126]

The opposition of Devonians to the renewed prospect of Home Rule for Ireland was another factor in the Conservatives' improved political fortunes between the two 1910 general elections.[127] Between 1885 and 1892, the question of Home Rule for Ireland had previously contributed to a decisive shift in the political support of Devon's population towards either the Conservatives or Liberal Unionists. When the issue returned to the political forefront during the 1910 general elections, both parties experienced a comparable swing in electoral support in the county. The strength of feeling amongst Devonians against Irish Home Rule was partly motivated by concerns about the influence of the Roman Catholic Church in Ireland. Opponents of Home Rule warned that self-government for Ireland could potentially lead to Catholic domination and the persecution of Irish Protestants. As a result, these critics argued that Irish Home Rule would overrule 'British Rule' since it was the alarming prospect of 'Rome Rule'. Similarly, some Devonians regarded Home Rule for Ireland as a sinister Catholic plot to destabilise the United Kingdom, just as the Spanish Armada threatened to destroy Protestant England in 1588.[128] When framed in this manner to tap into the folk memory of the Spanish Armada's defeat, these critiques of Home Rule for Ireland resonated amongst the county's population.[129] Moreover, Irish Home Rule held a unique relevance among the people of Devon due to the county's geographical proximity to Ireland. The opposition of many Devonians towards Home Rule for Ireland can therefore be considered a response to the 'strategic dangers of having an alien Power so close to its exposed coasts.'[130] However, when Asquith's government put forward the Home Rule Bill in 1912, tensions among Unionists and Nationalists escalated to near breaking point. In the following two years, the resulting Ulster Crisis had worsened to such an extent that many contemporaries feared in 1914 that the tense situation in Ulster could precariously instigate a civil war in Ireland.

Local government and Devon's local elite

Similar to other counties in England, local government in Devon was an interdependent system of organisations that sought to arbitrate over government affairs within the county's boundaries. The highest tier of this administrative framework was Devon County Council (DCC), established after the Local Government Act of 1888.[131] DCC was responsible for governing general matters in the county. The three county boroughs of Exeter, Devonport, and Plymouth followed after the DCC. There were also borough and town councils for larger individual towns such as Barnstaple, Honiton, Ilfracombe, Tiverton, and Tavistock. The next tier comprised councils that administered larger areas of Devon's urban and rural districts, the Urban District Council (UDC) and the Rural District Council (RDC), respectively. Finally, there were parish councils for individual localities. While these governmental bodies formed a hierarchy, county government in Devon was not a single entity. Instead, it acted as an interdependent system since it comprised different tiers within a chain of command that relied upon one another and worked together.[132] Local government also provided opportunities for Devon's civil society to extend an influence upon the socio-cultural fabric of life in the county.

At the apex of Devon's civil society were the county's landowners, civic dignitaries, clerics, political figures, and other local notables. By the early twentieth century, these distinguished personages influenced public, political and social life in Devon. A crucial figure in the county's civil society and a member of Devon's landowning aristocracy was Hugh Fortescue, who became the fourth Earl Fortescue after his father died in 1905.[133] Alongside his duties as a peer of the realm in the House of Lords, Fortescue oversaw the running of both the Fortescue family home, the Neo-Palladian country house of Castle Hill and its adjoining estate near Filleigh in the idyllic North Devon countryside.[134] The fourth Earl came from one of the county's most revered families, and he was a highly respected notable figure in his own right.[135] Fortescue possessed an industrious work ethic and maintained the family's noble traditions concerning public service. The fourth Earl's diligence and dedication were especially apparent during his tenure as the Lord Lieutenant of Devonshire from 1904 to 1928.[136] The office of Lord Lieutenant was a prestigious and historical office that originated in county government. By the time Fortescue was appointed Devon's Lord Lieutenant, it was still a significant public role conferred by royal appointment. As the monarch's representative in the county, Earl Fortescue represented King Edward VII and later King George V in Devon through his term in the post.[137] In addition, the office of Lord Lieutenant retained connections with local military units due to the 1908 army reforms of Richard Haldane, Secretary of State for War. In the case of Devon, Fortescue was chairman of the county's Territorial Forces and presided over the county's Territorial Force Association.

Alongside his duties as Devon's Lord Lieutenant, Fortescue also occupied his time with local government entities in the county. From 1904 to 1916, he acted as Chairman of DCC and the Devon Quarter Sessions.[138] He was also a prominent Freemason and Master of the Devon and Somerset Stag Hounds.[139] Through these combined engagements, Fortescue exerted considerable authority upon the socio-cultural fabric of county life before 1914. As David Parker has summarised, the fourth Earl Fortescue personified the 'traditional role of wealthy estate owners as social leaders, patrons of morally sound institutions, leading supporters of charities and local guardians of law and order.'[140] Meanwhile, the wife of the fourth Earl, Lady Emily Fortescue, held similar influence across the county with her involvement with several local societies with female membership, including the Women's Institute and the Devon Nursing Association.[141]

Another prominent social figure who wielded significant influence in Devon was the Tiverton industrialist Sir Ian Heathcoat-Amory who became the second baronet Heathcoat-Amory of Knightshayes Court on 29 May 1914.[142] Heathcoat-Amory managed the family's textile manufacturing business, John Heathcoat & Company, and the operations of their lace factory in Tiverton. Since his family were enlightened employers, Heathcoat-Amory endeavoured to work with his workforce to provide a harmonious and benevolent relationship between employer and employee.[143] In addition, both the Mayor of the mid-Devon town of Tiverton and the recorder for Tiverton, Alfred T. Gregory and Sir Trehawke Kekewich, were civic worthies of local life in the mid-Devon town.[144] Meanwhile, in Exeter, James George Owen was a crucial dignitary in the city during the Edwardian era.[145] Whilst he was the High Sheriff of Exeter from 1910 to 1911, Owen gained greater civic authority when in November 1914, he became the city's Mayor and held the post until 1919. Owen's appointment as the Mayor of Exeter also meant that his wife, Janie Kirk Owen, became the Mayoress of Exeter. Alongside their Mayoral positions, Owen and Gregory were influential figures in Devon's civic society since they were editors of local newspapers.[146] Although Gregory was the owner and editor of the *Tiverton Gazette*, Owen was a notable newspaper magnate.[147] As the managing director of the Western Times Ltd, Owen possessed several Devon newspapers based in Exeter, which included the conservative-leaning *Devon and Exeter Gazette* and the liberal-inclined *Western Times*.[148]

At the same time, Plymouth had important provincial newspapers based in the city. One notable example of this was the conservative-leaning *Western Morning News*, which covered the news for both Devon and Cornwall. Plymouth also had a newspaper consortium, the Western Newspaper Company, which published the *Western Daily Mercury* and *Western Evening Herald*, and the managing editor was the newspaperman and writer Robert Alfred John Walling.[149] Alongside these larger newspaper consortiums, other Devon tabloids covered the news across the county. For instance, two newspapers covering the news in North Devon were the liberal-leaning *North Devon Journal* and the conservative-inclined *North Devon Herald*, both based in Barnstaple.[150] By contrast, the *South Devon Weekly Express* in Chudleigh covered the news in South Devon. There were also newspaper titles, such as the *Brixham Western Guardian* and the *Teignmouth Post and Gazette*, that covered the news for specific towns and their surrounding localities.

Conclusion

By 1914, many of Devon's residents defined their identity as Devonians through the unique features of the county's beautiful landscape and coastlines. Although idealised representations of the county reinforced these idyllic qualities, Devon was more than just a picturesque holiday destination. The county's peripheral location within England meant that the people of Devon had a 'clannish' nature where local cultural codes such as the county's landscape and Devon's food products were prestigious aspects of Devon that also made their native county unique. Devon's history, especially its lauded seafaring past, was a source of pride for many Devonians, informing a sense of local identity and local patriotism in the county. Devon's illustrious forebears, such as Drake and Buller, were used as examples in promoting a county identity and local patriotism in Devon. These figures from Devon's past and their contributions to the history of England and the British Empire were crucial threads in a narrative of Devonian exceptionalism.

Figures from Devon's local elite were instrumental in the civic campaign during the late nineteenth and early twentieth centuries to educate Devon's population about who they were. Alongside these notables, organisations in the county's civil society also sought to inculcate local patriotism and disseminate a spirit of local pride across Devon more widely. Due to the county's distinctive composition, Devon had a tremendous amount of local variation within the county's borders. Whilst there were large urban centres, Devon was still a predominately rural county by 1914. Despite the growth of Devon's holiday sector and the presence of other industries, agriculture remained the largest industry in the county. The prominence of agriculture in Devon meant that the county possessed a unique farming culture. At the same time, Devon's coastlines ensured that the county had a distinct maritime culture with strong ties to the Royal Navy.

Notwithstanding their geographical remoteness from London, the county's population were not entirely uninformed about outside events. Indeed, the constitutional crisis resulting from Lloyd George's 'People's Budget' and the question of Irish Home Rule significantly influenced the political choices made by many Devonians at the ballot box. Nevertheless, politics in the county were still primarily local due to the prominence of local issues. In many respects, the notable figures who comprised Devon's local elite reflected a distinct social hierarchy. By engaging in local civic organisations and other associations, these figures from Devon's civil society exercised and maintained a distinctive influence upon everyday life in the county by 1914.

Chapter 2

Mobilising for War, 1914

On 28 June 1914, in the Bosnian city of Sarajevo, Serbian terrorists killed Archduke Franz Ferdinand, the presumptive heir to the Austro-Hungarian throne. The Archduke's assassination generated a tense diplomatic situation, later known as the July Crisis of 1914, that enveloped the countries that constituted the rival Alliance blocks of the Triple Entente and the Central Powers.[1] During that July, the Royal Navy Reserve fleet was engaged in a test mobilisation at sea. However, before these naval exercises concluded, Admiral Prince Louis of Battenburg, the First Sea Lord, cancelled the dispersal of these reservists on 26 July in light of the deteriorating international situation.[2] Two days later (28 July), Winston Churchill, the First Lord of the Admiralty, ordered the Fleet to go to its war stations.[3] In Sidmouth on 1 August, Stephen Reynolds was deeply concerned that the Navy people he knew had not yet returned from the July naval exercises. The fact that he had received no news about them added to the sickening suspense he felt about the July Crisis.[4] Since the local Naval reserves were still at sea, it was clear to Reynolds that, contrary to reports in the press, the British mobilisation was 'undoubtedly very complete.'[5]

Although the Royal Navy was ordered to its war stations, this was not yet the case for the Territorial Forces. On 1 August 1914, the Secretary of the Devon Territorial Force Association, Colonel Smith Rewse, informed Earl Fortescue that there was no need for him to come to Exeter because there seemed, at that time, to be no prospect that the Territorials would receive the order for mobilisation.[6] By contrast, the East Lancashire Territorial Association viewed the situation more alarmingly since they held an emergency meeting on the same day. During their meeting, the Association ordered the necessary provisions required for their Territorial soldiers to be ready when they received the order for mobilisation.[7] Yet, notwithstanding the uncertainty of what would happen with the July Crisis, Reynolds thought it would likely blow over and leave 'Europe all the better for this glimpse into her mad idiocy of armaments.'[8] While Reynolds tried to reassure himself that common sense would prevail in the face of potential catastrophe, the July Crisis worsened later that day when Imperial Germany declared war against Tsarist Russia.[9]

In the twilight hours of 2 August, Morland John Greig, the Master of the Devon and Somerset Stag Hounds, and Exford resident Mr Aston arrived at Castle Hill in Filleigh to inform Devon's Lord Lieutenant that Germany had declared war against 'both France and Russia.'[10] This news was partly accurate because Germany had not yet declared war on both countries. Germany would later declare war against France on 3 August.[11] Yet, during the evening of 2 August at Castle Hill, Greig and Aston also wanted to update Earl Fortescue about the rumours they had heard concerning the Asquith Government's attitude and intentions on how Britain would respond.[12] However, by 3 August (the August Bank Holiday), many contemporaries had accepted the possibility of conflict as a certainty rather than a subject of speculation.[13] Like others across the United Kingdom on 3 August, Reynolds concluded that war seemed 'almost inevitable.'[14] Despite the fine weather that day, the Mayor of Tiverton, Alfred T. Gregory, confessed that indulging in the frivolous pursuits associated with a regular Bank Holiday was inappropriate when faced with the likelihood of war.[15] After the declaration of war on 4 August, eminent figures from Devon's civil society, such as Earl Fortescue and Alfred T. Gregory, acted as intermediaries of the war experience. Like the civic figures who constituted the local elite of Sussex, Devon's notables sought to mobilise the county's resources and convert Devon into a county at arms.[16]

The transition from peacetime to wartime

During the early days of August, the calling up of fishermen and other seafarers who were members of the Royal Naval Reserve and Royal Fleet Reserve continued in earnest. These naval reservists hurried from Devon's coastal communities to their nearest train station, where they would travel to Plymouth and Devonport.[17] For the families of these Reservists, it was a painful experience to bid an emotional farewell to their departing menfolk at their local railway station. Stephen Reynolds shared the sadness these families felt as they witnessed the departure of these Reserves at Sidmouth's railway station on 3 August. However, Reynolds also had an epiphany when he realised the magnitude of this event, which would have a more profound and devastating significance for the fishing communities he had long campaigned for. Reynolds lamented on 4 August that his work over many years to improve the lives of fishermen would probably be smashed by 'this accursed international insanity.'[18] The arrival of the Naval Reserves into Plymouth from Devon, Cornwall and further afield, ready to report at Devonport Barracks, meant that Plymouth and Devonport were buzzing with activity on 4 August.[19] Plymouth resident F. Ashe Lincoln remembered their arrival into the city that day to join with their fellow mariners from Plymouth. Similar to what Reynolds had seen at Sidmouth's railway station, Lincoln noticed that the wives of these Naval Reserves from the city were tearful at seeing their husbands heading off to their mobilisation stations.[20]

At 8 am GMT on 4 August 1914, the German Army invaded Belgium. In protest against Germany's violation of Belgium neutrality, the British government issued an ultimatum to Berlin that the German Army needed to withdraw from the country by 11 pm GMT the same day. If this condition was not met, then Britain would enter a state of war against Germany. The government's ultimatum heightened the drama whether Britain would remain neutral or declare war on Germany. In the countdown to the ultimatum's deadline, individuals and large crowds across the United Kingdom urgently sought the latest updates throughout the day. At 7 pm in the East Devon town of Ottery St Mary, the veteran British diplomat and Chairman of Ottery St Mary UDC, Sir Ernest Satow, noticed that many people in the street were reading the *Express & Echo* to get the most up-to-date reports on the crisis.[21] Many people were so anxious for verified information on the Crisis that they decided to wait outside the offices of local newspapers for the latest updates. In Exeter's High Street, eager crowds gathered around the office of the *Western Times* so that they could read 'every item of news as it was posted in the windows.'[22] However, some individuals sought to exploit these preoccupied people waiting for news in the city's High Street as eight cases of pickpocketing were later reported to the City's police.[23] Simultaneously, Exeter's police force were deeply concerned about the behaviour of the crowds waiting for news in the city's streets. As a precaution against any potential disturbances that could occur on 4 August, the Exeter Constabulary issued six of their police officers with firearms.[24] As a guardian of civil order in the city, the Mayor of Exeter, William Kendall King, sought to restore calm in this time of great uncertainty. At a special meeting of the City Council on the evening of 4 August, King prescribed how the city's populace should behave during this anxious crisis. In his address, he evoked the city's history hoping that this would inspire the people of Exeter to act responsibly. He hoped that the current generation of Exonians would prove themselves 'citizens of our great heritage, our King and our country.'[25]

The German invasion of Belgium also meant the local Territorials stationed in the county received their mobilisation orders. During the evening of 4 August, the 5th Territorial Battalion of the Devonshire Regiment marched from their camp at Woodbury Common through Exeter on their way to Exeter St David's railway station. Upon their arrival in Exeter at 8 pm, thousands of men, women and children lined the city's High Street to give the departing Territorials a great send-off. Simultaneously, these farewells were demonstrations of Devonian exceptionalism and county pride. As the Battalion passed through Exeter's Queen Street, members of the crowd raised the 'cry of "Good old Devon"'.[26] These declarations reaffirmed the local patriotism and the sense of loyal reliability associated with the county's military units. An hour later, a similar scene demonstrating the strength of local ties was evident when the 4th Territorial Battalion of the Devonshire Regiment turned and saluted the statue of Sir Redvers Buller as they marched past it.[27] The fact that these men paid tribute to the memory of Buller revealed the local character of the Battalion and their connection to Devon's military history. The strength of county pride in the Devonshire Regiment was also apparent amongst several people who had rushed to St David's station to bid the departing 4th Devons an emotional farewell. A favourite cry from these people was 'Up with the cream and down with the sausage!'.[28] Although this exclamation was a declaration of pride in the local food of Devon cream, it also served as a rallying cry of local patriotism and how this unique dairy product was linked with the county's Regiment. Indeed, the Devonshire Regiment was associated with the county's dairy industry and distinctive food products, such as Devonshire Dumplings or 'Devon cream'. Another way to view these sentiments is that they were expressions of Devonian exceptionalism in that the men of Devon were the cream of the nation's manhood, and the cream always rises to the top. Due to the pride associated with the superior quality of the Devon cream, the troops of Devon would prevail against the forces of Imperial Germany, symbolised as a quintessential German food item: the sausage. Since Kaiser Wilhelm II did not possess a strong stomach, the quality of the 'Devon cream' would, according to one postcard celebrating the Devonshire Regiment, cause him to experience indigestion (Figure 5). These rousing sentiments of local pride reinforce Pierre Purseigle's suggestion that contemporaries utilised local cultural codes to humiliate the enemy and underpin the 'local vision of an intrinsically inferior German'.[29] Another example of this from Britain was in Northampton, where, due to the pride associated with the town's shoe industry, the Northampton made shoe was of better quality than the poorly produced German shoe.[30] Ultimately, these examples demonstrate how local communities saw themselves in wartime, playing their part through their own unique contribution to the war to secure the prospect of victory against the weaker German enemy.

After the *Devon and Exeter Gazette* columnist had witnessed the conduct of Exonians who participated in these farewell ceremonies for the troops heading off to war on 4 August, he reflected that enthusiasm was a sufficient 'but a weak word to use' to describe the scene.[31] Although contemporaries like this correspondent described these crowds cheering on departing local troops at railway stations as enthusiastic, this was not jingoistic and unrestrained enthusiasm for war. The large crowds who enthusiastically cheered the departing troops at train stations in Britain, France and Germany were not celebrating the arrival of war.[32] Instead, these groups of people were enthusiastic because they attempted 'to give the soldiers a good send-off.'[33] Since those who witnessed these crowds made individual assessments based on what they saw, it is essential to reflect on the definitions that contemporaries used to define how these crowds reacted to these events. The words they used, such as enthusiasm and excitement, to describe the emotions of these groups need greater scrutiny as to what these descriptions as ideologically loaded terms constitute. A testimony demonstrating this was from Earl Fortescue when he witnessed the send-off for the local Territorials at Exeter St David's railway station. Based on what he saw during the evening of 4 August, Fortescue noted in his diary that he deemed the behaviour and attitude of the men and the people present to be 'quite satisfactory.'[34] From this assessment, Fortescue considered that the conduct of these groups was a fitting and proportionate response given the occasion of wishing the troops farewell. Another example was from Alfred T. Gregory, who later recalled that it was a 'thrilling scene' to watch the town's population present a jubilant send-off to the departing Army and Navy Reservists at Tiverton railway station on 5 August.[35] Rather than demonstrating excitement for war, Gregory's observation may indicate that he considered the sight of these people wishing these local reserves farewell to be greatly inspiring and reassuring to his patriotic sensibilities. The application of specific descriptions by observers like Earl Fortescue, Alfred T. Gregory and individual newspaper correspondents to determine how people and groups responded to the war can help to understand the nuances of these responses.

Through the night of 4 August 1914, crowds waited eagerly and nervously for news in cities and towns across the United Kingdom. Newspaper correspondents witnessed and recorded how these crowds responded once they received the news that Britain entered a state of war against Germany after the British government's ultimatum expired at 11 pm GMT.[36] In Exeter, correspondents for both the *Western Times* and the *Devon and Exeter Gazette* recorded that the crowds in the city reacted enthusiastically to the news.[37] In his coverage of the night's events, the columnist for the latter newspaper described the scene as one where 'the enthusiasm knew no bounds, cheer succeeded cheer, hats were thrown into the air, and everyone went wild with excitement.'[38] However, like the descriptions of enthusiastic and excited groups at railway stations on 4 August, the label of 'enthusiasm' used to describe how the crowds in Exeter behaved that night does not indicate naïve and jingoistic enthusiasm for war. On the contrary, the correspondents from these two Devon newspapers interpreted the cheering and excitement of these crowds as evidence that this behaviour demonstrated their patriotism and solidarity with the nation.[39] Indeed, the cheers and patriotic singing of enthusiastic Exonians had woken other citizens living on the city's high street from their slumber. Based on what he witnessed, the columnist for the *Devon and Exeter Gazette* believed that the city had 'fully lived up to the character of the centre of the patriotic West.'[40] However, the actions of the Exeter crowds (cheering and singing the national anthem) may instead constitute a form of catharsis, a release of pent-up suspense or unbearable tension built up during the July crisis. Catriona Pennell suggests that this may explain the behaviour of crowds in cities like Cardiff, where they sang and cheered to convey their relief that the uncertainty was over.[41] The *Devon and Exeter Gazette* columnist proposed that the behaviour of the Exeter crowds that night was indeed a discharge of tension and anxiety. According to the paper's writer, Exeter had set a noble example of controlling her feelings during the past few days of great uncertainty. Yet on the evening of 4 August, now Britain's position was clear, the city had proven her resolve and given 'way to a patriotic outburst.'[42] In Exeter, the displays of jubilation could also reflect how these citizens were pleased that by setting the ultimatum against Germany, Britain had proven her resolve by holding firm and standing up against an aggressor.

Early recruitment efforts in Devon

Following the appointment of Earl Kitchener as Secretary of State for War on 5 August 1914, a campaign to raise a new volunteer army began in earnest.[43] To co-ordinate this campaign across the United Kingdom, the War Office dispatched a circular on 7 August that appealed to all Lord Lieutenants, along with the Territorial Associations, to use their influence to help secure recruits for Kitchener's New Army from their respective counties.[44] As Devon's Lord Lieutenant, it fell to Earl Fortescue to fulfil this new wartime directive and promote voluntary recruitment in the county.[45] Alongside Fortescue, eminent dignitaries from Devon's civil society participated in efforts to encourage the county's eligible men to join the Forces. One key civic representative who directed recruitment efforts in the county's towns and cities was the local Mayor since they were often the public face of voluntary recruitment in urban localities across the United Kingdom.[46] As the Mayor of Tiverton, Alfred T. Gregory was one Mayor who fulfilled this role and attempted to convince military-age men to enlist at open-air recruiting meetings. In his petition for recruits, Gregory used the famous appeal of Italian general Giuseppe Garibaldi to persuade volunteers in the struggle for Italian independence in 1860. Gregory asked the eligible local men whether they could rise to the challenge since the war was the defining moment of their lives: 'I offer you, not pay, or plunder, not even fame: you will have to face hardship, peril, possibly wounds, and perhaps even death. It is the test of your manhood. Will you come?'.[47] Gregory recalled that this recruiting strategy was very effective since it convinced many of the best eligible men in the surrounding countryside to volunteer.

In provincial recruitment campaigns across the United Kingdom, notable figures incorporated local identities in their appeals to encourage eligible men to enlist. These civic dignitaries hoped that adding this local authenticity would enhance the sincerity of their petitions. Figures from Devon's civil society also tailored this local character into their recruitment appeals to try to mobilise the county's eligible men. One way that Devon's local elite attempted to do this was to evoke the pride associated with the county's status as Devonshire and promote a spirit of Devonian exceptionalism. By establishing links with the county's history to the present moment, these figures laid down the gauntlet to the current generation of Devonian men to rise to the challenge and uphold the county's patriotic traditions. Fortescue employed this historical continuity as a recruiting strategy in a letter read aloud to those present during a recruitment meeting in the East Devon town of Topsham on 20 August. To the local men in the audience, he hoped they would remember with pride the part that their forefathers had played in the defeat of the Spanish Armada in 1588. With this noble historical precedent in mind, Fortescue believed the men of Topsham would undertake their duty to defend the nation at this crucial moment. Indeed, he expressed his confidence that the patriotism of these men was as strong in 1914 as it had been amongst their Elizabethan forebears.[48] In a letter read aloud during a recruitment meeting in the north Devon town of Bideford on 4 September, the town's former Mayor, Hugh Stucley, also evoked the contribution that Bideford had made against the Spanish Armada to encourage local men to enlist. He stressed they should be under no illusion since the danger was 'quite as real now' as when the King of Spain threatened England in 1588.[49]

Another way Army recruiters across England played on the strength of local identities was to use prominent local military figures from the nation's past as patriotic role models. For example, recruiting authorities in the counties of Norfolk and Cambridgeshire utilised Horatio Nelson and Oliver Cromwell in their respective recruitment campaigns to convince local men to enlist and protect their communities.[50] In Devon, the county's local elite evoked the figures of Sir Francis Drake and Sir Redvers Buller as great men of Devonshire for the same purpose.[51] On 20 August 1914, John Shirley Steele-Perkins, the Sheriff of Exeter, proposed the formation of a new military unit named after Buller to capitalise on his popularity in the county.[52] Provisionally titled 'Buller's Foot', this special Battalion would, according to Steele-Perkins, be a valuable asset for voluntary recruitment in the county because the name of 'Buller made the blood thrill in every Devonshire heart.'[53] Thanks to the efforts of Earl Fortescue and others, the military authorities agreed to this proposal in early September, and the 8th Battalion of the Devonshire Regiment was named 'Buller's Own'.[54] Alongside Fortescue, Army recruiters tried to convince men from the county to join 'Buller's Own'. At a recruitment meeting in Bideford on 4 September, Colonel R. A. Moore Stevens urged the town's menfolk to come quickly so that Buller's Battalion could be filled with 'true, brave Devonshire men.'[55] The efforts of Fortescue and others appear to have succeeded as Lieutenant Colonel Alexander G. W. Grant informed Fortescue on 30 September that whilst recruits were still coming in, Devon men comprised around 90 per cent of the Battalion.[56] The unit's connection to the Buller family was reinforced when Buller's only daughter, Georgina Buller, presented a bulldog to the Battalion in December to act as the unit's mascot.[57] The dog, Billy, was also known as 'Buller' or 'Buller's Bulldog'.[58]

In the case of Devon's Elizabethan privateer, the recorder for Tiverton, Sir Trehawke Kekewich, evoked the legend of Drake's drum for recruitment purposes. He adapted this story of Devon's folklore to merge local identities into a narrative of historical obligation. As Drake's descendants, the county's men knew instinctively that the beat of his drum was a rallying sound for them to undertake their duty to defend England as it had been to previous generations of Devonian men. Due to the grave peril that the nation now faced, Kekewich claimed that he could imagine Drake standing on Plymouth Hoe furiously beating his drum, calling upon the young men to fulfil their birthright as true Devonians and enlist.[59] The following year, a *Devon and Exeter Gazette* correspondent used the legend surrounding Drake's drum to strengthen his argument that there should be more martial music at recruitment events. He believed that a musical accompaniment, especially the rhythm section, would instinctively rouse the patriotism of Devonian men: 'For in the throb of the drum, the men will hear the voice of Drake and the spirit of the old sea-fighter will impel them, their games finished, to go forth and beat the Germans, too.'[60]

In the eyes of his peers, the sight of an eligible man deciding to enlist was a symbolic gesture worthy of commendation and praise. Contemporaries who were ineligible for military service sought to congratulate the men who volunteered since they had made the 'right' choice to fulfil their duty and present their patriotism in the correct way. At a recruitment meeting in Exeter on 23 November 1914, the twenty-first Baron Clinton, Charles Hepburn-Stuart-Forbes-Trefusis, applauded the patriotism of the Devon men who had already enlisted. Since these keen men realised the significance of the crisis, Clinton judged that they were 'full of patriotism, [and possessed an] understanding [of] what patriotism means.'[61] On a local level, the congregation of Ottery St Mary's congregational church wanted to commend their Vicar, Reverend S. J. K. Mills, who had decided to enlist after he was motivated to do so by two of Lloyd George's speeches.[62] On the day of his farewell party (3 December 1914), a Senior Deacon, W. Godfrey, presented Mills with a parting gift of a watch to mark the 'noble[,] self-sacrificing patriotism underlying his decision' to volunteer.[63] Similar displays of public commendation to men who volunteered for military service were evident in the Dorset coastal village of Charmouth. After the outbreak of war, a regular ceremony took place outside the local Coach and Horses hotel where the village band would play for every local man who enlisted.[64] This ritual was a valuable means for the local community to visibly praise and support the decision of each man who joined up. Acts of positive support sought to reinforce the validity of the man's decision since he wanted to fulfil their 'obvious' obligation to the nation.

By contrast, the eligible men who decided against joining up could receive a different token. The item given to these men or other eligible men still wearing civilian clothes was a white feather that acted as a visual mark of shame. The white feather could also act as a deterrent whereby a man of military age did not need to fear the public humiliation of receiving a white feather and being branded a coward if he decided to enlist. Dispensing these white feathers were typically the women volunteers of the White Feather Brigade, also known as the Order of the White Feather.[65] Although the campaigns of the White Feather Brigade did find support amongst notable figures in Devon, some Devonians considered it presumptuous and inappropriate to give white feathers to eligible men to pressure them to enlist.[66] Nevertheless, Army recruiters in the county, like Captain Cuthbert Bearne, believed it was a valid recruiting strategy. Upon seeing any eligible man not yet in uniform during recruitment events, Army recruiters encouraged young women to 'buttonhole' these men with white feathers.[67] However, to present an eligible man with a white feather was also a very public and visible means to superintend their patriotism. Like a police constable on patrol looking out for those committing a crime, some women empowered with their white feathers were on the lookout for military-age men still in civilian clothes. Once they found a man who matched this appearance or who they suspected was avoiding military service, they could present him with a white feather. In some cases, women could confront and interrogate the man about why he was not in khaki or had refused to volunteer.[68] In Cornwall, the Mayor of Truro, Isaac Roskelley, proposed that ladies in the city should take on a superintending role when giving white feathers to men unwilling to volunteer. For every young man who did not come forward, he encouraged these women to send them white feathers and keep a register of their names.[69] Yet rather than confront these reluctant men directly, some women in Devon employed more secretive methods to challenge them without reprisals. Instead, they delivered anonymous letters and postcards to the homes of local eligible men which contained abrasive messages or demanding explanations as to why they had not yet enlisted.[70]

Although voluntary recruitment was initially brisk in Devon, the county's recruitment totals at the end of two months were disappointing.[71] The War Office's statistics reveal how Devon's enlistment figures compared to the recruitment returns of ten other counties across England by 10 October 1914. The War Office used the number of recruits that each county had raised against the size of their populations to calculate the percentage this number of recruits represented for each county. In the case of Devon, the county had raised 4,414 recruits which was 0.62 per cent of a total population of 701,944. The adjacent county of Cornwall had a worse percentage than Devon, raising just 922 recruits, representing 0.28 per cent of a population of 328,098. However, Devon's recruitment totals compared unfavourably with those from the neighbouring and less populated counties of Somerset and Dorset. Whilst Somerset had 3,194 recruits which was 0.82 per cent out of a population of 388,847, Dorset had 3,219 recruits, representing 1.44 per cent of a population of 223,266.[72] From a review of these War Office figures, Devon had one of the lowest contributions of Army recruits of any county in England.

Many Devonians, like former soldier W. H. Bolt, reacted to the county's low recruitment returns with disbelief and dismay since they viewed these figures as a reflection of Devon's patriotism.[73] These concerns were not unfounded. Since Devon's notable figures viewed Devonshire as one of England's most loyal and patriotic counties, they envisaged the county's recruitment figures would naturally set an excellent standard. The Recorder for Exeter, J. Anderson Foote KC, summarised this expectation on 6 October 1914 when he suggested that Devon 'ought to do better [in recruitment] than any other county.'[74] However, the county's lacklustre recruitment returns dashed these hopes. Devon's civic figures believed that these statistics had damaged the reputation of Devonshire for steadfast loyalty, whilst others interpreted them as a sign that the county was less dedicated to the war.[75] Kekewich concluded that the county's recruitment returns had shown that the eligible men of Devonshire had not done their duty. Although Devon's men possessed a competitive spirit in sport, these totals demonstrated that these men lacked this competitiveness in volunteering. As a result, Kekewich believed that while Devon enjoyed achieving victory against Somerset in games, Somerset was now beating Devon in the 'war game'.[76] Earl Fortescue also believed that the county's low recruitment figures had shown that Devon was letting the side down since he acknowledged that Devon had 'nothing to be proud of in the matter of recruiting.'[77] The Irish Parliamentary Party MP for East Mayo, John Dillon, later used the embarrassment associated with Devon's recruitment numbers to reinforce his claim that Ireland enthusiastically backed the war up to the spring of 1915. The depth of Ireland's commitment, Dillon contended, was demonstrated in the proportion of recruits from the country's rural districts where the populations of these areas had recruited 'far more freely than in Devonshire or Cornwall.'[78]

In localised recruitment campaigns in counties like Essex, Army recruiters employed the notion that a county should raise its 'fair share' or 'proper quota' of recruits as a recruiting strategy to stimulate pride in the county's contribution to the national cause.[79] If Devon contributed its 'fair share' of recruits for the Army or had raised more than this proportion, the county would have, in the eyes of Devon's local elite, proven its patriotism in a practical way. However, whilst Fortescue had taken a leading role in trying to 'raise Devon's proper quota' of recruits for the military, the county's lacklustre recruitment totals revealed that Devon had not made a proportionate contribution to the national cause.[80] In his public address at Tiverton on 1 December 1914, Fortescue used the perception that Devon had not raised its 'fair share' of recruits to embarrass the county's eligible men who had not come forward. He stressed that in Devon's rural districts there were 5,000 single men and 4,000 married men who had decided against volunteering despite having the opportunity to do so. In light of Devon's disappointing recruiting statistics, Fortescue wanted the audience to understand the consequences of the county's menfolk refusing to volunteer. Since Devon had fallen short of contributing her fair share of recruits in this first call, Fortescue suggested that 'other people's superior patriotism' had to compensate for Devon's deficiencies.[81] The Lord Lieutenant of Norfolk and the third Earl of Leicester, Thomas Coke, expressed similar frustration towards the eligible men of some rural parishes in Norfolk who had chosen not to enlist during the autumn of 1914.[82]

Just as Devon's notable figures interpreted the county's recruitment totals as a reflection of Devon's patriotism, this interpretative framework also applied on a micro level for individual localities in the county. The combined number of men from a specific locality already serving alongside those called up as reservists or who had volunteered after 4 August 1914 indicated that location's loyalty or patriotism. Devon localities with high numbers of men serving in the colours despite their small populations served a vital function in the discourses of patriotism. Fortescue touched upon this perception when he declared that there were parishes in the county that had demonstrated 'true Devonshire patriotism' due to their loyalty to the national cause.[83] Parishes heralded as exemplars of such patriotism included the East Devon parishes of Combpyne and Rousden. Despite the small number of inhabitants in both parishes, they had done better than other similarly sized localities since over 15% of their respective populations were under arms.[84] Alfred Croft, a resident of the west Devon village of Bere Alston, was so proud that his parish had no less than 100 men serving that he wanted to publicise the achievement in a letter published in the *Western Morning News*. Croft claimed that, alongside the 27 men who had recently enlisted, the total number of men already serving from the village was evidence of Bere Alston's 'patriotic spirit', which was 'matched, no doubt, in many another parish in Devon.'[85]

The county's newspapers were also instrumental in publicising the 'patriotic spirit' of these Devon parishes. For instance, the *Brixham Western Guardian* congratulated the south Devon village of Ashprington for its contribution to the military. The fact that 28 men were under arms from such a small populace of 421 people was, according to the tabloid, a 'striking testimony to the patriotism of South Devon', which would set a 'fine example to villages across the county' to follow.[86] Contemporaries hoped that by promoting localities with high numbers of men serving, such as Ashprington and Bere Alston, these locations represented examples of patriotism to emulate in a campaign of patriotic commendation. The ambition of this campaign was to create a sense of competition amongst Devon's localities where parishes would endeavour to reach such heights of patriotism. As a result, this competitive spirit between the parishes would bring these locations up to a good standard and improve Devon's recruitment returns more generally. Yet a survey of the number of Devon men under arms revealed that the figures varied across the county. Two locations that had poor results in this survey were the west Devon parish of Broadwood Kelly and the north Devon village of Milton Damerel. In both localities, under half per cent of their respective populations were in the colours.[87] However, some in Devon did not agree that promoting localities with high levels of recruitment was such a good idea. In a letter to the editor of the *Devon and Exeter Gazette*, writing under the initials of K. B., the author complained that 'far too much importance was made of the number of men from different parishes' in the county.[88] The author explained that, in their view, it was a counter-productive recruiting strategy since men living in localities with such high numbers could conclude that they did not need to enlist: 'The feeling that so many men have gone from "my" parish is wrong, as it makes slackers feel comfortable and think they can stay at home.'[89] Devon's newspapers also publicised localities with poor numbers of men serving as 'unpatriotic' examples and branded these locations in a naming and shaming campaign as 'backward places' or 'black sheep parishes.'[90]

The county's newspapers and figures from Devon's local elite sought to reinforce the dichotomy between patriotic and unpatriotic examples when they championed families with more than one son who had enlisted as exemplars of great patriotism. On 23 November 1914, Fortescue informed the people present at a recruiting meeting in Exeter about a single family from Barnstaple who had sent six brothers to join the colours. Upon hearing the applause from the audience commending this family, he also revealed there were families in the north Devon parishes of Filleigh, Iddlesleigh, and Morchard Bishop who had shown similar fortitude since they, too, had more than one son serving in the military.[91] In turn, the mothers of these families, like Mrs Martha Ainsworth from Loughborough in Leicestershire, who had six sons under arms, were championed publicly.[92] Like the commendation of specific Devon parishes, the publicity of families and mothers with more than one son in the Army or Navy also acted as instances of Devonshire patriotism.[93] When a recruiting party stopped at the Dartmoor village of South Zeal on 20 April 1915, Army recruiter Lieutenant Larden highlighted in his address one local family with six sons serving as 'an excellent example of true patriotism.'[94] The promotion of these families and mothers as 'patriotic' examples was an integral part of the system of voluntary enlistment, intended to shame families or mothers whose sons had not volunteered.[95]

Yet, many mothers in Devon did not welcome the prospect of their menfolk going off to war. For mothers involved in family-run businesses such as farming, the absence of these men would inevitably create problems. In the worst-case scenario, the death of these men could also mean the end of these family-run enterprises. When faced with this threat to their livelihoods, some mothers were matriarchal figures who sought to shelter their sons from Army recruiters or refused to permit their menfolk to volunteer. On 1 September 1914, Edrica de la Pole encountered one such mother and local shopkeeper, Mrs Triggs in the South Devon village of Kingston. Despite de la Pole's attempts to discuss the subject of recruitment with her, Mrs Triggs firmly refused to allow her son to join up.[96] Another mother who objected to de la Pole's efforts to convince her son to join up that day was Mrs Mary Freeman. De la Pole heard later that Ernest Freeman had told his mother about de la Pole's attempt to recruit him. Upon hearing this, Mrs Freeman 'expressed a wish to "see the lady".'[97] Based on Mrs Freeman's request to "see the lady", she probably wanted to discreetly scold de la Pole for trying to persuade her son to enlist and warn her not to interfere with their family's affairs. Moreover, since Ernest was the son of the landlord of a public house in Kingston, Mrs Freeman probably wanted to ensure that Ernest remained at home to help with the family business. Like Mrs Freeman and Mrs Briggs, some Devon mothers resented the efforts of the county's notable figures to recruit their menfolk and regarded them as nosy, intrusive busybodies.

Another Devonian parent who resented the outside interference of those seeking to gain recruits was Richard Miles from the village of Croyde in North Devon. On 9 December 1914, Sergeant H. Williman, the recruiting officer for the Ilfracombe district, visited Miles' cottage. Although Miles claimed that his three eligible sons were not at home, he objected to the prospect of them joining the Army. Aggrieved by Williman's persistence as to when he could see his sons, Miles swore at Williman and told him to leave. However, after departing from Miles' cottage, Williman stood patiently beside his bicycle at the corner of the road. Williman was almost certainly waiting to catch Miles's sons before they returned home so he could try to convince them to enlist in the Army when they were alone and away from their father. However, unlike Mrs Triggs, Miles attempted to protect his sons from being recruited by unconventional means as he came out to confront the recruiting officer armed with a large stick. When Williman tried to dissuade Miles from acting this way, Miles erratically battered his stick against the wall and warned Williman: 'That is how I will serve you, if you ---- well dare to come near my door'.[98] In the heated exchange between the two men, Miles thrashed the ground close to Williman with his stick and repeated his defiant outburst: 'That is how I will serve you or any of the King's ---- officers, who dare to come near my door.'[99] In response, Williman warned Miles that he would report him to the Commanding Officer. Undeterred by this rebuke, Miles proclaimed: 'To ---- with him, too.'[100] Williman issued Miles with a final warning that he should not use such language in the presence of a King's officer. Nevertheless, Miles concluded his offensive tirade when he declared in a tone of defiance: '---- and ---- the King.'[101]

Although Williman's encounter with Miles was an extreme confrontation, there were similar instances where Devonians challenged those seeking to convince military-age men to enlist.[102] In the South Devon seaside town of Dawlish, Army recruiters encountered some ladies who sought to undermine their appeals for recruits with the cutting remark: 'You are sending the young fellows away to have their heads shot off.'[103] However, Army recruiter Captain Cuthbert Bearne, utilised the wording of their snide remark in his retort when he claimed that these men were going to war to prevent these ladies' heads from being blown off.[104] Speakers during a recruiting meeting at the Dartmoor town of Bovey Tracey on 19 September 1914 experienced similar protestations when local resident Albert Call felt compelled to shout '---- them; why don't you go yourself?' whenever the speakers mentioned the Germans.[105] Also attending the meeting was local police Constable Frost, who warned Call to stop these outbursts. Nevertheless, Call continued to shout and interrupt the speakers as the meeting continued. A similar example of a man seeking to disparage Army recruiters occurred at a recruitment event in the village of Brookland in Kent on 23 August.[106] Like Call in Bovey Tracey, labourer Alfred Ovenden belittled the efforts of Army officers trying to convince eligible men to enlist when he told them to 'do the fighting themselves.'[107] Although it was his responsibility as Devon's Lord Lieutenant to garner recruits for the Army and the Territorials, Fortescue recognised that he too could face individuals seeking to undermine his efforts to convince the county's eligible men to enlist. After hearing his appeals for recruits, he acknowledged that some might conclude: 'It was all very well for Lord Fortescue to say "Go out and fight and risk his life. Why doesn't he go himself?"'[108] However, Fortescue had prepared a strategy to counter such direct personal challenges that some individuals could level against him. Whilst he could not enlist due to his age, Fortescue contended that he was doing all he could to help the war effort like many older gentlemen across the county. At the same time, Fortescue addressed the perception that he acted like an armchair patriot, directing Devon's eligible men to volunteer whilst he would never face combat because he was 'safe' from military service. Fortescue stressed that if he were a younger man, he would prefer to go off to war and use a rifle in the trenches than undertake office work and make speeches at home. Indeed, even if he could not serve as an officer, Fortescue declared that he would be content to go as a private soldier if he were younger.[109] Fortescue also wanted to point out that his two sons, Viscount Ebrington and Denzil Fortescue, were serving in the Armed forces: the former with the Royal Scots Greys and the latter in the Royal North Devon Yeomanry, respectively.[110]

Based on their behaviour towards Army recruiters, both Albert Call and Richard Miles were charged with using obscene language. On 29 September 1914 at Newton Abbot Petty Sessions, Call stated that his uncontrollable behaviour during the recruitment event at Bovey Tracey was motivated by his hostility towards the Germans. Since he had only sworn at the Germans, Call claimed that he did not intend to cause any harm. However, the fact that Call had disrupted Army recruiters by shouting 'Why don't you go yourself?' in response to their appeals for recruits indicated that he deliberately sought to challenge and undermine their authority.[111] The chairman of the Petty Sessions, A. J. Murrin, was appalled by Call's conduct. In light of the urgent need for recruits, he concluded that Call's behaviour was 'most unpatriotic and offensive.'[112] Later, on 30 December, the Bench of Braunton Divisional Petty Sessions came to a similar verdict with the conduct of Richard Miles. The Bench fined Miles 10 shillings for using obscene language and expressed the view that his hostility towards Williman was a 'disgrace to any Englishman.'[113] Meanwhile, at Ashford police Court in Kent, Ovenden was, like Miles, fined for his conduct at the recruitment event in Brookland but under the charge of 'obstructing recruiting officers.'[114] However, the Magistrates involved in the case were so appalled by Ovenden's behaviour that they believed fining him was not a proportionate punishment for his offence since they regretted that they could not send him to jail.[115]

Through their coverage of the legal proceedings involving Call and Miles, Devon's newspapers offered commentary on the verdicts of the two men, which included value judgements about the defendants' lack of patriotism. On 1 October 1914, the *Devon and Exeter Gazette* published one such commentary in their coverage of Call's trial. The paper shared Murrin's view that Call's excitable behaviour was not 'patriotic conduct.'[116] The newspaper's commentary went further when it questioned why Call's hatred towards the Germans had not spurred him on to volunteer to fight against them. When the same paper covered Miles's trial, it was also critical of his attitude towards Williman. As an Army representative, it was Williman's 'business ... to obtain recruits', and the way that Miles had treated him was clearly 'unpatriotic' behaviour.[117] The reporting in the local press of Devonians who objected towards recruitment, like Call and Miles, allowed these news outlets to arbitrate upon these responses as instances of patriotic or unpatriotic behaviour, thereby contributing to the discourses of patriotism in the county.

During the autumn of 1914, Army recruiters and members of Devon's local elite attempted to explain why the county had low recruitment totals for the Army. Charles Sandbach Parker, the Unionist candidate for the Barnstaple Division, concluded that recruitment numbers were low in this part of North Devon due to 'a lack of loyalty and patriotism' amongst eligible local men who were not interested in volunteering unless it paid them well.[118] One man who questioned whether there were enough incentives for young unmarried men in North Devon to enlist was John Andrew, the Surveyor of the Roads for Barnstaple RDC. When Andrew raised this question during the Council's meeting on 8 December 1914, the Council's Chairman, George Christopher Davie, replied that there were the 'inducements of patriotism, if nothing else.'[119] However, Andrew contended that he did not see it in those terms. Stunned by Andrew's statement, Davie declared that he was grateful that the rest of England did not share Andrew's views because if there was 'no patriotism we should soon get the Germans over here.'[120] In his defence, Andrew stressed that they could get more eligible men to volunteer if these men were offered better terms and well provided for if they were injured or killed. Nevertheless, fellow Council member Reverend John Dene was outraged by Andrew's remarks and was baffled why Mr Andrew, or any Englishman, should express such reservations about military service. In Dene's opinion, every eligible man should come forward since there were existing provisions for men if they were wounded or killed. However, Dene had misconstrued Andrew's comments as unpatriotic since non-enlisted men could easily take them out of context and use them as excuses against volunteering.[121]

To Edrica de la Pole, the men of Kingston seemed determined to remain at home rather than enlist. She had come to this conclusion after she attempted a recruitment campaign in the South Devon village on 1 September 1914. Despite her best efforts, including the pledge of a five-shilling bounty to every man who joined the Army before 7 September, de la Pole was unsuccessful in persuading the men of Kingston to enlist. In her diary, de la Pole noted that she feared that the only way that these men would undertake military service would be through conscription.[122] The reluctance of many men to enlist from Devon's rural areas, like Kingston, indicates that they were not well informed about the war since local concerns often eclipsed the war's significance.[123] However, de la Pole learned two days after her unsuccessful recruitment drive that the indifference and stubbornness of some men in Kingston towards the war was more profound than she initially encountered. She had heard that some local men from the village had refused to join six others to take turns watching the coastline for any threats. In a tone of despair, de la Pole recorded in her diary that this development was 'just [like] the recruiting difficulty [all] over again.'[124] On 14 September, the *Western Morning News* published a letter from an anonymous author claiming young men in Plymouth were also indifferent towards volunteering. After asking these men why they had not enlisted, the author noted that the most frequent response to this question was that the Army did not want them due to the recent arrival of 250,000 Russian troops in France.[125] These men had capitalised on the farfetched rumour that approximately 10,000 to 250,000 Russian troops had travelled through Britain to the Western Front to support the British and French armies in the autumn of 1914.[126] Indeed, the author was disgusted that these men justified their decision against enlisting based on the illusion of '250,000 phantoms'.[127] As a result of encountering these dismissive men, the concerned author hoped that Plymouth would not hold the record for the number of slackers.

Some contemporaries believed Devon's low recruitment numbers were due to the county's farmers and their sons not coming forward. To Army recruiters, the number of men involved in the county's agricultural sector, including Devon's farmers, their sons and the labourers who worked on their farms, represented a significant source of potential recruits. However, the fact that many men from Devon's rural areas had decided against volunteering fuelled speculation that the county's agriculturalists had not provided their fair share of recruits compared to other communities in the county. Fortescue suggested on 23 November 1914 that whilst there were notable and honourable exceptions, farmers sons from Devon had held back and 'not come forward as freely as the sons of others' in the county.[128] One Army recruiter agreed that not enough farmers' sons had enlisted but also suggested that Devon's farmers had deliberately put difficulties in the way of their men to make it more challenging for them to volunteer.[129] Statements from notable figures and Army recruiters about farmers sons not enlisting prompted speculation in Devon's newspapers as to whether the county's farmers were unpatriotic.[130] The hostility towards Devon's farmers for not contributing their fair share of recruits was evident at a recruitment meeting in the mid Devon town of Cullompton on 2 December. When the Secretary of the Tiverton Farmer's Union, John Lewis, spoke during the proceedings, he faced heckles from the audience that included abrasive taunts and demands to know where the farmers' sons were and why they were not joining up.[131] However, Devon's farmers refuted accusations that they were to blame for Devon's low recruitment returns.[132] One Devon farmer wrote to the *Western Times* complaining against the sweeping assertions printed in the newspapers. These had, in his view, made the county's farming community 'appear to the English nation as being unpatriotic.'[133]

Yet, when faced with prescriptions from public figures that their eligible men should volunteer, Devon's farming families faced a distressing predicament.[134] Like French farming families concerned about how wartime mobilisation would influence their business practices, Devon's agriculturalists worried about the future of their farms with the loss of their men folk.[135] One anxious Devon farmer told his son that he would have to sell the cattle if he decided to join the Army. Although he loved his King and Country, the farmer's son decided not to volunteer if it meant the loss of the herd. Nevertheless, he was determined to help the nation on the farm and worked with his father to sow double the amount of wheat in the fields. As a result, this led to a decrease in the acreage of oats by one-half. Whilst growing more wheat helped domestic food supplies, it was a poor economic decision for their family business. By contrast, if they had kept the same acreage to grow oats, the resulting crop would have yielded a better monetary return. Since the farm had taken this financial hit to grow food for the national interest, the farmer's son proposed in a letter to the editor of the *Devon and Exeter Gazette* that this selfless act demonstrated their patriotism because he asked rhetorically: 'Then, are we not patriotic?.'[136] In the eyes of Devon's farmers, the importance of providing more food for the nation at this critical time contributed to a discourse of patriotism which justified their decision not to enlist. At the same time, this justification also provided them with a convenient means to continue their peacetime occupations and ensure the survival of their farms during the war. However, when considering the urgent need for recruits, Devon's local elite and the county's newspapers remained unconvinced about the merits of such explanations against volunteering.[137] Nevertheless, Devon's agriculturalists were not alone in declaring that they demonstrated their patriotism through the hard work of producing food for the nation. In New Zealand, a farmer from Woodville claimed later in 1917 that he was stirred by 'patriotic motives' to undertake the exhausting but crucial task of growing eight acres of wheat in difficult to farm bush land.[138]

Another explanation for the low number of recruits was that recruitment efforts took longer to organise in Devon than in other counties. Bonnie White suggests that Devon initially lacked dedicated and centralised recruiting agencies to coordinate a recruitment campaign effectively. Unlike Devon, both Somerset and Cornwall had established Parliamentary Joint Recruiting Committees for their respective counties shortly after the outbreak of war.[139] A Parliamentary Recruiting Committee (PRC) for Devon and recruiting committees that covered divisions across the county were eventually established in late November and early December 1914, respectively, with Earl Fortescue acting as the Committee's President.[140] The sluggishness towards organising recruitment efforts was also evident in the west Devon town of Okehampton. On 25 November, the recruiting officer for north Devon, Lieutenant Colonel Alexander, asked Okehampton's Borough Council why they had yet to form a Civilian Recruiting Committee. Although he had hoped that the Council would have taken the initiative to set one up, Alexander had heard that they were not inclined to do so since they had 'let the matter drop.'[141] However, in their reply, the Council members attempted to clarify why the Council had decided to pass on establishing a recruiting committee. They claimed that 'no useful purpose would be served by forming a [Civilian Recruiting] Committee' since the town's political associations were already active in local recruitment efforts.[142] Nonetheless, upon reading their letter and from what he had heard previously, Alexander may have concluded that the Council had used the activities of Okehampton's political organisations as a convenient excuse to justify not having to undertake recruiting work themselves. By contrast, Alexander's appeal achieved greater success with the town council of South Molton since they did not show such obstinance against establishing a recruiting committee, agreeing to form one on 9 November.[143]

Yet, like Okehampton Borough Council, the parish council of the east Devon coastal village of Beer employed a similar defence against setting up a recruiting committee in 1915. The Council members declared they did not believe civilians should press men to join the Army since the time had come for conscription and the pay and allowances were insufficient. Based on these arguments, they concluded there was no need for a Committee since Beer had 'done as much as, or more, than it could be expected to.'[144] However, local politics may have influenced the Council's decision. The Secretary of the Honiton Division Joint PRC, William Rising Bray, believed that the reason for the Council's refusal to form a committee was to avoid potential conflict between council members since 'certain officials at Beer had sons of military age not serving, and when the leaders refused the others backed out.'[145] Army recruiters experienced similar difficulties with local government bodies in Ireland after the Central Council for the Organisation of Recruitment in Ireland appealed for cooperation to promote recruitment in their respective administrative areas. Niamh Gallagher has shown that the situation on the ground was incredibly complicated because, whilst some local councils disregarded the request entirely, other bodies were divided on how to respond.[146]

Yet Lieutenant Colonel Alexander's letter from 25 November 1914 revealed another issue hampering recruitment in Okehampton. Sergeant Newbury, a local Army recruiter, had encountered difficulties putting up recruitment posters in the town. In some instances, the prints that Newbury had affixed 'had been torn down.'[147] Second Lieutenant T. R. H. Smyth of the 3rd East Yorkshire Regiment had a similar experience in May 1915. Smyth had attached posters to doors, windows and farmers' gates in the East Yorkshire village of Holme-on-Spalding-Moor to promote a forthcoming fourteen-day recruitment march. However, like Newbury had experienced in Okehampton, Smyth discovered that many of his recruitment posters had been taken down.[148] Army recruiters encountered the same phenomena in County Tipperary, Ireland, but when residents took down recruitment posters or vandalised them, local authorities considered that these incidents represented anti-recruitment activities. Indeed, the local police arrested and charged individuals they caught defacing or removing these posters.[149] Although the removal of recruitment posters in Devon and Yorkshire can prompt speculation about whether these actions signify anti-recruitment activity or opposition to the war, there are potentially other reasons why local residents took down or vandalised these prints. In Holme-on-Spalding-Moor, Smyth concluded that the taking down of recruitment posters did not indicate anti-war sentiment in the area. Instead, he believed that the local populace removed these posters because they were annoyed by them.[150] Keith Grieves suggests that the removal of recruitment posters in rural areas during the early stages of the war was a 'sign of [the] otherness of the English countryside.'[151] For rural communities, these posters were deemed unsightly and unsuitable for a country environment. The sight of them affixed to surfaces such as trees or farmers' gates may have been off-putting and irritated local inhabitants.[152] These individuals may have felt justified in taking these posters down if Army recruiters had 'imposed' or fixed these 'inappropriate' prints onto private property without asking for permission to do so from local landowners. Although Okehampton was one of Devon's urban areas, it is plausible that some inhabitants were so irritated by the sight of these recruitment posters that they decided to remove them. In the Warwickshire town of Atherstone, local resident Mary Ellen Briggs felt compelled to take down a recruitment poster on 31 August 1914. Although a local man had permission to put up the print appealing for recruits on a wall in Coleshill Road, Briggs firmly objected to seeing it displayed opposite her breakfast-room window. Armed with a knife, flannel and a bucket of water, she took matters into her own hands and stripped the recruitment poster off the wall. On 29 September, the local magistrates summoned Briggs to appear before Atherstone police Court for pulling down a public notice. Briggs explained that she had removed the recruitment poster because it was, in her view, 'the most unsightly poster in Atherstone.'[153] However, the Chairman believed that she had behaved very foolishly and had committed 'a most unpatriotic act.'[154] In response, Briggs argued that her loyalty was not in doubt, claiming she was as loyal as anyone. The Chairman disagreed and replied that removing the recruitment poster demonstrated otherwise.[155]

Another factor contributing to the difficulties Army recruiters experienced in Devon was that it was a traditional recruiting ground for the Royal Navy. Indeed, when canvassing for potential recruits, Army recruiters faced significant competition from the recruitment campaigns of the Navy and Royal Marines.[156] This tension between rival recruitment efforts was also evident in Cornwall, where local newspapers reported that many eligible men had not answered the call to enlist in the Army but instead yearned to join the Navy.[157] For fishermen in Devon and Cornwall, joining the Navy or Naval Reserve was the more sensible option in light of their maritime experience. The drive of the young fishermen of Brixham to join the Navy was apparent to a correspondent for the *Western Times*, who reported on 19 November 1914 that these men responded with 'exceptional fervour' to the recruiting drive for the Royal Naval Reserve.[158] Since Devon possessed a strong maritime tradition, some contemporaries concluded that this explained why the county had low recruitment returns for the Army because Devon's eligible men had joined the Navy rather than the Army.[159] The *North Devon Herald* later summed up this belief when it described how 'Devonshire had sent a large proportion of her hardy sons to uphold the flag of England on the seas.'[160] One London newspaper criticised insinuations of 'disappointing results' for Army recruitment in Devon and Cornwall as 'outrageously unjust' because these two 'patriotic old counties' contributed more men to the Navy than 'all the other counties of England combined.'[161] However, Earl Fortescue disagreed with this statement's accuracy and felt compelled to address it in his speech at a recruitment meeting in Tavistock on 4 December. Whilst he wished the newspaper's claim was true, Fortescue argued that it distorted the facts. Moreover, he suggested that the declaration was merely an excuse for both counties not achieving better results for the Army.[162] Although the newspapers did not publish the number of men that volunteered for the Royal Navy, Fortescue did keep a record of approximate recruitment figures in Devon for the Navy, Regulars, and Territorials. From 4 August to 7 November 1914, around 550 men had joined the Royal Navy in the county.[163] By 4 March 1915, this figure increased to approximately 1,122 men and 133 boys who had joined the Royal Navy, Royal Marines, and Naval Reserves.[164] In comparison, Fortescue calculated that 8,827 men had enlisted into the Regular Army and 9,072 men had joined the Territorials in Devon by April 1915.[165] However, Fortescue's figures account for the number of men who signed up at recruiting offices in Devon for the various branches of the Military rather than record where these men had come from. Presumably, Devon's menfolk who decided to volunteer went to their nearest recruiting office in the county. At the same time, men who lived in districts that bordered Devon from neighbouring counties could travel to Devon's recruiting offices, such as men from east Cornwall travelling to Devonport to sign up for the Royal Navy. Nevertheless, it is clear from Fortescue's figures that Naval recruitment efforts were not the primary reason why Devon's recruitment totals for the Army were low.

The fact that the county had lacklustre recruitment results led some contemporaries to lament that the eligible men of Devon were not the true descendants of Devonshire's patriots of the past.[166] Reverend Dr John T. Trelawny-Ross, a resident of Ham near Devonport, believed that the county's menfolk who decided against volunteering had shunned their noble Devonian heritage. Indeed, he questioned in bewilderment whether the response from these men towards recruitment efforts was 'worthy of "Glorious Devon" and her far-flung role of history-making and empire-building heroes?'[167] By evoking the county's prestigious past in their critiques, notable figures like Trelawny-Ross used Devon's history as a yardstick to measure the patriotism, or lack thereof, of the county's eligible men. For example, Trelawny-Ross highlighted the glorious patriotic response of Devon's men in 1803 to the nation's requirements and compared this to the lacklustre one from their descendants in 1914. This stark contrast between the responses of these two generations led him to conclude that the men of Devon in 1914 had fallen far from the standards of patriotism set by their forefathers in 1803.[168]

Devon's newspapers also employed the county's past in their criticisms against eligible men who avoided military service. On 27 November 1914, the editor of the *Devon and Exeter Gazette* complained that a large number of single men in the legendary 'Shire of the Sea Kings' had failed to grasp their traditional responsibilities as Devonian men to defend Britain. The newspaper enquired whether these men wanted the shameful message proclaimed across the nation and throughout the British Empire that Devon was 'not doing her part' to provide recruits for the Army.[169] Due to this predicament, the newspaper printed a stern warning to Devon's slackers that they needed to come forward to avoid dishonour and preserve the county's grand traditions of the past.[170] Fortescue echoed these comments when he warned the county's menfolk that the eyes of history were upon them at this crucial moment. It would be an everlasting reprimand to them, if Devonshire was to be 'found low on the list among those who have made contributions to the needs of their nation' in the history of the war.[171]

Alongside these critiques from local notables and newspaper columnists, other contemporaries complained about the eligible men who decided against volunteering in letters published in Devon's newspapers. One such complainer submitted letters to the *Brixham Western Guardian* under the pen name of 'Buller's Bull Dog', labelling the men of 'enlistment age' who ought to come forward but had not done so as 'stay-at-homes.'[172] These 'stay-at-homes' had not yet realised that singing patriotic songs and waving or wearing flags were only token gestures that would 'not help Britain and the Empire to come out of this gigantic struggle with honour and security for generations to come.'[173] Based on what he saw of these self-absorbed 'knuts' of Brixham, 'Buller's Bull Dog' argued that these men should not delude themselves in thinking that these ostentatious acts demonstrated their patriotism. As eligible men engaging in gestures that were inadequate substitutes for military service, the author believed that they 'ought to wear white feathers in their buttonholes instead of those dainty little patriotic buttons.'[174] Letters written under pseudonyms, like those of 'Buller's Bull Dog', acted as denunciations against young eligible men unaware that volunteering was their patriotic duty. In wartime Austria-Hungary, citizens utilised denunciations to demonstrate their patriotism and define it in opposition to the unpatriotic behaviour of their neighbours.[175] Tamara Scheer suggests that the pen names that authors used for their denunciation letters are inherently worthy of consideration. The fact that these nameless individuals chose to sign their letters submitted to the Habsburg War Office under aliases such as 'Patriot' showed they volunteered their ongoing support to detect forms of behaviour deemed 'subversive' and try to become official informants.[176] In the case of the letters submitted by 'Buller's Bull Dog' to the *Brixham Western Guardian*, the fact that the author selected a locally distinct pen name rather than use a typical pseudonym like 'Patriot' served a significant purpose. By signing these letters 'Buller's Bull Dog', the author believed that the newspaper's local readership would recognise that this referred to the canine mascot for the Battalion that bore Buller's name. Using this military-related alias allowed the authors to strengthen their patriotic credentials and reinforce the local authenticity of their rebukes against the unpatriotic conduct of the county's 'eligibles.'[177] Although contemporaries submitted anonymous letters to the local press rather than to an institution monitoring public opinion, these messages functioned as a way in which Devonians attempted to superintend the patriotism of eligible men. Even Earl Fortescue received one such letter from an anonymous Tiverton resident in 1915. The nameless author wanted to inform Devon's Lord Lieutenant about several 'slackers' present in the mid-Devon village of Sampford Peverell who had refused to enlist and blithely spent their time since the beginning of the war enjoying leisure pursuits.[178]

Unlike 'Buller's Bull Dog', John Stocker, an Alderman and Justice of the Peace (JP), was prepared to put his name to a letter denouncing the eligible men in Exeter who remained at home. Published in the *Devon and Exeter Gazette*, Stocker concluded that these men did not possess 'sufficient patriotism to enlist.'[179] Rather than volunteer, these Exonian men went to concerts where they cheered and sang along to patriotic songs such as 'God Save the King', 'Britons Never shall be Slaves,' and 'Rule Britannia'. Stocker believed that eligible men should not engage in these distractions since they were a false substitute for military service. Like 'Buller's Bulldog', he had seen through these hollow gestures where these men merely paid lip service to the war rather than participate in their true patriotic duty. For eligible men who engaged in such cheerleading from the sidelines, Stocker pessimistically claimed that these acts constituted the point where the patriotism of these men ended.[180] The vicar of Lynton parish church, Reverend T. N. Munford, also criticised those who remained at home rather than enlist. In his sermon on patriotism, Munford asserted there could be no equivocation at this crucial moment since the 'true patriots were those who volunteered for service, and not those who enthusiastically cheered them.'[181] Another JP, J. C. Chapman, expressed a similar complaint about Devon's eligible men in the south Devon seaside town of Torquay in December 1914. Whilst these men had no responsibilities at home to stop them from volunteering, it appeared to Chapman that they had 'lost their patriotism in their devotion either to laziness or football.'[182] Letters from Devonian men above military age, like those from Stocker and Chapman, were a form of armchair criticism against the county's eligible men, complaining that they were devoid of patriotism. One anonymous writer blamed football rather than laziness for the loss of patriotism amongst many of the county's eligible men in a letter printed in the *Western Times* on 27 November. Writing under the pen name of 'An Englishman', the writer complained that football matches were such a distraction for these men, it was not surprising to him that Earl Fortescue complained about the lack of interest in recruitment in Devon: 'Full of enthusiasm for a couple of hours' football pleasure: a despondent countenance at the appeal for a patriotic spirit.'[183] Trelawny-Ross came to a similar judgement about the priorities of eligible men since they took a greater interest in football than the nation's fate.[184]

After the declaration of war, national and local newspapers also criticised football matches since they were deemed an unpatriotic activity that hindered Army recruitment. When faced with hostility and pressure from local patriotic individuals, regional football clubs in rural Australia closed the football competition in August 1915.[185] By contrast, Exeter City Football Club resisted similar calls because the Club adhered to the rules of the Football Association. However, Exeter City's decision to continue to play football into the rest of the season was controversial. In a letter published in the *Devon and Exeter Gazette*, Sidmouth resident F. T. Colclough was bewildered that the city's inhabitants would allow football to be played in wartime. In his view, the decision had shamed Exeter's 'loyal and faithful' reputation. Moreover, Colclough lamented that it was a shame that some young men from the city could not be sent to Canada or any of the colonies to reassess their priorities and learn what 'true loyalty and patriotism mean.'[186] Like other football clubs in Britain during the autumn and winter of 1914, figures from Exeter City were engaged 'in a public relations battle with their detractors.'[187] The Club's Secretary, Sidney Thomas, attempted to defend the Club's decision in a letter published in the *Devon and Exeter Gazette* on 4 September 1914. Although football games attracted large crowds that included military age men, Thomas stressed that cancelling football as a wartime measure would not spur these men to enlist. However, in an addendum to the letter, the newspaper's editor clarified that Thomas's justification did not weaken the arguments against football from the standpoints of patriotism and decency.[188] Sir Roper Lethbridge, a past president of the Devonshire Association and the former Conservative MP for Kensington North, was also unconvinced by Thomas's defence. In a letter submitted to the *Devon and Exeter Gazette*, Lethbridge criticised the stance taken by Exeter City's secretary and disparaged the men who continued to play football as unpatriotic since they belonged to 'white feather teams.'[189] On 3 September, the newspaper published an item against Exeter City that evoked the same unpatriotic imagery associated with the white feather. However, unlike Lethbridge's letter, the columnist proposed a solution to shame the military age men who would rather watch football games than enlist. Under the pen name of 'onlooker', the columnist advocated that a group of ladies be stationed outside St James Park football ground in Exeter and bestow a 'white feather to each of the unpatriotic idlers' when the next match occurred.[190]

Amidst the public backlash against football matches, the *Devon and Exeter Gazette* used football to attempt to control the definition of what constituted patriotism for the county's military-age men. On the day of a momentous football match between Exeter City and West Ham at St James Park (5 September 1914), the paper published a cartoon depicting two figures: the first was an Exeter City football player holding a leather football, and the second was Lady Britannia wearing a band decorated with the word 'Patriotism.'[191] The football player is about to resume playing the game but he is stopped by Lady Britannia. As they exchange glances, she stares back at him disapprovingly. Lady Britannia holds onto the football player with her left hand while her right hand presents him with a rifle. Titled 'Rifle or Football – Which?' (Figure 6), the illustration conveyed a stark visual message that Lady Britannia did not view football as a patriotic activity in this time of war. Like the *Devon and Exeter Gazette* illustration, the popular journal *Punch* published a poster on 21 October that employed a similar anti-football message. The 'Greater Game' poster contains an authority figure, Mr Punch, looking harshly towards a Professional Association football player holding a football in his hand during a football match. Before he can resume playing, Punch reprimands the footballer for his selfish decision to earn money on the football field when he could gain his honour on the battlefield.[192] However, unlike the 'Greater Game' poster, the 'Rifle or Football – Which?' newspaper illustration presented a powerful message about patriotism for eligible men who blithely participated in this peacetime pursuit. By thrusting a gun towards the footballer, Lady Britannia challenged the man of military age and directed him to accept the right patriotic course of action to enlist. Lady Britannia's gesture also carried greater authority since she was the nation's indisputable guardian wearing the ribbon of patriotism.[193] Therefore, Lady Britannia in this cartoon was depicted as an arbiter of patriotism. Alongside the illustration's representation of patriotism, the newspaper attempted to further shape and control the definition of patriotism through the layout of items presented on the page. Below the cartoon on page 4 of that edition of the *Devon and Exeter Gazette* was a photograph of recently enlisted men, including five from the newspaper's staff, with the caption: 'For King and Country'.[194] Hence, through this contrast of items, eligible men across Devon, whether footballers or not, should fulfil their patriotic duty to defend the nation by joining the colours.

A project that sought to motivate the men of Exeter to enlist was a special Battalion of the Devonshire Regiment that consisted solely of men from the city. During early December 1914, the recently inaugurated Mayor of Exeter, James George Owen, attempted to stimulate the martial spirit of Exeter and induce men aged between 18 and 36 to volunteer in the unit, provisionally named Exeter's Own. The *Devon and Exeter Gazette* hoped that this special military company would stir the city's young men who had not yet 'realised their duty to King and Country' to enlist and give them the opportunity to serve alongside local friends.[195] Earl Fortescue also had high hopes for Exeter's Own, believing that it would succeed like the recently formed Buller's Own Battalion. Moreover, he was confident that Exeter's Own would act as a model for other localities across Devon to raise individual companies or units of local men.[196] However, the reality of trying to get men from the city to join up to serve in Exeter's Own dashed these grand aspirations. In the words of a *Devon and Exeter Gazette* journalist, the responses from the citizens of Exeter were 'miserable in the extreme.'[197] At the final recruiting event for Exeter's Own on 12 December, Owen revealed the inadequate results of the week's campaign. Whilst they had intended to recruit 250 men from the city for Exeter's Own (the 11th Battalion of the Devonshire Regiment), only eight men had volunteered. After hearing the embarrassing result, one audience member shouted the damning accusation of Shame. Upon hearing this, Owen agreed that it was a shame.

Owen claimed that if Exeter had successfully raised a company of 250 men, the city would have confidently presented its loyalty and patriotism 'in [a] real and practical manner.'[198] However, the shockingly low number of recruits for Exeter's Own had instead revealed a lack of patriotism amongst the city's young men. The fact that hundreds of eligible men remained in Exeter led a *Western Times* correspondent to lose his patience with these men and the reasons they may have used to justify their decision against volunteering. In light of the humiliating result for Exeter's Own, he believed that the ties and responsibilities of these men at home were insufficient excuses 'for holding back.'[199] Based on their reluctance to serve, the correspondent even questioned whether the city's menfolk possessed the characteristic pluck and grit of 'Devon's sons.'[200] The *Devon and Exeter Gazette* was equally disparaging of these men when the paper claimed that the cowardly men of Exeter had shunned their loyalty to Devon's noble traditions and failed to uphold the city's loyal and faithful reputation.[201]

In his address, Owen referred to a recent incident that shocked him and demonstrated the complete disregard towards military service felt by some of the city's menfolk.[202] On the evening of 21 November, two men of military age stood outside the offices of Owen's Exeter based newspaper, the *Express and Echo*. After reading a recruiting notice in the office window, one of the men remarked to his companion with a contemptuous laugh: 'Let the b…ers want'.[203] A columnist for another of Owen's newspapers, the *Western Times*, was so appalled by the man's 'unpatriotic' behaviour that he had shown himself to be 'no Devon.'[204] Another correspondent for the same paper went further in his criticism in that any man in the county who had the opportunity to enlist but preferred to stay at home was 'no true Devon.'[205] Following this line of argument as put forward by these newspaper writers, the county's men needed to stay true to their Devonian roots. By volunteering, these men would prove that they were a 'true' Devonian man or man of Devon.

Later in December 1914, the *Western Times* published a letter from an Exeter sailor who was outraged that only a handful of men had volunteered for Exeter's Own. The fact that hundreds of eligible men remained in the city, participating in carefree leisure pursuits, such as going out with girls and watching football matches, pained him deeply. He advocated that Exonians take drastic measures to make these menfolk reconsider their priorities. Rather than dispense white feathers to these men to indicate their cowardice, the people of Exeter should follow the example of the young ladies of Newcastle and '"cut" every young fellow who will not join up.'[206] An editorial in the *Devon and Exeter Gazette* utilised the imagery of the white feather to criticise the men of Exeter who declined the opportunity to undertake military service. Since these Exonian men would not fulfil their duty voluntarily, they preferred the 'feather bed of the craven to the hero's reward of the battlefield.'[207]

Charities in Devon

Following the declaration of war, the British population sought to support the war effort through war-related philanthropy.[208] In Devon, figures from the county's civil society successfully marshalled Devonians to support the war effort through charitable groups and philanthropic activities.[209] A charity that achieved significant success in Devon during the war was the Devonshire Patriotic Fund or Devon Patriotic Fund (DPF). Created under the initiative of Earl Fortescue on 7 August 1914, the DPF sought to provide relief and assistance to the 'wives, families and other dependent relatives of Sailors and Soldiers (Regulars and Territorials) belonging to the County, and to aid in the care of their sick and wounded.'[210] A reason to explain the DPF's success was that the charity directly supported the families of the county's soldiers, sailors and reservists.[211] Tammy Proctor has suggested that local charitable groups created a 'nexus of activity for the war effort that tied civilian volunteers imaginatively to the war itself.'[212] The DPF was one such charity that allowed the people of Devon to demonstrate their commitment to the war. Another reason why the DPF enjoyed such success in Devon was that it provided Devonians who were outside the requirements of military service with a valuable opportunity to present their patriotism. One example of this were donations to the DPF from the villagers of Bere Alston who had raised over £100.[213] Amongst like-minded non-combatants, fundraising and relief work also helped to reinforce a sense of community identity on the British home front. Alongside the efforts of women and men unable to serve in the military, children could also support wartime charities by promoting their activities and acting as fund-raisers.[214] Accordingly, humanitarian politics with the notion of 'moral' citizenship 'based upon voluntary action was now elevated to the level of national politics and equated with patriotic service.'[215] Patriotic fund societies were also established further afield.[216] In Australia, Aboriginal women supported the war effort by donating their handmade crafts to raise funds for the Patriotic Fund. Canadian indigenous women employed similar strategies to raise money to support the war effort through their own Patriotic and Red Cross Societies.[217]

For women across the combatant countries, involvement with war-related philanthropy, whether through fundraising or giving handmade goods, was an appropriate means to demonstrate their commitment to the war and a symbolic way to claim citizenship in the wartime community. The recognition of the unique contribution that women could make to the war through charitable efforts was particularly evident with knitting since it was an inclusive activity.[218] French women and girls undertook knitting since it was recognised as an 'act of patriotic sacrifice.'[219] Knitting was also profoundly significant for women across the United Kingdom since the activity of knitting demonstrated a woman's solidarity with the 'nation and their willingness to participate in the war effort.'[220] After a request from Lord Kitchener in the autumn of 1914, Queen Mary launched an appeal to supply 300,000 pairs of socks and 300,000 (knitted or woollen) belts for men in the armed forces by the beginning of November 1914.[221] In Devon, Lady Fortescue submitted a request to Devon's newspapers to publish a letter to help promote Queen Mary's appeal across the county. In her letter, she expressed her hope that the women of Devonshire would come forward and knit garments. Simultaneously, men could also play a part in this enterprise since they could donate money to help pay for the wool used for these knitted garments.[222] To further motivate these readers to help with this initiative, Lady Fortescue asked them to think of the county's menfolk serving in the Devonshire Regiment along with those Devonian men serving in other regiments. Indeed, many women in the county crafted these items as poignant gifts for their loved ones serving as combatants overseas. Originally, Lady Fortescue hoped that the people of Devon could contribute at least 3,000 socks and belts. However, the response from the county's population went well beyond Lady Fortescue's original estimate since she received 5,000 pairs of socks and 1500 body belts in just six weeks.[223] After deducting the poorly made socks, she received 2,341 pairs of socks, 1,070 belts, and a donation of £20. For Lady Fortescue, this was a very satisfactory result. In her letter to the *Western Times* on 24 November 1914, she wanted to relay how pleased Queen Mary was with 'the generous help she has received from Devon.'[224]

Alongside home-made comforts, like knitted clothing, the women of Devon also presented more unusual gifts for the war effort. On 3 November 1914, the *Western Times* printed a letter from a Devonian sailor serving on HMS *Devonshire*. In his letter, the sailor wanted to relay to the newspaper's readership that the 'Women of Devonshire' had presented them with a silver drum.[225] According to the sailor, the drum was now part of daily routines on the ship where it was 'used to beat to quarters, the drummer parading round the decks, beating the roll, whenever the men are required at their stations for action.'[226] However, the men serving on board HMS *Devonshire* also decided to add their own character to this gift. The sailors named the item 'Drake's Drum', evoking the legend from county folklore. Just as Drake's Drum functioned as a mythic rallying point for Devon's men to come forward, this new drum from the women of Devon also served as a symbolic connection for these men with their home county.

Conclusion

When the Territorials of the Devonshire Regiment marched off to war on 4 August, the crowds of Exeter sought to give them a good send-off. After witnessing such demonstrations of support and patriotism from the city's residents, newspaper columnists and figures from Devon's local elite believed these scenes were proportionate to the day's events and in keeping with their patriotic sensibilities. Through declarations of county pride such as 'Good Old Devon' and 'Up with the cream and down with the sausage', the people of Exeter sought to reassure the departing soldiers of the Devonshire Regiment that the men of Devon would prevail against the forces of Imperial Germany and uphold the county's patriotic traditions. However, civic figures from Devon did not feel the same sense of pride when it came to the initial results of voluntary recruitment efforts in the county. Although members of Devon's civil society outside the requirements of military service sought to direct Devon's eligible men to undertake their duty and broadcast prescriptions that they should join up, many eligible men were reluctant to volunteer. Frustrated and disappointed by Devon's poor recruitment returns, Devon's notable figures complained about the county's military-age men who remained at home and their lack of patriotism. Whilst some women in Devon presented white feathers to young men still in civilian clothes, other figures sought to superintend the patriotism of eligible men in scalding letters printed in the county's newspapers. The resulting armchair critiques and denunciations reveal how the county's residents resented the patriotic failings of the current generation of Devonian men. However, for many eligible men in the county, local priorities such as the survival of family businesses overruled many appeals to enlist. Although Buller's Own achieved great success, symbolising the idealism and high hopes of the county's local elite, the attempt to replicate its success with a military unit for the city of Exeter proved disastrous. Compared to the disappointing experiences of voluntary recruitment in Devon, war-related philanthropy enjoyed much greater success as a form of wartime mobilisation in the county. Charities like the DPF found significant popularity in the county since they resonated with the humanitarian sensibilities of Devon's population. Through knitting items, financial donations and other charitable activities, individuals in the county outside the requirements of military service presented their humanitarian patriotism, fulfilled their wartime obligations and claimed moral citizenship in the wartime community on the Home Front.

Chapter 3

The Totalisation of the Conflict? 1915

During the evening of 19 January 1915, German Zeppelins crossed the North Sea and attacked the Norfolk towns of Great Yarmouth and Kings Lynn. The bombs that these Zeppelins dropped on the two towns caused devastation and inflicted civilian casualties.[1] Like the earlier bombardment of Scarborough and Whitby by the German Navy in December 1914, contemporary observers reacted with shock and outrage to the news that German Zeppelins had attacked British non-combatant populations. Indeed, Susan R. Grayzel suggests that civilians in southern England found it challenging to understand the meaning of these Zeppelin raids.[2] One citizen in Devon who struggled to come to terms with the purpose of these attacks was Plymouth preacher James Thomas Rogers. Writing in his journal, Rogers believed that the Zeppelin raids could be 'described as fiendish murder' because these attacks had 'no effect upon the operations of the war.'[3]

Whilst Rogers noted that the German Navy had not yet launched an attack against the British mainland as far west as Devon, Earl Fortescue believed that further raids were possible. At a recruitment meeting in the South Devon seaside town of Paignton on 6 January 1915, Fortescue stressed that Devon's seaside towns were also potentially exposed to the threat of naval bombardment. In Fortescue's view, the German Navy would 'no more hesitate to bombard Torquay or Paignton than they did Whitby and Scarborough if they thought they could do so without running too much risk.'[4] There were military-age men in Devon who realised after the assaults on Whitby and Scarborough that the county's seaside towns were equally susceptible to attack from the German Navy. One man who had this realisation was Torquay resident Norman D. Cliff. Since he believed the German Navy could attack the South Devon seaside town, Cliff felt compelled to enlist in January 1915 to defend his home 'in the only way that seemed possible.'[5] However, many military-age men in Devon did not share Cliff's motivation to enlist.

For members of the county's local elite, the indifference of Devon's men towards the prospect of undertaking military service was embarrassing and extremely regrettable. The reluctance of these men reinforced the view held by many in the county that the current generation of Devonian men lacked the sense of duty and innate patriotism of Devon's legendary men of action. Although the county's contribution to the Army in 1914 had fallen short of what Devon's local elite had expected, these notable figures did not give up trying to convince the county's military-age men to volunteer. During 1915, Devon's local elite participated in a new and more coordinated recruitment campaign that they hoped would bring the county's recruitment returns to a better standard.

The Route Marches and attempts to reinvigorate recruitment

To increase the supply of Army recruits from Devon, the county's PRC organised a series of touring recruitment rallies in coordination with the Military Authorities. Described by contemporaries as route marches or recruitment marches, these touring recruitment campaigns travelled across specific areas of Devon with a detachment of the Devonshire Regiment, accompanied by bandsmen and recruiting sergeants. Each route march would advance along a designated route in a district during a week. During their scheduled timetable, the military procession would stop and pass at specific towns, villages, and hamlets on the journey to their final destination.[6] These timetables also included open-air recruitment meetings organised at the various locations where the route march would stop. To raise awareness of these recruitment tours, Devon's PRC promoted the route marches with posters and arranged for the county's newspapers to publicise the schedules of these events.[7] Notables from Devon's civil society also supported the route marches.[8] This support ranged from financial contributions with private subscriptions sponsoring the events to material assistance where individuals loaned their char-a-banc cars to the event for transport purposes.[9]

The people involved in the route marches set out with the ambition these events would win over Devon's eligible men.[10] Their determination was apparent in how the newspapers covered these touring recruitment events as a form of outreach. In their coverage of the route marches in both

Devon and Cornwall, the *Western Morning News* presented these events as a travelling religious movement: a crusade for more recruits. In Cornwall, one of the newspaper's correspondents claimed that these participants had eagerly taken up their task, akin to the spirit of the old Crusaders: 'Convinced of the unassailable justice of their cause, they are going forth to impart their faith and zeal to their fellows.'[11] The same tabloid also characterised those involved in the route marches that travelled Devon's districts as Devonshire's own 'khaki crusaders.'[12] These 'khaki crusaders' included parliamentarians (both from Devon's constituencies and further afield) and dignitaries from the county's civil society who sought to rouse the patriotism of Devon's reluctant men and convert them into willing recruits.[13] The *Teignmouth Post and Gazette* summarised the patriotic ambition of the route marches in that these events would 'fan into flame that spirit of patriotism which exists – although in many cases latent – in every true Britisher, and they will, indeed, realise that their King and country need them.'[14] Devon's civic figures and Army recruiters attempted to stimulate this spirit of patriotism through their speeches and addresses to convince men of military age to enlist. An example of this was when Lieutenant Macmillan spoke at an open-air recruiting meeting in the south Devon village of Stokeinteignhead on 2 September 1915. Although the local eligible men were absent from the event, he sought to inspire their patriotism and guide them toward the right patriotic course of action. He proposed that these missing men still had the chance to redeem themselves by presenting 'their patriotism in the correct way' by volunteering.[15]

Another fundamental way that Army recruiters and notables from Devon's civil society attempted to awaken the patriotic spirit of eligible men on the route marches was through the presence of the soldiers from the Devonshire Regiment. They hoped seeing these troops from the county's Regiment on public display in their uniform would have a motivating effect. These soldiers would act as male role models, inspiring Devon's non-enlisted men to volunteer. The *Eastern Morning News* expressed a similar hope for the route marches that passed through the city of Kingston-Upon-Hull in the East Riding of Yorkshire. The paper hoped that the sight of recently enlisted soldiers would practically demonstrate the benefits of Army training to non-enlisted local men and inspire them to volunteer.[16] On 29 January 1915, the *Devon and Exeter Gazette* reported that the visiting soldiers proved to be effective recruiters on Devon's route marches.[17] As men recently returned from fighting at the front, their appeals encouraging other military-age men to enlist would hold greater authenticity since they were already serving in the Army rather than men unable to undertake military service.[18] Therefore, this connection between military-age men would hopefully help to win over the county's men who had not yet enlisted. Devon's local elite and Army recruiters also referred to the Devonshire regiment in their addresses to inspire the county's eligible men to join up in order to serve in the county's regiment: Devon men for the Devon Regiment.[19] When a recruiting march stopped at Ilfracombe on 1 June (Figure 7), William Henry Andrew, the Chairman of the North Devon town's UDC, urged the young men of the seaside town to 'do their duty to King and Country, and to honour the Devon Regiment as it deserved.'[20]

At the south Devon village of Shaldon on 2 September 1915, Lieutenant Macmillan mentioned the Devonshire Regiment in his appeal to encourage the county's eligible men to enlist. However, Macmillan used the Regiment to try to get these local men to think not in terms of self-interest but along the lines of fellowship amongst Devonians. Even if the local young men possessed 'no patriotism', Macmillan argued that these men should still 'volunteer out of consideration to the men of their own county regiment.'[21] Devon's local elite also framed their appeals using the theme of local solidarity, presenting the Devonshire Regiment as an emblem of Devon's identity and heralding the Regiment's soldiers as exemplars of Devonian masculinity. These figures emphasised that Devon men should fill the ranks of the 'Devons' to ensure that the county's Regiment maintained its Devonian character. Thus, they stressed that Devonian men should enlist to uphold the fair name of Devonshire and take up their rightful place in the county's Regiment.[22]

Crediton author Edith Dart felt such a sense of pride in the county's regiment that she crafted a glowing tribute to the military unit in her poem *The Devons*. Through the courageous actions of the men serving in the Devonshire regiment, Devon's sons had upheld 'our dear land's name.'[23] The county's men serving in Buller's Own were also praised in a poem published in the *Devon and Exeter Gazette*. On the battlefield, the poem asserted, the brave lads of Buller's Own had charged through the hazardous 'hell fire' zone for the 'Glory of Devon'.[24] Alongside poems praising local military units, the county's newspapers also published poems encouraging local men to volunteer by championing local identities. One poem that attempted to do this was Dudley Clark's poem *For Dartymoor*. It proclaimed that the men of

Dartmoor should enlist alongside other Devon men to defend their unique part of the county. To help ensure that the poem's employment of local identity resonated amongst the men of Dartmoor, Clark wrote *For Dartymoor* in the verbal style of the Devonshire dialect: 'An I must fight wi[th] Devon men Vur Dartymoor, our Dartymoor [sic].'[25] Another poem that attempted to convince the county's men to volunteer by tapping into the strength of local identities was *Wanted: Not Conscription – Volunteers* by Ilfracombe resident B. Reed. Rather than utilise the Devonshire dialect or refer to the county's unique landscapes, Reed's poem used Devon's distinctive food products to evoke this Devonian identity. If Devon's sons decided to enlist, the gallant 'Devonshire Dumplings' would 'procure the [highly prized] "clotted cream"' and demonstrate that Devonia did not lack 'Patriotic fame.'[26]

On the route marches and recruitment events in 1915, Devonian exceptionalism returned as a significant theme in the appeals of Devon's local elite and Army recruiters to motivate the county's men to enlist.[27] Devon's PRC also evoked this spirit of Devonian exceptionalism and integrated it into a patriotic narrative of historical obligation in a recruitment pamphlet called *The War: An Appeal to Devon Men and Women*. According to the booklet, Devonshire was a county of brave men who, stirred by a tremendous intuitive sense of patriotism, had demonstrated their loyalty to the nation throughout British history. The men of Devon had fought valiantly against the Spanish Armada, against Napoleon's Army at the Battle of Waterloo, and against the Boers in the Second South African War.[28] Since their heroic forefathers played their part at pivotal moments in Britain's distant and more recent past, the pamphlet prescribed that the present generation of Devonian men needed to carry on this patriotic lineage by coming forward to fight against the Kaiser's Army.[29] Thus, with the eyes of history upon them, the booklet laid down the gauntlet to these men with its bold expectation that they would prove themselves worthy of their noble Devonian heritage: 'We believe you will write Devon's name large across the pages in which will be told the history of the great war'.[30]

Between January to June 1915, Devon raised around 500 recruits each month for the Regular Forces and a comparable number for the Territorials.[31] The county's route marches contributed to these recruitment returns since some of the touring recruitment events did yield a certain degree of success.[32] The first route march that toured north Devon from 12 January to 15 January was one such encouraging result for Army recruiters as they managed to secure around 48 to 60 recruits.[33] On 26 February, Earl Fortescue highlighted another route march in the county that had achieved good results. Fortescue claimed there were many places on the recent recruitment tour where the 'patriotism of young men began and ended with the wearing of a tricolour feather.'[34] He evoked this opposition of feathers – a white feather indicating a man's cowardice and the other containing more patriotic colours (the red, white and blue of the British flag) to commend these men for enlisting and demonstrating their patriotism. However, on several route marches in the county, there were locations where recruits were conspicuous by their absence. When a route march arrived at the south Devon village of Kingskerswell on 1 September, a correspondent to the *Western Times* observed that no local men had come forward. Despite the lack of recruits, he was confident that the efforts of Army recruiters had not been in vain. Using a farming metaphor, the correspondent expressed his confidence that the 'patriotic seed sown' by Army recruiters on the route march would likely produce recruits in the future.[35] There were instances where these patriotic seeds did bear fruit since some men decided to join the Army several days after the touring recruitment event.[36] Nevertheless, the route marches that toured Devon's districts in 1915 were largely ineffective in convincing many eligible men in the county to enlist because, as Fortescue recalled later, 'few recruits presented themselves.'[37]

A route march highlighted by contemporaries as a disappointment was the one that travelled through east Devon in early June 1915.[38] On 14 June, the route march's first day, a detachment of the 3rd Devons arrived at Ottery St Mary. After the troops received food and refreshments, an open-air recruitment meeting occurred in the town square. However, despite the great turnout, a *Devon and Exeter Gazette* correspondent noticed that the speakers' appeals failed to motivate the eligible men in the audience to enlist. Only one local man came forward that day, but he was deemed unfit for military service after a medical evaluation.[39] Sir Ernest Satow was among those who witnessed the meeting in Ottery St Mary's town square. Following the day's disappointing result, Satow reflected upon the efficacy of local recruitment efforts up to that point in his diary. After hearing that there were, allegedly, at least five military-age men in the local area who decided against enlisting, he concluded that they had clearly drained the district of all the willing men.[40]

In their reporting of the further stages of the east Devon route march during that week, the county's newspapers focused on the notable lack of recruits and the disappointing experiences of Army recruiters. The recruiting party told a *Western Morning News* correspondent that based on the meagre results of the east Devon route march, it was 'hard work and good money wasted.'[41] A *Western Times* columnist suggested that whilst it was no fault of those involved in the recruitment-march, the touring recruitment event had 'proved to be a fiasco.'[42] Meanwhile, a journalist for the *Devon and Exeter Gazette* criticised the young men who decided to stay at home rather than enlist. These reluctant men, he insisted, needed to come forward during the last stage of the route march to 'prove their patriotism'.[43] Accordingly, it was up to the men of east Devon to demonstrate that the district had 'not [fallen] behind other parts of the county in patriotism.'[44] Six months prior, the same newspaper launched a similar challenge to the men of West and North West Devon following comments from Fortescue that the areas between Launceston and Hartland Point could do much better regarding recruitment numbers. The paper proposed that it was 'up to the people of West and North-west Devon to prove that, despite their screened positions in a geographical sense, they realise the need for patriotism and self-sacrifice.'[45]

The critical coverage about the route march in the county's newspapers spurred the Vicar of the east Devon village of Alfington, Reverend Gerald McCarthy Lewin Reade, to write a poem that expressed his frustrations with the county's eligible men. Poems that touched upon the failures of local recruitment, like those written by Reade, sought to add pressure on military-age men who were reluctant to volunteer.[46] When faced with the threat that German soldiers could commit atrocities on English soil, Reade condemned the local farmers and tradesmen for not coming forward on the east Devon route march to protect the nation against this nightmare scenario.[47] In a later poem, *England's Call, the Empire's Response - Duty of Devonians*, Reade criticised the county's agriculturalists and male shopkeepers. By staying at home, these groups of men had shown that they were too 'poor in spirit for the brave man's part.'[48] Reade referred to Devon's famous historical men of action to underscore the failings of these frightened heedless men. Although descended from "worthies" like Drake and Grenville, Reade complained that the present generation of Devonian men who, through their reluctance to volunteer, had shown they were 'poltroons' and lacked the inherent patriotism of their forebears.[49]

Although Army recruiters and figures from Devon's local elite employed the county's past to inspire Devonian men to enlist, there were instances where these historically framed appeals did not achieve the desired rousing effect. At the north Devon village of Parkham on 17 February 1915, Fred Howard, a recruitment canvasser from the Central Recruiting Committee, presented his appeal for recruits using the figure of Drake and the fable of Drake's drum. During his address, Howard urged the village's eligible men to volunteer 'in the name of Drake' because, as Devon men, they should not let 'Drake's Drum' beat in vain.'[50] However, a *Western Times* correspondent noticed that the reception of Howard's appeal from the audience at Parkham was 'colder than the chilly moorland blast.'[51] Notwithstanding the indifference of the locals towards Howard's speech, the efforts of Army recruiters had not gone entirely to waste as one eligible man from Parkham did come forward. Howard later used Devon's history in his address when a recruitment march arrived at the mid-Devon hamlet of Staple Cross on 15 July. In his 'rousing appeal' for recruits, Howard evoked the words of Queen Elizabeth I, who said that 'Devon men had hearts like Lions', alongside the brave actions of the Devonshire Regiment in the South African War.[52] However, Howard's stirring words did not motivate any eligible men to come forward, even though several were present at the event.

Another instance where Army recruiters used local identities to motivate eligible local men to enlist was when a route march came to Widecombe-in-the-Moor on 21 April. Although the Dartmoor village held the 'stigma of being a black spot on the map of Devon' since it had not contributed a single man to the war, Army recruiters wanted to remove this disgrace by recruiting the fifty eligible men left in the locality.[53] In an attempt to do this, the procession of the military band played the song 'Uncle Tom Cobleigh' as they and the soldiers marched towards the village square. By performing this distinctly Devonian song, the military band tried to rouse the local men to enlist with a fitting tribute to Widecombe-in-the-Moor. The recital also reinforced their Devonian credentials since their performance of 'Uncle Tom Cobleigh' acted as a historical link to when the soldiers of the Devonshire Regiment sang the popular folk song as they marched off to fight in the South African War.[54] Nevertheless, despite playing 'Uncle Tom Cobleigh' to try to win over the local men, the recruiting party came away from the village empty-handed since no men came forward to enlist.[55]

On 27 February 1915, the *Western Times* reported that recruitment in Devon was still very varied, being characterised as a 'mixture of ignorance, apathy and enlightened patriotism'.[56] Indeed, despite the work of Devon's

PRC during the first three months of the year, Fortescue admitted on 31 March that voluntary recruitment efforts in the county remained 'very uphill work.'[57] The struggle to get recruits for the Army was particularly evident in Plymouth. Fortescue conceded that the Royal Navy's recruitment campaign and the considerable number of the local population employed at the Royal Naval Dockyard at Devonport had made getting recruits for the Army and Territorials in the city a more significant challenge.[58] Like the city of Plymouth, some areas of Devon continued to have low recruitment numbers. Fortescue suspected that the strong presence of nonconformity in north and north west Devon had contributed to the poor recruitment returns for these areas.[59] However, John W. Gulland, Liberal MP for Dumfries Burghs and a treasurer for the PRC, suggested that areas of Devon that had not done well in recruiting were 'not exclusively Nonconformist and Liberal'.[60] Indeed, Gulland revealed that 'some of the most Church and Tory Divisions [in the county] have also a very low percentage.'[61] In his letter to Colonel Western, Fortescue revealed that small market towns and watering places in Devon, predominately, had done well. While Torquay claimed to have sent 2,000 men to the forces, roughly 5 per cent of the town's population, this was not the case for Exeter, which had a lower percentage despite the citizens of the city doing their best to encourage local men to enlist.[62]

The newspaper coverage of the route marches across Devon revealed the difficulties recruiting sergeants, soldiers, and the county's notable figures encountered when they were trying to canvass for recruits.[63] One example of these difficulties was when the recruitment march that was touring through the division of Tavistock arrived at the west Devon village of Halwill on 18 February 1915. Charles A. Millman, a Liberal representative from the Central Recruiting Committee, tried to convince one young farmer to enlist and asked would he wait until the Germans invaded before he volunteered. In response, the agriculturalist replied provocatively: 'What difference would it make to me if they did come? … Let them, I don't care I have nothing to lose.'[64] However, the recruiting party met similar responses from other eligible men as they continued their tour through rural west Devon. The columnist for the *Western Morning News* described the shared disclination of these men towards volunteering as the 'great refusal.'[65] Indeed, he believed that the responses from these men were absolutely disgraceful 'to Devonshiremen [sic].'[66]

The following day, Millman encountered another eligible man at the west Devon village of Bridestowe who dismissed his appeal by replying: 'We've got no time for that rummage. Let someone else do it if they like.'[67] Disgusted by this man's response, a *Devon and Exeter Gazette* correspondent hoped that the cowards who articulated such a 'patriotic' answer would 'receive nothing but contempt from their more patriotic fellows.'[68] Since these indifferent men brushed aside these appeals to enlist, the *Devon and Exeter Gazette* lambasted them as 'unpatriotic villagers.'[69] Some Army recruiters also faced individuals who deliberately belittled their earnest appeals for recruits. When asked if he would like to join up, one prickly farmer in the west Devon village of Ashwater turned the tables on the Army recruiter by demanding if he were to enlist: 'Will Lloyd George pay my rent?'[70] However, it later came to the attention of the *Western Morning News* correspondent covering the recruitment march that the farmer in question was not sincere in his protestation because he owned his farm and was not a tenant farmer. In Cornwall, Army recruiters faced similar ridicule and confrontation from local populations on the route marches that toured the county in March and April.[71] During a route march in the Launceston Division in April, Millman encountered one young eligible man who tried to undermine his authority when appealing for recruits. Like the unexpected challenge from the farmer in Ashwater, the young man attempted to destabilise Millman and catch him off guard when the eligible man asked mockingly: 'Why can't the Pensioners go out and fight.'[72]

The indifferent and provocative responses from Devon's eligible men determined to 'stay at home' were deeply humiliating for those unable to serve, including many of the county's women. When several young men in the villages of north Devon refused to join up during a route march on 17 February 1915, a *Western Morning News* correspondent noticed that the local girls viewed these eligible men with contempt. However, he was astounded by the patriotism of the district's women. When the route march passed through the north Devon village of High Bickington, one woman in the crowd declared that she would be willing to volunteer as she would 'love to have a go at the Germans.'[73] In response to the lady's declaration, a seasoned soldier remarked that the local women possessed 'far more pluck than the men.'[74] Based on the enthusiasm of these women, the *Western Morning News* correspondent claimed that Army recruiters would encounter little difficulty to enrol 'a whole regiment of the fair sex.'[75] In the masculine system of voluntary recruitment, these incidents were deeply symbolic attempts by women to shame the county's menfolk and interrogate their masculinity since the sight of women 'offering to enlist, or calling men cowards, were explicit attacks on their patriotism.'[76]

Army recruiters on the route marches faced individuals who interfered with their efforts to convince military-age men to volunteer. Labourer William Quick was one man who disrupted the work of Army recruiters during the evening of 16 July 1915 in the mid Devon village of Hemyock. Whilst intoxicated, Quick argued with three soldiers from the third Battalion of the Devonshire Regiment trying to persuade young men to enlist in the local public house. Although one soldier threatened to report Quick for an offence under the Defence of the Realm Act, he ignored the soldier's warning and harassed them later that night. Whilst the recruitment meeting was taking place in the local school, Quick challenged the soldiers waiting outside to fight him.[77] As Quick was about to strike one of the soldiers, the honorary secretary of the Tiverton Division of the Devon PRC, Joseph Gould, stepped in between the soldier and Quick to receive the full force of the blow. After getting back on his feet, Gould reported the altercation to the local policeman. In light of Gould's account alongside the testimony from the local PC, Quick was fined 40s. for being drunk and disorderly at the Cullompton Petty Sessions on 3 August.[78]

During the route marches and other recruitment events in 1915, there were instances where hardly any military-age men were in attendance, or they were mostly conspicuous by their absence.[79] When a recruiting march arrived at the north Devon village of Shebbear on 16 February 1915, the local Vicar, T. E. Fox, was appalled that thirty-six local eligible men were not among the villagers present to greet the troops of the 3rd Devons.[80] A correspondent for the *Devon and Exeter Gazette* noticed that the eligible men of the west Devon village of Sourton were also noticeable by their absence when a recruiting party came to the locality on 19 February as part of the recruiting tour through the district.[81] At a recruitment meeting in the South Hams town of Modbury on 22 April, Edrica de la Pole observed that the local eligible men were conspicuously absent from the event.[82] Later, when a *North Devon Journal* correspondent covered a recruiting march that toured north Devon in early June, he noticed that at all the villages the recruiting party had travelled through, the 'young men of military age were mainly conspicuous by their absence.'[83] Recruiting officer Lieutenant Macmillan noted a marked absence of eligible men when a route march arrived at the south Devon village of Stokeinteignhead on 2 September.[84] Correspondents for Devon's newspapers observed that the sons of the county's agriculturalists were among the military-age men missing at recruitment events.[85] Army recruiters also encountered this in Cornwall since there was a 'marked absence of farmers' sons' on the Cornish route marches, and farmers' sons seldom appeared at evening recruitment meetings.[86] However, some contemporaries suspected that the absenteeism of military-age men at recruitment events in Devon was not coincidental. After he noticed only a few military-age men attending an open-air recruiting meeting in Barnstaple on 4 June, a *Devon and Exeter Gazette* columnist concluded that many eligible men deliberately dodged recruitment events. He suggested these missing men had intentionally sought convenient excuses to justify their absence from the event.[87]

By looking for ways out of appearing or making other arrangements to coincide with recruitment events, non-enlisted men used these pretexts to render themselves opportunely unavailable to attend.[88] Previously, on 12 February, the Mayor of Bideford, Sidney Redclift Chope, expressed his belief that if the county's PRC organised recruiting meetings in the district, the local men they wanted to recruit would likely be absent from such events.[89] Although some contemporaries suggested that Devon's young agriculturalists were simply too shy to appear at recruitment events, others believed their well-timed absence was due to the tactical machinations of their fathers.[90] These farmers had deliberately overloaded their sons with work on the farm to ensure that they remained on the property when local recruitment meetings occurred.[91] This strategy allowed these farmers to monitor their son's movements and remove any possibility that they could attend the event. The fact that the county's farmers and their sons had not come forward had a detrimental impact on voluntary recruitment in Devon since it had, in turn, provided other classes including labourers with a justification not to volunteer.[92] When trying to obtain recruits in south Devon in the autumn of 1915, Army recruiters also encountered men, especially the local farmers, who still justified their decision not to enlist because other men were not prepared to make any sacrifices and continued to amuse themselves as usual. Based on the reports of these reluctant responses, Earl Fortescue acknowledged that, unfortunately, there were 'many people who will jump at any excuse for not doing their own duty.'[93]

Since military-age men were nowhere to be seen at recruitment events or route marches, recruiting officers believed these missing men had gone into hiding before the recruitment party arrived.[94] Army recruiters speculated that these men had hidden away in places out of sight, such as nearby corners, hedges, houses, and farm buildings.[95] These men would remain concealed in these hiding places until the recruitment event finished or the route march had moved on. Only when they believed that the 'danger' had passed did these men consider it safe to emerge out of hiding. In French Guinea, the young men of the village of Kindia employed similar strategies by hiding in the mountains, the forests and the bush to evade French Army recruiters. Although these men concealed themselves during the day, they ventured out of their hiding spots to return to the village in the middle of the night.[96]

Yet Earl Fortescue warned Devon's eligible men against hiding away from recruiting officers. By using such evasion tactics, he claimed that these men were doing more to facilitate the introduction of compulsory military service than all the politicians who advocated for it in Parliament.[97] Local notable John Yeo Tucker also cautioned the eligible men who remained in the north Devon village of Braunton against hiding away in country lanes because it was their obligation to defend the nation.[98] When a route march stopped at the south Devon village of Churston on 30 August, Sergeant Rendle noticed that the local eligible men were conspicuous by their absence. However, rather than chastise these men for hiding away, he instead made fun of them for doing so. Rendle sarcastically proclaimed that if these men joined up, they could use their skills for concealment to 'take cover in France [just] as well as they took cover from those recruiting meetings [then] the Germans would never hit them.'[99]

Although some eligible men had 'taken cover' in nearby 'safe' locations, there was the possibility that they could be found and shamed. On 14 January 1915, a soldier of the 3rd Devons discovered one man in hiding when his detachment of soldiers travelled on a route march from the north Devon village of Witheridge to South Molton. As they marched past a roadside cottage, the soldier noticed a terrified young man inside, peering at them through the window. After he was exposed, the man remained inside the residence, preferring to stay behind the safety of the glass window. As a result, the soldiers humiliated him for not venturing out to face them. A correspondent for the *Western Morning News* also mocked the petrified man when he asked was the man simply afraid to leave the cottage and 'face the music?'[100] A similar incident occurred when a recruiting party arrived at the north-west Devon village of Ashwater on 17 February. On the day of the recruiting event, three eligible men had decided to hide in a nearby barn. When the men peeked through a crack in the barn door to observe the proceedings, they were found by two soldiers who subsequently routed them out of the building.[101]

The fear of being caught by Army recruiters probably triggered the flight of two eligible men during a route march in Cornwall on 21 April 1915. As a battalion of the Duke of Cornwall's Light Infantry (DCLI) marched on the road to the Cornish hamlet of Albaston, the soldiers saw two male figures ahead of them in the distance. However, when both men realised the troops were coming towards them, they fled and hid in a henroost. After witnessing the evasion tactics of these two men, Colonel Williams referred to this event in his speech when the recruiting party arrived at Albaston. If the natural reaction of these men was to run away when faced with the sight of the DCLI, he questioned how they would respond 'if the Germans came?'[102] There were also instances where eligible men fled to avoid getting caught by Army recruiters in Devon's urban areas. At a large outdoor recruitment meeting in Exeter on 2 October, eligible young men from the city were present during the event. Although a few men joined up after being canvassed by recruiting sergeants, a *Devon and Exeter Gazette* correspondent noticed that many of these men 'took cover as soon as the be-ribboned men appeared.'[103]

To some observers, the sight of these eligible men seeking to avoid or hide away from Army recruiters led to speculation that these men were afraid and cowardly. A *Devon and Exeter Gazette* correspondent accused the men of the south Devon village of Chelston of cowardice when a recruitment march arrived at the locality on 31 August 1915 because they 'remained out of sight until the danger was past.'[104] However, there are potentially other reasons to explain why some eligible men wanted to stay clear of Army recruiters and were missing during recruitment events. In November, a journalist for the *Western Times* reported that military-age men in Exeter were averse to attending public recruiting meetings in the city due to the 'fear of being pounced upon and asked to join.'[105] Many eligible men across the county avoided recruitment events because they shared this concern. They wanted to avoid being caught and cornered by Army recruiters who would challenge them on the spot about why they had not volunteered. These sentiments are evident in the language used by the correspondents for Devon's newspapers to convey the encounters between Army recruiters and eligible men. It is revealing that these writers described the Army recruiters 'tackling' eligible men (Figure 10), how some military-age men 'took cover' whilst others fled from Army recruiters at recruitment events because they were afraid of being 'pounced upon'. These descriptions give the impression that eligible men felt that Army recruiters pursued them since they were hunting for recruits. Once Army recruiters found a man who they believed was of military age, they would seek to tackle and question him in the hope that they could get him to enlist.[106] On 2 September, two ladies employed such interrogatory tactics against a farm labourer they believed was conveniently absent when a route march arrived at the south Devon village of Coombeteignhead. Since the farm labourer had only appeared after the recruiting party had moved on, the women accused him of being a coward and tried to pressure him to enlist. However, these ladies' efforts were to no avail. Based on their exchange, a *Western Times* correspondent reported sarcastically that the farm labourer was determined not to enlist because 'Pushing the rake was more important to him than pushing back the Germans.'[107]

Like the farm labourer at Coombeteignhead, eligible men faced continual questioning about why they had yet to volunteer. On 8 January 1915, Devon's newspapers printed a list of five questions that military-age men needed to ask themselves since they had not yet enlisted.[108] Devon's PRC used these five questions as a recruitment strategy to elicit guilt amongst non-enlisted eligible men who had not yet joined up in their pamphlet, *The War: An Appeal to Devon Men and Women*.[109] Recruitment posters distributed across the United Kingdom also encouraged non-enlisted men to reflect on why they were still at home. One poster utilised a quotation from Lord Kitchener asking the man whether he was satisfied with the sincerity of his reasons against military service (Figure 9). However, the justifications that eligible men used against volunteering did not just have to satisfy themselves because, as Adrian Gregory has rightly pointed out, when faced with public pressure to enlist, any fit man of military age would need 'to rationalise to himself and others why he was not in uniform.'[110] In their conversations with eligible men on the route marches and other recruitment events in Devon, Devon's local elite and Army recruiters listened to their explanations why they were not in khaki and, in many instances, tried to counter their reasonings against joining up. On 22 April, Lieutenant Larder encountered one eligible man who declared that he would only enlist after the local farmers had come forward. However, Larder countered this man's defence. Larder proposed that if the man volunteered, he would set an example to the agriculturalists who had yet to enlist. After hearing Larder's proposition, the non-enlisted man knew that his claim would not dissuade Larder from trying to recruit him. Realising that Larder had defeated his argument, the cornered man turned upon the Army Lieutenant and refused point blank to enlist 'with a quite unnecessary coarseness.'[111] A correspondent for the *Western Morning News* concluded, based on how the man reacted to Larder's enquiry, that this man's justification was only a pretence that had unsuccessfully camouflaged his disclination to face his duty.[112]

After hearing the explanations from eligible men against joining up, Army recruiters judged the validity of these rationalisations. Army recruiters could have remained unconvinced by the reasonings of these non-enlisted men in light of the urgency to garner recruits, dismissing them as weak excuses or, in some instances, unpatriotic. Based on their experiences talking to men unwilling to volunteer, recruiting officers had shown little sympathy towards some of their justifications. Indeed, they referred to some men's reasonings in their addresses and mocked them as ridiculous excuses. Lieutenant Larder quoted one justification he had heard that did not stand up to scrutiny and was simply laughable in its absurdity. According to Larder, the young man from the east Devon village of Stockland claimed he could not enlist because he had chickens to look after and pooh-poohed Larder's suggestion that women or children could tend to his poultry instead.[113] Since Army recruiters ridiculed some men's justifications against military service, other military-age men may have concluded that they were better off not attending these meetings for fear of having their own explanations subjected to similar shaming. Considering the reporting in Devon's newspapers of sensational confrontations between eligible men and individuals trying to garner recruits, some men in the county may have decided against attending recruitment events because they did not want to experience such awkward public interrogations of their reasons against enlisting.

Holsworthy solicitor, Apsley Petre Peter, was so frustrated by the explanations that eligible men used to get out of volunteering, such as 'I will wait until I am fetched', that he had formulated a strategy to force these men to reconsider their objections towards military service.[114] In a letter to Earl Fortescue on 19 May 1915, Peter proposed that the legislature should direct efforts to publish the names of men judged by local authorities to be eligible for military service from their respective areas. Similar to how Devon's newspapers identified and shamed individual parishes with low numbers of men serving in the colours, these named men would hopefully face the same public humiliation. However, according to Peter, the men listed on these posters would then be given 'a chance to voluntarily enlist or establish ground of exemption say to the satisfaction of a body like the justices, who know all the circumstances & can hear what is advanced.'[115] With the legal experience of these judicial figures, this body would be qualified to take on the invidious task of adjudicating upon the sincerity of these men's justifications against military service. Accordingly, Peter believed this intimation, along with the 'moral suasion', would be a very effective system to make these reluctant men think carefully before expressing objections towards undertaking their duty.[116]

The Mayor of Exeter was probably aware that many eligible men sought to avoid humiliating cross-examinations from Army recruiters when he dispatched a letter in March 1915 to every non-enlisted man in the city in a renewed attempt to raise 150 recruits for Exeter's Own. Included with Owen's letter was a form that provided each Exonian man who felt uncomfortable expressing their justifications against military service in public with an 'opportunity to state confidentially the reasons, if any, which prevent him volunteering.'[117] Although it is unclear how many of the city's male citizens responded to Owen's appeal, the survey most likely did not achieve the success that Owen had hoped for since he later revealed on 9 November that the second attempt to form Exeter's Own also ended in disappointment.[118] The questionnaire probably did not convince a majority of Exeter's menfolk to document their reasons for not volunteering. Upon receiving the form, some men may have unconsciously objected to completing it since they believed it was none of Owen's business to ask for their rationalisations against enlisting. Other Exonian men could have ignored or disregarded the form entirely by throwing it in the bin. A similar example of the disinclination to discuss recruiting in Exeter was evident in May when the Devon PRC organised a house-by-house canvass in the city. When canvassers called upon several houses of men they wanted to recruit, their wives and sisters 'shut the doors in the face of the canvasser.'[119]

In January, notable Charles Alfred Thomas Fursdon spearheaded a comparable letter campaign to stimulate recruitment in the mid-Devon parish of Cheriton Bishop. After he received authorisation from the Parish's Joint Committee to write an appeal to eligible men in the local area, Fursdon sent out 54 letters. If the Committee did not receive a reply to the letter by a specific date, a Committee member would call upon the man for an answer. However, based on the responses that the Committee had received by 18 January, Fursdon was pessimistic about the scheme's result, predicting that no men would volunteer.[120] Yet, in a letter to Earl Fortescue, Fursdon revealed that this was not his only difficulty. By being part of this scheme targeting local eligible men, Fursdon had also experienced resentment from the locals against him personally 'for having taken the matter up'.[121] Like the reproaches that Edrica de la Pole encountered when she attempted a recruitment campaign in Kingston in September 1914, Fursdon discovered that some Devonians strongly resented other people trying to recruit their eligible men, viewing the endeavours of these individuals as ordering these men about. Indeed, the refusal to accept the prescriptions of others did not apply to just recruitment as Fursdon believed that amongst the Parish's population, there was a 'violent feeling against being "dictated to by any local Committee".'[122] Alongside the opposition from some Devonians who unconsciously objected to being 'dictated' by individuals on these committees, other Devonians encouraged eligible men not to enlist. Bricklayer James Wheat revealed to Satow in April 1916 that he would have joined up the year prior but had decided against it because 'people [had] advised him not to.'[123]

In the case of why some farmers' sons were absent at Devon's recruitment events, they may have wanted to avoid being cornered or given the third degree by those seeking to recruit them who would likely contest the merits of their justifications against volunteering.[124] James Parker, the Labour MP for Halifax, was dismissive of the arguments put forward by the county's farmers to avoid their 'obvious' duty to volunteer. When he travelled with the Devons on their recruitment march to the mid-Devon village of Oakford on 13 July 1915, he was forthright in his criticism against the rationalisations made by the county's agriculturalists against military service. Parker argued it was 'all humbug' to use the question of food supplies to back up their assertions since the majority of the army's food was not homegrown but instead imported from overseas.[125] In light of the pressing need for recruits, Fortescue equally disputed the validity of claims from Devon's eligible agriculturalists that by producing food, they were 'doing the nation's work as much as if they enlisted.'[126] Indeed, he asserted that the rationalisations from farmers against military service were 'a very convenient doctrine for people who preferred to remain at home.'[127]

For those involved in the route marches, it was hard to avoid such value judgements when the county's farmers framed their rationalisations against military service that concentrated on their self-interests. On 17 February 1915, Army recruiters encountered an agriculturalist who expressed his objection towards volunteering in more self-centred terms. When a recruitment march came to the north Devon village of Parkham, a young farmer explained to a correspondent for the *Western Morning News* that he would not enlist. The farmer claimed that since he and his friends were farmers' sons, they had decided to stay at home in order to 'look after the grub and the money.'[128] Upon overhearing the young farmer's selfish declaration, Millman decided to tackle him. Millman directed the young agriculturalist's gaze to the detachment of troops in the village. As Millman pointed to one of them, he interrogated the farmer. Millman stressed that the soldier had done his share by going to the front, and he asked the farmer: 'Won't you join and help the others.'[129] However, the farmer was unmoved by Millman's line of reasoning. The farmer replied that he had never requested the man to go off to fight and brazenly declared that he would not join 'so there.'[130] Unable to hide his irritation with the young agriculturalist's bad-mannered reply, Millman proclaimed out of sheer frustration that the farmer 'ought to be kicked!'[131]

These responses during the route marches and other recruitment events reinforced the image that Devon's farmers and their sons were unpatriotic and selfish shirkers. On 3 June 1915, Army recruiter Lieutenant Larder touched upon the perception that the county's agriculturalists prioritised their own self-interest over the national interest. Although they objected to sending their own sons off to war, Larder claimed they did not seem to mind other mothers' sons who were at the front 'losing their lives, fighting for them and their property.'[132] Indeed, based on his exasperating experiences trying to convince them to enlist, Larder went so far as to suggest that the county's farmers were a disgrace to Devon.[133] Although there were honourable exceptions, Fortescue acknowledged that the county's farmers had discouraged recruitment both 'by precept & example.'[134] The efforts of agriculturalists to obstruct voluntary recruitment were particularly evident in the thinly populated and mainly agricultural districts of west and north west Devon.[135] The former Liberal MP for Plymouth, Thomas Dobson, launched a scathing indictment against the county's farmers in his address at a recruitment meeting in Tiverton on 15 July. According to a *South Devon Weekly Express* correspondent, Dobson directly confronted the eligible agriculturalists attending the event. Dobson argued that since the local farmers were still at home and not yet in khaki, they were 'not acting the part of true patriots.'[136]

Army recruiters encountered one farmer who was directly hostile to their efforts to recruit his sons when a route march called at the mid-Devon village of Huntsham on 15 July. Two soldiers from the recruiting party decided to visit a farm on the Huntsham Court Estate, they encountered two brothers' eligible for military service and endeavoured to convince them to enlist. However, after the third brother confronted and interrogated the soldiers, their father emerged and joined the tense altercation.[137] The farmer was adamant that his sons would not go off to war voluntarily and ordered the soldiers to leave the premises since they were not welcome on the farm. However, one of the soldiers stood his ground. He explained to the farmer that he did not understand the point of 'fighting again for the slackers at home.'[138] After hearing this, the local farmer became enraged and expressed his antagonism towards the soldiers in more strident and insulting terms. To get the men to clear off, he admonished them, warning them not to interfere in matters which did not concern them and to stick to what they should be doing: 'You [both] ought to be back in the trenches; not here mucking about. I don't care a damn if the Germans do come.'[139] The local farmer was probably insulted by the insinuation that his sons were slackers and was irritated that the soldiers had not left his property. Yet, despite this scandalous outburst, the soldier pleaded with the farmer to reconsider his objection to his sons volunteering: 'Don't you think you ought to have some regard for your women and children?'[140] However, the farmer was unshakable in his opposition. Provocatively, he retorted that he could not care less about what would happen to the women and children if the Germans did invade: 'I shall be dead before they touch the women folk, who must look after themselves.'[141]

When the two soldiers reported the shameful incident to the organisers of the route march, local recruiter Fred Howard accompanied them on their return to the farm. However, like the soldiers experienced earlier that day, the farmer was aggressive towards Howard. The farmer defiantly declared that the two soldiers had no right to come onto his farm and interfere with his sons. Indeed, he put his foot down on the matter: 'I said they should go [off to war] when I say they shall go. I have to live, and there are others round here earning more money than my men. I want you off the premises.'[142] Before he left, Howard warned the farmer that he could be arrested 'for insulting the King's uniform and hindering recruiting' under the Defence of the Realm Act.[143] However, the farmer seemed to be unmoved by the threat of prosecution. Based on the farmer's resistance and responses towards those seeking to recruit his sons, the farmer sought to protect his sons from the 'meddling' clutches of any Army recruiters trying to take them away.

In their coverage of this confrontation between Army recruiters and the farmer from Huntsham, Devon's local newspapers were unanimous in their condemnations towards the agriculturalist. Alongside the *Western Times*, the *Western Morning News* questioned the farmer's 'patriotism' in inverted commas.[144] The *Devon and Exeter Gazette* was especially critical of the farmer in their commentary on the quarrel. Based on his conduct, the paper claimed that the farmer's attitude should surely 'make the parishioners of Huntsham blush.'[145] The incident also made the pages of the weekly national newspaper *John Bull*. Disgusted by the farmer's behaviour, the publication questioned whether the farmer was really a man since his conduct had shown that he was a 'barbarian' whose selfishness shamed the local male population. The tabloid claimed that whilst Devonshire was not a county of slackers, it was clear that Huntsham held a nest of them, and this nest needed to be 'smoked out' without delay.[146]

A project that sought to reverse the negative perception of farmers was to raise a special 'Farmers Battalion in the Western Counties' modelled upon the principle of the class battalions of Kitchener's New Army.[147] Otherwise known as the Pals' Battalions, these were military units of locally raised men that achieved great success in urban areas, particularly those in the north of England. These units effectively combined 'local and personal loyalties with national patriotism in a manner which proved irresistible to tens of thousands of potential recruits.'[148] In Sussex, the Conservative MP for Eskdale, Claude Lowther, successfully raised a local unit modelled on the Pal's Battalions, originally known as the 'Southdowns' but later renamed 'Lowther's Lambs.'[149] However, attempts to raise Pal's Battalions did not attain the same success in Devon. Based on the lacklustre result for Exeter's Own in December 1914, Fortescue concluded that this method of localised recruitment did not appear to 'have any particular attraction in the county.'[150] Despite these misgivings about raising Pal's battalions in Devon, Fortescue put his reservations to one side during the summer of 1915 when he was actively involved in efforts to form a farmers' battalion. If the military unit were successful, it would demonstrate the patriotism of Devon's farmers and show that they were producing their fair share of recruits. Amongst Fortescue's private papers, the evidence indicates that the project did gain momentum as it received the support of military representatives and figures from the landed gentry.[151] However, despite Fortescue's efforts, the farmers' battalion did not go beyond these correspondences since the War Office rejected the conditions to create the unit.[152] A comparable attempt to emulate the success of the Pal's Battalions amongst eligible agriculturalists was made in Shropshire. However, Nicholas Mansfield reveals this effort to raise a special farmers' battalion 'was a dismal failure.'[153]

The Derby Scheme in Devon

By May 1915, the declining number of recruits across the United Kingdom had contributed towards public opinion shifting towards introducing some form of compulsion.[154] For the newly formed Asquith Coalition government, it was clear that an assessment of the nation's manpower resources was in order. To achieve this audit, the Coalition government introduced the National Register Act that entailed a compulsory census of all citizens between 15 and 65 years of age 'to state whether they could and would perform work of national importance.'[155] Although National Registration was presented as a survey of all citizens, the Local Government Board (LGB) copied the information supplied by men of military age onto a separate pink form that detailed their occupations. While men engaged in government work or employed in essential industries were classed as 'starred', men not engaged in essential industries were classified as 'unstarred' or not starred. Essentially, the National Register sought to determine the number of available unmarried men left across the United Kingdom. Local councils undertook this audit and sought volunteers to survey their districts with the relevant National Registration forms in August 1915. The Chairman of St Thomas RDC, J. H. Ley, expressed his confidence that in a 'patriotic County like Devon … [they] … would be able to find plenty of voluntary workers' to complete the survey.[156] Each individual would receive a National Registration card to confirm that they registered under the National Registration Act. However, Army recruiters utilised the data collected from the National

Register for an intensification of voluntary recruitment called the 'Group System', otherwise known as the Derby Scheme.

Named after Edward Stanley, the Director-General of Recruiting and the 17th Earl of Derby, the Derby Scheme was a registration scheme that applied to England, Wales and Scotland but not to Ireland and ran from 16 October until 15 December 1915. Initially, every unstarred man received a copy of a letter from Lord Derby appealing to him to enlist in the Army and informing him of what the Derby Scheme entailed. If an unstarred man decided to enlist, he had the option to either volunteer immediately or 'attest' his willingness 'to accept military service when called upon to do so' later.[157] The unstarred men who chose the latter option became attested men. They were now, in effect, Army reserves and organised into various groups depending on their marital status and age.[158] Unmarried men were registered in groups 1 to 23, whilst married men were ranked in groups 24 to 46. By separating attested men into their designated groups, the single men in the first 23 groups would be called upon to serve before the married men registered in the second 23 groups.[159] However, if an attested man wanted to postpone his call up to a later date, he could apply to be transferred from his originally designated group to a later one, thereby deferring his call-up. At the same time, an attested man could request to be recorded as a 'starred' man if he believed he was indispensable to industry. These appeals would receive a fair hearing at a local tribunal established by local government entities, whose members decided whether to allow an attested man to become 'starred' or agree to postpone their call-up by moving them to a later group.

Many contemporaries presented the Derby Scheme as the last chance to save voluntary recruitment. On 21 October 1915, the *Western Morning News* reported that if all the men required for the military were to come forward and make the Derby Scheme a success, it would make the introduction of conscription unnecessary and be a 'wonderful triumph for pure patriotism.'[160] In Devon, Earl Fortescue was actively involved with the Derby Scheme. At recruitment meetings across the county, he acted as an intermediary, answering queries from those attending about specific points about the Derby Scheme.[161] Moreover, he also discussed the Scheme with Lord Derby.[162] Alongside Earl Fortescue, figures from Devon's civil society participated in the Derby Scheme, volunteering to act as canvassers for recruits across the county. Arthur Steele King, the Vicar of the east Devon village, recommended to John Ford, the Lord of Branscombe Manor, that canvassers ought 'to be men of tact, ability and over military age!'[163] Although many canvassers matched these characteristics, women also acted as canvassers. Taking on the role of canvasser provided individuals who were ineligible for military service with the chance to present their dedication to the war effort publicly. Austin M. Harvey, the assistant Unionist agent for the Torquay Division, played his part in the Derby Scheme by acting as a canvasser in the district since he could not join up on medical grounds.[164] At one recruiting meeting in Herefordshire, E. F. Bulmer, the Vice-Chair of the South Herefordshire Joint PRC, secured 137 men to attest with a local magistrate attending to certify each man's signature.[165]

Devon's PRC gave these volunteers a card pamphlet that presented a letter from Earl Fortescue for every individual who agreed to take on the role of a canvasser and notes acting as guidance on how they should carry out the canvass. Canvassers received a white card that authorised them only to conduct a canvass of 'unstarred' men.[166] Based on the information collected with the National Register across Devon, there were 56,000 unstarred men in the county.[167] Canvassers also received blue cards that contained the names of men of military age in the areas they were assigned to canvass. Canvassers would visit the homes of unstarred men in their assigned areas, similar to the practice of political agents calling upon residents' during a general election campaign to encourage them to vote. The blue cards also 'constituted the authority of the canvasser to carry out his or her work.'[168] For instance, canvassers in the mid-Devon town of Chudleigh needed to visit the residences of 161 men, whilst canvassers in the south Devon town of Kingsteignton had to call at the homes of 222 men.[169] By contrast, the East Devon parish of Dunkeswell had 30 men who had to be canvassed.[170]

When canvassing for recruits, Army recruiters and canvassers promoted the Derby Scheme to unstarred men as their final option to join the Army voluntarily. If the Scheme were to fail, they would face conscription into the Army. When faced with this predicament, many men in Devon did volunteer. On 16 November 1915, a local recruiting officer in Exeter informed a *Devon and Exeter Gazette* correspondent that many of the city's young men now realised that they could no longer escape military service because of 'the patriotism of their married comrades.'[171] Similarly, William Frederic Connor, the vicar of the north Devon village of Bishops Nympton, informed Earl Fortescue on 17 November that one young man had told him that he and a friend would probably enlist in Barnstaple to 'escape the disgrace of conscription.'[172] In Kingston, Edrica de la Pole spoke with a local man acting as a canvasser on 20 November, and he revealed that six men had decided to enlist as a result of his efforts. Amongst these men was Ernest Freeman, the pub landlord's son whom de la Pole had 'tackled' but failed to convince to volunteer in September 1914.[173] However, like de la Pole, the canvasser also experienced some local obstinacy. The canvasser revealed that one local man, Jack Triggs, remained elusive. Since he was 'one of the worse slackers', de la Pole believed Triggs would have to be fetched.[174] By 8 December, de la Pole noted in her diary that although 33 local men had joined up for the Derby Scheme, two local men had not even tried.[175]

The Vicar of Sheepstor, Reverend H. Hugh Breton, informed Earl Fortescue after a local man had canvassed the Dartmoor parish in November 1915 that nearly all the local eligible men had come forward without complaint. Encouraged by how well the 'uneducated but kindly peasants of Dartmoor [had] responded', Breton believed that the Derby Scheme would achieve even greater success in towns where men had 'better facilities for judging the extremely critical state of our national affairs.'[176] By contrast, James Bucknell, a farmer in Knowstone, believed that volunteering for the Derby Scheme was 'going to be very bad' in the north Devon parish.[177] In his letter to Earl Fortescue on 15 November, Bucknell reported that the Group Scheme was causing great dissatisfaction locally due to the discrepancies of the 'starred' system since some local farmers' sons were 'starred' whilst others were not. Based on the inconsistencies and unfairness of who was starred and who was not, Bucknell wished that an 'amendment [was] put to it and all served alike.'[178] A resident from Dawlish submitted a similar complaint anonymously to the *Western Morning News*. The author, writing under the pen name of Justice, complained that whilst two local farming families had all their sons starred, there were other families who, despite having sons in the military, their remaining sons were unstarred: 'This gives rise to much ill-feeling [locally] as you may imagine, and is on the face of it unfair.'[179] Even the canvassers' card acknowledged that mistakes had been made in the National Registration both in the men who had been starred and those who were unstarred.[180] There was also the complaint that the information submitted for National Registration was incorrect as Fortescue informed Lord Derby about 'dishonest starring.'[181] The canvassers note also informed that canvassers should note down cases where they suspected a man had 'never been registered, so that the necessary steps may be taken to bring their names to the notice of the Authorities.'[182]

Yet, when visited by canvassers, an unstarred man also had the option to refuse to undertake military service. If canvassers encountered men who refused to enlist, they made discreet enquiries asking the man about why he had taken this decision.[183] Once the canvasser interviewed the man and obtained the reasons behind his refusal to enlist, they recorded this information with the possibility that it 'might be tabulated and sent to headquarters in London'.[184] In November 1915, when undertaking a canvass in the Essex village of Little Clacton, female canvassers encountered 13 men who refused military service. The replies that these men gave to these ladies against enlisting varied significantly, including one man whose father refused to permit him despite wanting to volunteer.[185] By contrast, when Charles A. Millman undertook a canvass in the parish of St Cleer in south east Cornwall, most eligible men he met refused to enlist. In a letter to the *Western Morning News*, Millman judged that these men advanced no sound reasons against military service but rather a copious amount of idle and empty excuses. Sickened by his encounters in St Cleer, Millman concluded that these 'shirkers' were 'entirely lacking in patriotism, and concerned only for the safety of their own miserable skins.'[186] Although canvassers were authorised to make enquiries about why men refused to enlist, they could also face confrontation when conducting their enquiries. Eligible men in rural Essex had an aversion towards women canvassers since they did not like how they pestered them.[187] In the face of any possible challenges, Fortescue tried to reassure anyone who wanted to take up the role of Canvasser on 22 October 1915. Probably mindful of the previous confrontations between some Devonians and Army recruiters, he stressed that individuals who undertook canvassing work had the 'distinct advantage of having official cover for what they were doing, and anyone who attempted to interfere with the canvasser would render himself liable to a serious charge.'[188] Alongside the problems with starring, contemporaries believed that men had evaded registration.[189]

After meeting with canvassers on 18 November, Fortescue wrote to Lord Derby to relay the Derby Scheme's progress in the county. Although the canvas had made considerable progress in the 16 parishes of the east Devon district of Honiton, Fortescue revealed that the result in terms of recruits was 'small.'[190] Canvassers encountered similar difficulties in the constituencies of Tiverton and Newton Abbot. In Tiverton, one-third of the cards had not yet returned, whilst 25 to 30 per cent of those canvassed in the district were 'willing to join.'[191] Although the percentage of those in Newton Abbot willing to join up was the same as in Tiverton, canvassers noted that over half of the recruitment cards had not been returned. Representatives for the urban constituency of Torquay informed Fortescue that one quarter of the cards had 'not been returned: recruits were about 33 per cent.'[192] Meanwhile, in North Devon, half the cards had been returned in South Molton, whilst in Bideford between one-third to half of the cards still had not been returned. However, in both localities, the promises to enlist from men stood at approximately 17 per cent. While in Torrington, these pledges were below average.[193] According to the statistics collected by the Recruiting Officer for the Sub-area, among those signing up to the group system, there was a 'slight preponderance of married men, about 55 per cent as against 45 per cent of single.'[194] Fortescue informed Lord Derby that in the county's rural districts, especially, everyone was indispensable.[195] Indeed, Fortescue acknowledged further difficulties with the Derby Scheme 'in this part of the world besides Barnstaple' because there were 'really grave difficulties in the way.'[196]

On 19 November, Earl Fortescue acknowledged based on the results so far that it seemed that 'the canvassers obtained were unfortunate selections or else they had been unfortunate in regard to the people they had been up against.'[197] Other men in Devon also challenged the Derby Scheme canvassers. At a meeting of the Totnes Division PRC on 24 November, it was revealed that undoubtedly canvassing had been 'seriously interfered with, and this also militated considerably against obtaining recruits'.[198] In Newton Abbot, agitators had worked against the Scheme. Fortescue wanted to bring to Earl Derby's attention that there were some 'Trade Unions in the neighbourhood, Clayworkers, Railwaymen etc., some of the fiery spirits on which have organised opposition to recruiting and are pushing the propaganda of the Anti-Conscription Fellowship.'[199] According to Fortescue, the District Superintendent and an insurance company collector of the Pearl Assurance Company, William Bond, was at the heart of this opposition. Since he had taken control of the local trade and Labour Councils, Bond was running this opposition without restraint. To counter Bond's efforts to disrupt recruitment, Fortescue wondered whether the Labour Recruiting Committee could send one of their prominent members who would attend the meeting and hopefully 'stop the malcontents.'[200]

For the men who decided to 'attest' and postpone their enlistment, he could wear a 'khaki armlet'. Otherwise described as the 'Derby Armlet', the khaki armlet was a woollen armband made out of khaki cloth stitched with a red patch in the shape of a Royal Crown. Recruiting committees across Devon, like the Plymouth Recruiting Committee, distributed these khaki armbands to the attested men.[201] Upon receiving the khaki armlet, an attested man received a white card stamped with the armlet's number to correspond to the man it was assigned. Recruiting authorities advised attested men to wear these armlets whilst they waited for their designated group to be called up. Whilst wearing the armlet, the attested man needed to have the white card in his possession where 'he must produce it for inspection by any officer in uniform, any non-commissioned officer on duty, a recruiter in uniform, or by any police constable' to authenticate that the man was permitted to wear one.[202] The Admiralty created a version of the Derby armlet for those who sought to become reservists for the Royal Navy. It was a blue woollen armband with a red anchor patch stitched onto it. The men who received the Navy's blue armband also needed to abide by the same conditions as those who obtained the Derby armlet. Whilst wearing the Navy armlet, they needed to have their enrolment card or discharge papers since any police constable or Army recruiters could seek to authenticate that these men were authorised to wear it.[203]

For the attested man, the khaki armband served several functions. Philip and Julie Sprinks suggest that the attested man could wear the armband to demonstrate that they had attested, deterring 'the attention of zealous recruiting staff, public opprobrium or women with white feathers'.[204] The *Western Times* proposed that the armband should be recognised as a 'badge of patriotism.'[205] Although some men may have felt that they were 'parading their patriotism', a *Devon and Exeter Gazette* correspondent noticed that some attested men were more discreet in how they wore the armlet, adorning it like a wristband or on the cuff of their coats.[206] Some men may not have wanted to draw attention to the fact that they possessed a Khaki armlet because these armbands were a highly coveted item amongst male citizens still not in khaki. The *Western Morning News* reported that whilst 'khaki armlets' had appeared in the streets of Exeter by 9 December, there were problems with their supply. Men in the city had complained that they were still waiting for their armbands even though they had attested several weeks prior, whilst others who had only recently attested had already received their armbands.[207]

The khaki armlet could produce jealousy amongst those still waiting to receive their armlet or from men who were unable to secure one. On 9 December 1915, upon retrieving his overcoat from the cloakroom of a theatre after a performance in London, one civil servant discovered that his khaki armlet was missing, presumably stolen.[208] However, this was not an isolated case. The *Farnsworth Chronicle* reported on 22 January 1916 that several khaki armlets had either been lost or stolen. As a result, the article advised the rightful owners of these armlets to be careful with them, especially when hanging up their coats in public spaces.[209] The newspaper also stressed that men who wore the armband ran a risk since they could be targeted by men ineligible to wear it or face a heavy fine by authority figures for not wearing it. In London, one man decided that he would try to sell a khaki armlet to men who were not wearing them. During the evening of 19 January 1916, George Neal approached Charles Claridge and Robert Banns as prospective buyers just before they entered a Music Hall.[210] Neal asked Claridge where was his Derby armlet to which Claridge replied that he did not possess one since he had no right to wear it. Upon hearing this, Neal proposed to sell an armlet to Claridge for the price of six pence. Neal also noticed that Banns was not wearing an armband, so he offered the men the chance to purchase two khaki armlets 'for a "bob".'[211] However, after Claridge rebuffed his offer, Neal stormed off, declaring that 'he hoped the Germans would win, and that England were no good.'[212] The incident led Claridge to inform a nearby policeman, and when PC Wright arrested Neal, he discovered that he had two Khaki armlets in his possession: Neal's own and the other bearing the number 140,850. When Neal appeared before Marylebone police Court on 20 January 1916, he was charged under the regulations of the Defence of the Realm Act alongside the charge of being drunk and disorderly.[213]

Alongside suspicions that men had evaded registration, many contemporaries claimed that unstarred men had taken shelter in starred occupations as a viable way to avoid volunteering. *The Times History of the War* suggested that it was highly likely during the Derby Scheme that 'an enormous number of unmarried men entered "starred" trades with the object of escaping enlistment.'[214] Munition factories were one 'starred' trade that men entered in order to evade military service. Upon receiving Lord Derby's letter in December 1915, agricultural wheelwright and resident of Bishops Nympton, John Perryman, decided that he would go to work at a munitions factory in Taunton rather than enlist.[215] In rural Essex, many young men also sought employment in munitions factories to avoid the prospect of military service.[216] Indeed, Army recruiter Major William Brown regretfully admitted to Reverend Andrew Clark, the Vicar of Great Leighs, that this was a growing trend since increasing numbers of young men sought 'shelter in munition work.'[217] However, in Devon, contemporaries claimed that many eligible men in the county had sought employment at Devonport dockyard to go into 'hiding under the Dockyard umbrella' and escape enlistment into the Army.[218] Army recruiters suggested that this was also the case in Cornwall. The Vice-Chairman of the South-East Cornwall Parliamentary Recruiting Committee, Frank Hill Perry-Coste, claimed on 27 March 1915 that he had encountered ten eligible men from the south-east Cornish village of Polperro who had '"found sanctuary" in the Dockyard from being compelled to enlist.'[219] There may be validity in the claims that Devonport Dockyard was a lure for eligible men in Devon and Cornwall since the number of workmen in the Dockyard increased by 1,745 men in 1916 compared to number employed in 1914.[220] Upon entering the dockyard, the Admiralty issued the 'On War Service' badge to these men which provided them with exemption from Army enlistment and acted as a 'sufficient answer to the recruiting canvasser when he calls upon them as to their not being available.'[221] For unstarred men, employment in the dockyard as a 'starred trade' was also an attractive prospect in financial terms when compared to the wages for joining the Army or Navy.[222] Perry-Coste revealed this was the case for the ten men of military age from Polperro because they had decided to go to the Royal Dockyard to make 'as much money in a week as the men who had enlisted were getting in a month or six weeks.'[223]

Considering the vitally important work undertaken at Devonport Dockyard, Andy Gale suggests that the Admiralty went to great lengths to hold onto their workforce.[224] Indeed, it seemed a question of protecting their trained men. In a letter to Lord Derby dated 11 November 1915, Fortescue revealed that the Dockyard people would try to keep them all 'to save themselves the trouble of replacing these fellows by men over 40.'[225] The Admiral-Superintendent's secretary, R.F. Franklin, confirmed to the Plymouth Citizens Recruiting Committee on 19 November that the Admiralty wanted to ensure they did not lose these men. One of the measures that the Admiralty used to prevent the loss of these men was to prohibit canvassing in the dockyard because every military-age man was on

War Service.[226] Stephen Reynolds was concerned about where fishermen stood pertaining to the Derby Scheme. On 17 October, he wrote to H. G. Maurice about this matter. In Reynolds' view, the naval experience of Devon's fishermen meant that they should primarily be reserved for the Admiralty. Simultaneously, he complained that there was considerable difficulty in getting crews to fish for winter herrings and mackerel. If the Army were to take more fishermen, he warned that 'we shall be in an awful mess.'[227] However, the Admiralty suggested that fishermen were not expected to enlist under the Derby Scheme since 'they may be required as recruits for the Royal Navy Reserve.'[228]

During the last few days of the Derby Scheme, Devon's newspapers reported a rush for recruits in recruiting offices in Plymouth and Barnstaple. Recruiting offices in Tiverton and Cullompton experienced similar rushes. On 10 December 1915, 270 men came through the Tavistock recruiting office to be attested.[229] The *Western Times* reported on 17 December that the recruiting station in Bideford had responded magnificently to the Derby Scheme where close to 1,000 men had offered themselves during the previous few days.[230] Fortescue's statistics indicate that 1219 men volunteered for the Regulars and 1223 for the Territorials in November 1915.[231] However, for December's figures, Fortescue recorded 217 men had volunteered for the Regulars, whilst 539 men signed up for the Territorials that month.[232] Considering how busy recruiting offices in Devon were during the last days of the Derby Scheme, these last-minute rushes may have been placed into the figures for the following month since Fortescue noted that 13,516 men signed up for the Regulars whilst 14,586 men joined the Territorials in January 1916.[233]

Humanitarian patriotism

Although Devon's route marches generally did not garner large numbers of recruits, the county's residents outside the requirements of military service actively supported these events in a humanitarian way. In posters to promote these events, Devon's PRC appealed to a sense of Devonian ties. When the troops of the Devonshire Regiment came to visit individual districts across the county, local populations were encouraged to provide the troops with a 'hearty Devon welcome.'[234] Like the route marches that toured Scotland, non-combatants in Devon's communities gave a hearty welcome to the soldiers from the county's regiment.[235] In the districts and localities that the troops visited on the route marches, women and children came equipped with and waved British flags whilst other residents had erected large banners to demonstrate their support behind the war. However, these banners acted as displays of local solidarity and expressions of county identity. The people of Bovey Tracey made one such banner to coincide with a route march and demonstrate their pride in the Devonshire Regiment. When the soldiers of the 3rd Devons arrived in the town on 19 April, they saw a large banner stretched across the road with the message: 'Welcome the Brave Devons.'[236] The enthusiastic reception that local populations gave to soldiers on the route marches also included providing them with refreshments, food and other comforts.[237] For the inhabitants of Devon's villages, this hospitality also gave them a valuable opportunity to pragmatically present their patriotism.[238] One demonstration of this practical patriotism was the hearty welcome given to the soldiers of the 3rd Devons by the populations of the north Devon villages of Swimbridge and Landkey. When the route march stopped at both parishes on 3 June 1915, the local populations presented the troops with abundant gifts of apples, fruit, chocolates, and cigarettes.[239] The residents of the mid-Devon village of Washfield responded in a similar fashion when the soldiers arrived on 14 July and gave them presents of chocolates and cigarettes.[240] A correspondent for the *South Devon Weekly Express* considered these displays of support by Devonians to be appropriate since they had given the soldiers 'a true Devonshire welcome.'[241] By contrast, the *Devon and Exeter Gazette* hailed the showering of local troops with these provisions as acts of 'generous Devonshire hospitality.'[242]

Like the Devonians who provided generous hospitality to the soldiers on the recruitment-marches, Mrs Nellie S. King, the Mayoress of Exeter and other women volunteers offered similar hospitality to soldiers and sailors travelling through the city. When troop trains stopped at these stations, Mrs King and other volunteers from her War Depot were stationed on the platform and provided these travelling troops with lunchboxes, tea and other food stuffs. These items were either donations from the general public or bought with funds contributed to the Mayoress of Exeter's War Depot. When Mrs Janie Kirk Owen became the Mayoress of Exeter in November 1914, she continued the work of the War Depot to provide hospitality to travelling troops at Exeter's railway stations. By December 1914, the Depot's volunteers had handed out 11,564 lunchboxes to soldiers arriving at Exeter's railway stations.[243] The county's newspapers praised such achievements and the efforts of the Mayoress of Exeter and the other women volunteers to provide hospitality to the travelling troops. At the same time, this press coverage also contained letters of appreciation from the soldiers from Britain and the British Empire who received the hospitality of the Mayoress of Exeter's War Depot. In a letter originally published in the Johannesburg *Sunday Times* and later reprinted in the *Western Times*, a South African Scottish Regiment soldier wanted to relay how he and his fellow soldiers greatly appreciated the hospitality offered at Exeter. Upon their arrival at Exeter from Plymouth, they were welcomed on the station platform by the Mayoress of Exeter and her lady volunteers with gifts, including ham sandwiches, tea, cake and fruit. The soldiers were relieved to encounter and greatly appreciated the hospitality that they received.[244]

Margaret Darrow has suggested that charity work for the women of France was an integral part of the broader mobilisation of their femininity.[245] The activities of the Mayoress of Exeter and others to bestow humanitarian administrations to soldiers at Exeter were viewed, like the work of French women, as a 'modest extension of the care women provided to sons and husbands within the household.'[246] This sentiment of maternal care to the soldiers was evident in a letter published in the *Western Times* from a mother in Leeds whose son benefited from the Depot's Hospitality Fund. In her letter, she expressed her deep appreciation to the Mayoress of Exeter and her team for the kindness that they had shown to these men: 'It was good of you all to do what we mothers wished to do, and could not.'[247] Accordingly, she wanted to thank Mrs Owen 'for mothering my son in my place.'[248] A photograph captured the motherly care the Mayoress of Exeter provided to troops at Exeter's railway stations. In August 1915, Devon's newspapers published this photograph under the title of 'Mothering' Tommy Atkins.[249] In the picture, Lady Owen administers tea to the troops at the station platform. Alongside the image, a caption indicated that the fund would supply every man with refreshments, food and a packet of cigarettes.[250] Therefore, contemporaries recognised that this duty of maternal care represented a distinct and appropriate contribution that women could exclusively make to the war effort.[251]

For people in Devon, presenting food as gifts was a suitable way to support the war effort. The organisation that collected donations of eggs was the National Egg Collection for the Wounded (NECW) which sought to deliver 'newly laid eggs to wounded soldiers and sailors in base hospitals or collect funds to do so.'[252] In the county's rural communities, many regarded the collection of eggs as an appropriate means to present their patriotism since it resonated with their sensibilities. Mrs W. Sanders, the Mayoress of South Molton, despatched a consignment of 540 eggs donated by the town's populace to the NECW in late August 1915.[253] Similarly, the Bideford Farmers' Union Depot of the NECW announced in December that it had sent a total of 15,750 eggs from the district.[254] Donating an egg or eggs to the NECW was a popular activity for many Devonians since it was a very straightforward and pragmatic way to support the war effort.[255] Due to the simplicity of this form of wartime philanthropy, a correspondent to the *South Devon Weekly Express* issued a challenge to the people of South Devon. He proposed that since it was a practical way to support the war, the local population would 'never be so unpatriotic as to refuse' to donate their eggs.[256] On first impression, the donation of eggs may seem to be a trivial matter. However, to Devonians, the contribution of eggs to the war effort was a symbolic gesture. The egg was also a symbol of hope in the Christian faith. By writing messages, painting pictures, and pencilling their name and address onto these items, they became tokens of communication, as important as letters and postcards. Accordingly, these donated eggs represented an emotional mutual connection between loved ones serving overseas in the military or anonymous individuals.[257]

Conclusion

During 1915, attempts to reinvigorate voluntary enlistment and recover the county's patriotic reputation did not achieve universal success across Devon. The evidence from the route marches reveals that the county's notable figures and recruiting officials continued to face an uphill struggle since many Devonian men still unconsciously objected to the prospect of military service. The noticeable absence of many eligible men during recruitment events does not reflect cowardice on the part of these men. Instead, they wanted to evade being pounced upon or cornered by members of Devon's local elite and Army recruiters who judged upon their rationalisations against military service. Similar ambitions to revive voluntary recruitment were evident during the autumn of 1915 when Earl Fortescue, alongside other notable figures acting as canvassers, sought to make the Derby Scheme successful across the county. However, canvassers in Devon encountered issues trying to complete their surveys. Many eligible men sought to avoid enlistment into the Army entirely by entering into 'starred' professions such as Munitions or Devonport Dockyard.

Although the inconsistencies in the volunteering ethos of recruitment continued to linger, the people of Devon presented their patriotism in more practical ways. This practical patriotism was evident during the route marches, where many Devonians donated food items and other comforts to the passing troops of the Devonshire Regiment. These gifts acted as tokens of emotional support and an appropriate demonstration of their patriotism and support for the war effort. Another public display of this humanitarian patriotism was the hospitality that the Mayoress of Exeter, along with her volunteers, bestowed to the troops that passed through Exeter's railway stations. Simultaneously, a suitable and humanitarian way that Devonians presented their patriotism was with large amounts of eggs the county's residents gave to support the war effort.

Chapter 4

The Shift from Self-Mobilisation to Remobilisation, 1916

When the Asquith Coalition government reviewed the results of the Derby Scheme in the early days of 1916, it was clear that the Scheme had not achieved the success many had hoped for.[1] The statistics revealed that more married men had attested than single men.[2] The Derby Scheme failed to convince the chief male demographic that the Government hoped would register for the Scheme. Since this last effort to save voluntary recruitment failed, the Asquith Coalition sought to introduce conscription with the Military Service Bill targeting the unmarried men who had not come forward. However, before Parliament voted on this legislation, the Government reopened the Derby Scheme on 10 January 1916 for a few weeks to allow men to volunteer or attest rather than face conscription.[3] In the *North Devon Journal* on 27 January, the editorial stressed that unmarried men in North Devon affected by the Military Service Bill should take up the opportunity to use the grace period to come forward voluntarily before conscription came into operation.[4]

At the same time in January, the first groups of men who had registered as reservists under the Derby Scheme received confirmation that they were soon to be mobilised for military service. One man who had received his call-up notice was Bill, the son of the local blacksmith in Kingston. As a blacksmith, the Army needed Bill's 'shoes' skills to repair and replace horseshoes for the horses used by the Army.[5] However, when local notable Edrica de la Pole visited the local blacksmith in Kingston on 12 January, she noticed that Bill's father, Thomas, was 'rather fussy' about Bill's call-up.[6] De la Pole may have concluded that Thomas was rather fussy about it in an attempt to obstruct Bill's call-up. Thomas's inflexible, obstinate attitude may be rooted in the fact that his son was the last in the line of a family of blacksmiths in Kingston who supported the business for 150 years.[7] Like Devon's agriculturalists, Thomas understood the possible ramifications of Bill's call-up on the family business's future. Yet de la Pole was not impressed with the behaviour of the two men towards this development. It led her to conclude that these men found the 'War "all right" until it touches them – then they yelp.'[8] De la Pole's observation emphasises how some men-folk in Devon continued to regard the conflict with indifference. This attitude remained until the war directly impacted them. Then, once the conflict's interference was established and intruded upon the possibility of their survival through the war years, these men painfully protested against it. A day later, De la Pole heard news that local man Harry Triggs was holding back from military service because he had an aversion to killing. In her diary, she acknowledged that whilst this was a natural reaction, she despaired about Triggs' attitude. If all men followed Triggs and 'put in the same plea[,] it would be a bad job' since no one would be prepared to fight.[9] However, the impact of the war upon the lives of Devon's residents became greater in 1916 when compulsory military service was introduced and administered through a vast network of Military Service Tribunals.

Policing patriotism on Devon's Military Service Tribunals and the 'round-up' raids

On 10 February 1916, the Military Service Act (MSA) introduced conscription for unmarried men aged 18 to 41. Like the Derby Scheme, conscription applied to England, Wales and Scotland but not Ireland. In May, the Government amended conscription to apply to married men.[10] Conscription would not apply to men medically unfit for military service, the sole supporters of dependants, or those engaged in vital war work.[11] However, before they were called up, men had the right under the MSA to submit an application for exemption against conscription into the Army. The LGB established a network of local military service tribunals to arbitrate upon these appeals against conscription. Although established by local government authorities such as borough councils, town councils, UDCs and RDCs, individual military service tribunals comprised volunteers from their respective local areas. Typically, these bodies included five public dignitaries from local civil society, such as local councillors, justices of the peace and the local Mayor. For example, as the Mayor of Tiverton, Alfred T Gregory sat as the chairman of the town's tribunal panel, while the chairman of Barnstaple's Tribunal was the town's Mayor, Frank Ashton Jewell.[12] At the same time, the MSA absorbed the network of tribunals previously established for the Derby Scheme, and these bodies became military service tribunals. Similarly, the volunteers who were part of these Derby tribunals were reappointed to administer the applications for exemption against conscription.[13]

Military Service Tribunal panels contained a military representative and a representative of the Board of Agriculture and Fisheries who represented the interests of farmers and fishermen. Since these tribunals operated in a very local context, tribunal panel members held the heavy responsibility to adjudicate upon claims against conscription on a local level.[14] In reviewing the applications from those seeking exemption against conscription, Devon's tribunalists had to balance the competing priorities of their local communities, the Military's demands for additional men and whether the man was indispensable to the applicant's employer. At the same time, tribunal members considered the applicant's personal and family circumstances in their decision-making.[15] Ultimately, these local tribunal panel members had to decide whether local eligible men should or should not be conscripted into the Army. After reviewing the individual's application, the tribunal could grant a certificate of exemption from conscription, whether this was an 'absolute, conditional or temporary exemption', or dismiss their application entirely.[16] However, the MSA also established a new level of tribunal that served each county whereby individuals could appeal against the decisions made by their local Tribunals.[17] At the same time, the Military possessed the right to lodge appeals to challenge the exemptions granted by local tribunals.

In Devon, the body that reviewed these appeals was the Devon Appeal Tribunal. Established on 3 March 1916, this body covered the administrative boundaries of Devon and the two county boroughs of Exeter and Plymouth. To arbitrate upon these appeals, Devon's Appeal Tribunal comprised prominent local citizens from the county's civil society, such as Sir Ian Heathcoat-Amory, Sir Trehawke Kekewich, and Miss Mary Sylvia Calmady-Hamlyn.[18]

For some of Devon's tribunalists who evaluated these applications on what grounds these eligible men should gain exemption from conscription, it must have been jarring to see these men, who failed as male citizens to undertake their duty and enlist voluntarily, now attempt to justify their claims against conscription.[19] When reviewing an individual's application for exemption against conscription, some tribunalists on local tribunals and the Appeal Tribunal used the behaviour of the applicants or their employers to make value judgements about their patriotism or lack thereof. One employer whose conduct Devon's tribunalists deemed to be 'unpatriotic' was Mr Blatchford, who ran a furnishing and building merchants business. Blatchford was present during a session of the county's Appeal Tribunal in Exeter on 9 June 1916 to defend his employee, Clement A. W. Carveth, after the Military appealed against the decision of the Okehampton Tribunal to grant Carveth an exemption for six months. In his defence, Blatchford stated that out of his 44 employees, he had only requested an exemption for one man for the summer. To try to reaffirm the sincerity of his application, Blatchford claimed that he had shown 'his patriotism' by allowing other apprentices from his company to join the Army.[20] Indeed, employers who released their employees in this way were praised for their patriotism by Tribunalists. In the West Yorkshire town of Holmfirth, the military representative for the town's tribunal, Colonel Mellor, commended employers for their 'patriotic attitude' who decided to release their employees for the armed forces.[21] However, in Blatchford's case, the Devon Appeal Tribunal members remained unconvinced by his defence and decided that they would not overrule the Military's appeal. Blatchford reacted angrily against the verdict, declaring he would hold onto his remaining apprentices for as long as possible. Like other employers who faced a similar predicament, Blatchford probably resented how the Military could interfere with their businesses by appealing against the decisions made by local tribunals. Nevertheless, Heathcoat-Amory was not impressed by Blatchford's protest. Based on how Blatchford responded, Heathcoat-Amory used his behaviour to make a value judgement about his lack of patriotism by retorting, 'I am sorry your patriotism is so thin.'[22]

A similar incident that formed the basis for Tribunalists to make a value judgement about patriotism was during the appeal of unattested cattleman Preston Pugsley. Although Preston received a conditional exemption from the local tribunal in the north Devon village of Shirwell, the military had appealed his exemption. When the North Devon Panel of the Devon Appeal Tribunal reviewed the appeal on 12 July 1916, William Pugsley, Preston's father and employer, sought an extension for Preston's exemption.[23] After reviewing his appeal, the Panel granted Preston a final extension until 1 September. However, this result did not satisfy William. If this result were final, William declared that he would have no choice but to sell his livestock. Lieutenant Stirling, the Panel's military representative, was offended by William's blunt and self-centred response. He asserted that the Pugsleys did not seem to care about the war and were concerned only about their stock.

As a result, Stirling concluded that there did not seem to be a 'pennyworth of patriotism going.'[24] These stark value judgements from Tribunalists, like those expressed by Heathcoat-Amory and Stirling, about an individual's lack of patriotism reached a wider audience across the county when these hearings were reported in the local press. The *Western Times* was one newspaper that capitalised upon Stirling's comment in their coverage of the hearing with the sensational headline that there was a lack of patriotism 'alleged against appellants in North Devon.'[25]

In the eyes of contemporaries, one male figure who epitomised a selfish disregard towards the national interest, thereby lacking any sense of patriotism, was the Conscientious Objector since these men opposed military service based on their political or religious beliefs.[26] Under the terms of the MSA, a man claiming to hold such an objection to military service could apply for exemption from conscription on the grounds of conscientious objection. However, he needed to make his case before a tribunal panel to secure this exemption. Contemporaries suspected that many eligible men claimed to hold a conscientious objection to military service merely as an excuse to avoid going into the Army. For many men claiming to be conscientious objectors, the experience of facing a tribunal panel to obtain this exemption could be humiliating.[27] Like the notable figures who made up the tribunal panels of Carmarthenshire, Devon's tribunalists employed intense and probing questioning in their cross-examinations of men claiming to be conscientious objectors.[28] When viewed in the context of superintending patriotism, Devon's tribunalists employed interrogations against pacifists in the hope that these cross-examinations would expose these men as unpatriotic shirkers and bring them to face justice.

A man who faced such intense questioning since he professed to be a conscientious objector was casual builder Arthur Short Portbury. Although he belonged to no religious body, Portbury claimed he was a pacifist Christian and appealed against conscription on religious grounds. Although some conscientious objectors agreed to help the war effort through service in non-combative roles, Portbury refused to make any such undertaking since his objection to the war was absolute.[29] On 11 March 1916, the Exeter tribunal reviewed Portbury's application against conscription. The tribunal's chairman and the city's Mayor, James George Owen, cross-examined Portbury. Owen presented a hypothetical situation to Portbury where a German soldier who had landed on Devon's shores was torturing a woman. If Portbury saw such a horrendous scene, Owen asked Portbury if he would run away. However, Portbury shied away from answering Owen's question.[30] The fact that Portbury evaded answering Owen's direct question seemed to confirm before the Tribunal that Portbury was, in reality, a coward. However, traumatic speculative scenarios, such as those employed by Exeter's Mayor, were a typical feature of the questioning utilised by tribunalists across England and Wales against conscientious objectors in the hope that these awkward predicaments would expose their cowardice.[31] Subsequently, Portbury's defence did not convince the members of the Exeter Tribunal as they dismissed his application. They believed Portbury was motivated by self-preservation rather than a sincere conscientious objection against military service. Based on Portbury's conduct during the session, a correspondent for the *Western Times* concluded that this man was an 'inveterate coward' who had 'no love of country.'[32]

Nevertheless, Portbury appealed the decision of Exeter's tribunal to dismiss his application. When the Exeter Panel of the Devon Appeal Tribunal reviewed Portbury's appeal on 31 March 1916, the Panel members subjected Portbury to a further re-examination. On this occasion, Portbury's chief interrogator was Sir Trehawke Kekewich. The intense cross-examination that Kekewich employed against Portbury included asking whether he would eat bread or cheese as these items were full of life and that he was taking life by consuming these food items. The panel's military representative, Captain Vosper, also used this line of questioning against Portbury.[33] Although he opposed the prospect of taking human life, Portbury acknowledged that he had no objections to eating food items such as the meat of farm animals that had once teemed with life, which someone else had killed for food production. This line of questioning also presented Portbury as a selfish hypocrite. Just as he relied upon someone else to kill farm animals for food, he relied upon someone else to protect him and do the fighting for him. Accordingly, Portbury's inconsistent answers to these probing queries undermined the sincerity of his conscientious objection. As the presiding Chairman, Heathcoat-Amory concluded that Portbury's defence had not satisfied the Appeal Tribunal any more than Exeter's tribunal. Portbury declared in a final note of defiance that he would rather face prosecution than undertake military service.[34]

Based on the interrogative humiliations that pacifists like Portbury received at their local Tribunal or the county's Appeal Tribunal, other conscientious objectors were keen to avoid such ridicule. One conscientious objector who probably wanted to avoid being shamed before an Appeal Tribunal was Ralph R. Willott, an assistant in a music shop and member of the No-Conscription Fellowship. When the Newton Abbot Tribunal reviewed his application for exemption, they judged that Willott was a pacifist but should serve in a non-combatant corps.[35] Although Willott appealed against the Tribunal's decision, he later withdrew this application because he had decided to present himself to the Royal Navy.[36] By joining the Navy, Willott had effectively dodged conscription into the Army and avoided the humiliating interrogation and judgements from a Tribunal panel. To join the Royal Navy or the Royal Marines was a viable way for eligible men in Devon to avoid conscription. A key selling point of the recruitment campaigns for the Navy and the Royal Marines after the introduction of conscription was that it allowed eligible men to join since the voluntary system of recruitment for the Navy was still open.[37] One Devonian employer who assisted men to join the Royal Navy was Mr Glass Senior from the agricultural implement makers Messrs J. Glass and Son based in Okehampton. Before the Exeter Panel of the Devon Appeal Tribunal on 15 December 1916, Glass Senior revealed that he had trained twenty-five men in engineering with a view to joining the Navy. This route was successful as he claimed that all of them had passed for service in the Navy.[38]

Many Devonians viewed joining the Navy as preferable to conscription into the Army. Upon receiving his papers in 1918 to report for an Army medical examination in Exeter, William Stone, a resident of the South Hams village of Ledstone, was adamant that he would join the Navy at Plymouth instead. By employing this strategy, he honoured his family's naval tradition whilst successfully circumventing conscription into the Army.[39] Another way that men sought to outmanoeuvre conscription was by going into munitions work. On 7 October 1916, the military representative of Bideford's Borough Tribunal, Mr Fairbrother, asked local baker and caterer W. C. Friendship what had happened to the two men he had employed. Friendship replied that one of the men, Darch, had left his employment. Although Darch informed Friendship that he was going to join the Army, he had instead journeyed up to Scotland to undertake munition work.[40] The news of Darch's departure prompted Fairbrother to complain that this was another example of a 'man who slipped through the net.'[41]

Although conscientious objectors were more likely to be subject to intense cross-examinations before military service tribunals, some eligible men experienced similar interrogations with unexpected lines of questioning. One man probably caught off-guard by Tribunal members' questions was an engraver who, on 27 September 1916, had passed for general service at Plymouth Tribunal. However, the Tribunal's military representative suggested that the man had been 'clever enough to avoid military service by starting a business on his own.'[42] Probably shocked by this unexpected snide accusation, the engraver refuted the charge from the military representative. He claimed he had not set up the business as a strategy to avoid military service because he had opened his business fourteen months prior.[43] By employing surprising trick questions, figures on the tribunals hoped to get the truth out of those they suspected were not sincere in their applications for exemption. Like the engraver facing an unexpected charge at the Tribunal, some men probably felt as if they had to face a court comparable to the experience of a judge interrogating a suspect. The fact that some men faced such cutting accusations from tribunal panels gave the impression that Tribunalists were interrogating those seeking exemption as if they were criminals. They may have feared becoming trapped by tricky questioning from Tribunalists. Other men may have also suspected that Tribunal or an Appeal Tribunal panel members interrogated them, intending to deliberately catch them out, trip them up or humble them. Within this Tribunal setting, being questioned by older men, some young men who faced these Tribunals may have felt like they were back at school and interrogated or humiliated as if they were children (Figure 12).

Devon's tribunalists were also wary that some men presenting their applications may not have been sincere in the information they supplied in their applications. On 14 July 1916, the Dulverton local Tribunal received an anonymous letter from a resident in the Exmoor village of Simonsbath, which claimed that a recent applicant had gained exemption under false pretences by exaggerating the farm's acreage.[44] Although several tribunal members were wary about such material submitted anonymously, they agreed that the Clerk should write to the applicant to request further information. Like the Dulverton tribunal, some tribunal panel members wanted to substantiate the claims of those seeking exemption. On 10 October, the military submitted an appeal before the Plymouth tribunal against the conditional exemption granted to a refreshment housekeeper based on the information disclosed in an anonymous letter. The letter alleged that the housekeeper had sold the business but 'attended a few hours a day as an excuse for avoiding military service.'[45] Cornered by this allegation, the housekeeper explained that the sale had not yet gone through. Although the Tribunal's Military Representative, J. L. Wolferstan, wanted the housekeeper's exemption changed to a temporary exemption, the Mayor of Plymouth, Thomas Baker, said the tribunal would confirm their decision of conditional exemption and rely upon the man giving information once he had sold the business.[46]

Although Devon's tribunalists saw themselves as undertaking a necessary but challenging public service for the nation, some of Devon's residents, like some citizens in Essex, did not necessarily view the military service tribunals as entities dispensing 'local justice against unpatriotic shirkers.'[47] Devon's tribunalists faced local animosity because they had the authority to decide the fate of the men who applied for exemption against conscription, in effect possessing the power of life and death for these local men. The decisions made by Devon's tribunalists, along with their prescriptions to Devon's populace, may have heightened frustrations among men seeking exemption since they felt that they were powerless before the tribunal panels. In the west Dorset village of Marshwood, local resident Mr Lumbard probably felt powerless when he was left waiting after he defended his application for exemption to the local tribunal on 4 October 1916. Despite making his case, the Tribunal panel did not inform Lumbard of the result of his application. Instead, they told Lumbard that they would write to him with their decision about whether they would award him an exemption from conscription.[48] The fact that the tribunals possessed such power over the lives of citizens helps explain the antagonism some Devonians expressed towards the tribunals when they presented their appeals against military service.

Since the Military Service Tribunals now determined the manpower for the British Army, the men and women on these tribunals were in fact 'agents of the state [who] pursued military manpower in the face of individual opposition and economic interests.'[49] Since some decisions by Devon's tribunals emphasised dedicating manpower to military efficiency rather than local interests, there would be eventual criticism of an unsympathetic decision. James McDermott has suggested that uncompassionate responses towards applications for exemption helped to imbue some of the tribunal panels with a quality of 'otherness.'[50] The lack of sympathy from Tribunalists towards an individual's application against conscription also reinforces the suggestion that some contemporaries viewed the tribunals with suspicion. At the same time, eligible men who came before the tribunals may have suspected that the county's tribunals only wanted to secure men for the Army rather than grant exemptions. It was hard to ignore that many of the men and women who administered over their claims against conscription had previously 'worked tirelessly to take men from civilian life and place them in Khaki.'[51] Some believed that these tribunalists carried over this mindset in their work arbitrating the appeals against conscription since they scrutinised and judged upon the rationalisations that these men or their representatives used to justify to gain exemption from conscription.

This sense of 'otherness' about tribunalists led some contemporaries to view Devon's tribunalists and the tribunal proceedings in a conspiratorial light. One man who claimed that the county's Appeal Tribunal operated this way was William Bond, an insurance company collector of the Pearl Assurance Company in Newton Abbot. During the Exeter panel of the Appeal Tribunal on 18 August 1916, Bond attempted to defend two of the Pearl Assurance Company's employees after the Military had appealed their exemption by the Newton Abbot tribunal. After heated exchanges between the respective parties, the Appeal Tribunal panel upheld the Military's appeals. In response, Bond accused the Appeal Tribunal's military representative, Lieutenant Stirling, of being a bully because he 'browbeat' people.[52] Moreover, he denounced the tribunal's verdict as biased and predetermined. However, Stirling threw accusations back at Bond, suggesting that he went around to the local tribunals appearing for other people rather than 'doing his own work.'[53] Moreover, he warned Bond that he would 'come over the table' and show him what kind of a man he was.[54] Stirling asserted that Bond ought to be ashamed of his outburst, and Kekewich warned Bond to leave the court or, otherwise, he would be 'dealt with under military law.'[55] In their reporting on the tribunal proceedings, the *Devon and Exeter Gazette* was sympathetic to the tribunalists. The paper contended that the people on the tribunals had to undertake 'sufficiently arduous work without being insulted by men of the Bond type.'[56]

Yet, the relationship between the decision-makers on the county's Appeal Tribunal and those on Devon's local tribunals was sometimes fraught. Since local tribunals had the sovereignty to determine who should receive exemption from conscription, the tribunal system produced significant 'inconsistencies from region to region and hindered a coordinated approach to manpower.'[57]

The discrepancies in who gained exemption encouraged criticisms levelled against specific local Tribunals in Devon. The South Molton Rural District Tribunal was one such local tribunal. During an appeal of an unnamed tailor at the Exeter Panel of the Devon Appeal Tribunal on 28 July 1916, the applicant revealed that South Molton's Tribunal had granted an exemption to his brother, who worked as a cutter. Although Heathcoat-Amory was surprised that a cutter received an exemption, Lieutenant Stirling added this was not uncommon at South Molton since they granted exemptions to every man who came before them.[58] There may be validity in Lieutenant Stirling's claim as the *Western Times* criticised the South Molton Tribunal on 7 April for the large number of exemption certificates that the panel awarded.[59] Indeed, the *Daily Telegraph* also condemned the Tribunal for the same reason since the paper revealed that when the South Molton Tribunal last convened, they reviewed 111 applications for exemption. Out of the 111 applicants, the paper sensationally reported that 94 men received exemptions from military service, and only three men were conscripted.[60] Lieutenant Stirling later decried the South Molton tribunal in more damning terms during a sitting of the Northern panel of the Devon Appeal Tribunal on 16 August. He believed it was apparent that all the single men had gone to South Molton to get exemptions.[61] Based on the generous number of exemptions that the Tribunal granted, it was clear that South Molton 'was not producing, as it should, men for the Army.'[62] In their reporting of the sitting, the *Devon and Exeter Gazette* suggested that Stirling had made 'serious reflections' upon the lack of patriotism in South Molton.[63] If Stirling's claims were true, the newspaper prescribed that it was 'the duty of every patriotic man' in the area surrounding the North Devon town to 'give such information to the authorities as will secure the attendance of slackers at the military centres.'[64]

In Tiverton, local resident L. A. Sayer alleged that the town's Tribunal gave some men special treatment since 'certain others' had gained exemption.[65] Sayer's allegation of favouritism may reflect his grievance against Tiverton's Tribunal since the body had not granted him exemption and wanted to smear the Tribunal in the hope that this would strengthen his appeal. Rural populations in the southern states of the United States of America voiced similar complaints that 'men with "pull"' received preferential treatment at the local and district boards that administered the draft of American military-age men into the Army.[66] However, the 'certain others' that Sayer referred to may have come from the local farming community. On 18 July 1916, the military representative for the Tiverton Tribunal, Colonel Couchman, made a statement for his colleagues on the Tribunal. He stressed that when they considered the appeals from the local farmers, the Tribunal panel members needed to 'harden their hearts' and evaluate these cases objectively because agriculture would be useless 'if the Germans got the upper hand.'[67] Like the members of Tiverton's tribunal, other Tribunalists on Devon's rural tribunals were sympathetic towards agricultural interests. Earl Fortescue later suggested that due to the familiarity of these figures with farming, the people serving on the county's rural tribunals had 'given more weight to the needs of agriculture which they thoroughly understood than to the necessities of the Army which they only imperfectly appreciated.'[68] Therefore, Devon's rural tribunals often took a 'parochial view of the situation' when they made their decisions.[69] The Government shared Fortescue's frustrations against local tribunalists because they seemed to embody the 'inertial drag of local priorities.'[70] However, some contemporaries interpreted the predisposition of rural tribunals to be sympathetic towards local farming interests in more negative terms.

Columnist Harold Ashton touched upon this negative public perception of Devon's rural tribunals in a series of sensational articles published in the *Daily Mail* during the autumn of 1916. Like the farmers of the Yorkshire dales, Ashton claimed that the agriculturalists in mid-Devon sought to shelter their sons from conscription. One Devon farmer confided to Ashton that it was scandalous how his fellow agriculturalists underhandedly worked the county's rural tribunals through secret backhanded deals. As a result of the scheming machinations of Devon's farmers, Ashton implied that backroom deals between tribunalists and farmers agreeing on granting exemptions against conscription were commonplace across the county. Ashton suggested that Devon's agriculturalists had the power to manipulate the decisions of these tribunals in their favour because these panels comprised 'farmers or persons directly concerned with agriculture and landholding.'[71] Sir Ernest Satow also concluded that the local farmers held great sway over how the tribunal system operated after three Ottery St Mary Tribunal members resigned in early 1917. When the time came to fill these vacant seats, Satow proposed that E. J. Manley could serve as a possible replacement for one of the posts. However, Ottery St Mary UDC member H. D. Baddock was elected to fill one of the vacant seats on the tribunal instead. Reflecting on the vote, Satow believed Baddock had won due to the local 'farming clique.'[72]

Yet, in his articles for the *Daily Mail*, Ashton suggested that many rural tribunals in Devon were supposedly biased towards the county's farmers. Due to how widespread this phenomenon was across the Devon countryside, Ashton proposed that Devon was a county overflowing with 'clotted cream ... and exemptions.'[73] Since many Devonshire farmers were guided primarily by their wallets and not by loyalty to their nation, Ashton claimed they operated under the war cry of 'Purse before Patriotism'.[74] Newspaper articles, like those by Ashton and other correspondents, addressed the suspicion that rural tribunals did not experience the same level of accountability as urban ones due to a perceived 'civilisational distinction' between the behaviour of individuals in close-knit urban localities and those in provincial and sparsely populated rural areas.[75] After the *Daily Mail* published Ashton's article, Devon's newspapers reported and commented upon the article's allegations about the lack of patriotism in the county.[76] The *Devon and Exeter Gazette* suggested that the unpleasant reports from the county's tribunals seemed to confirm Ashton's allegations because there were still many single hardy young fellows undertaking work in the countryside that older married men could complete.[77] In a later edition, the newspaper suggested that Ashton's conclusion, where many farmers in Devon operated under the ethos of 'Purse before Patriotism', was not isolated to the county's agriculturalists. The paper advocated that a review of the exemptions that the tribunals had granted should be completed since the desire of men to shirk their duty was 'clearly apparent in a good many [Devon] districts', both town and country.[78]

The advent of conscription brought a new rationale to the Volunteer Training Corps (VTC), where the Corps provided exempted men with military training before they eventually faced combat in the Army. For the appellants granted temporary exemption at the Brixham Tribunal, one condition of their exemption was to attest and attend military drills with the local VTC.[79] As a local paramilitary volunteer defence force, the VTC comprised men who were usually outside the requirements of military service.[80] However, if the exempted man was medically unfit to serve with the VTC, they could either have this condition withdrawn or told to join the Special Constabulary.[81] Through service in the VTC, exempted men could still make a contribution to help the war effort. However, the tribunal panels that imposed this requirement upon a man's exemption from conscription had to enforce their compliance with this prerequisite of their exemption.[82] In the case of Brixham's Tribunalists, some men did not adhere to this condition of their exemption. Two such men who had not appeared at any of the Brixham's VTC drills were J. Lawe and H. Tulley. After hearing this news during their meeting on 3 November 1916, the members of the Brixham Tribunal requested both men to attend the Tribunal's next meeting or explain why they had not participated in any drills.[83] Despite the Tribunal's repeated attempts, Tulley was still absent at the Brixham VTC's drills and marches. Accordingly, the tribunal members decided to write to Tulley to state that unless he attended the training exercise of Brixham's VTC within a week, the Tribunal would have no choice but to withdraw his certificate of conditional exemption.[84] At the same time, the Tribunalists instructed the clerk to write to 'certain other members' to warn them that unless they attended drill regularly, the Tribunal would consider withdrawing their certificates of exemption.[85] From the perspective of the Brixham Tribunalists, they wanted to use Tulley as an example to other exempted men that if they neglected this obligation of their exemption, they could face the same disciplinary measure. Accordingly, the requirement for individuals to participate in Brixham's VTC was a challenging commitment for the Tribunal to enforce upon exempted men.

In the autumn of 1916, many contemporaries suspected that large numbers of military-age men had successfully evaded military service by avoiding national registration. Acting upon these suspicions, the War Office authorised local authorities across the United Kingdom to conduct a series of searches to find these men. For three weeks in September 1916, local police forces and the military authorities coordinated and carried out a series of searches, otherwise known as 'round-up' raids. These raids sought to catch male citizens of military age attempting to evade military service under the MSA. In the hope of finding and capturing these shirkers, local police forces and military authorities chose locations and events where these men were likely to visit or congregate, such as football stadiums, music halls and theatres. Once they had selected the locations where they wanted to conduct their searches, the military authorities and the police planned and implemented the following sequence for a typical 'round-up' raid. After announcing their presence in the building, the local policemen and military authorities searched the premises and challenged every man they believed was of military age to provide evidence of their exemption by showing their registration cards, exemption

Figure 1. Portrait of Stephen Reynolds by Henry Lamb. (*Sidmouth Museum*)

Figure 2. Portrait of Hugh Fortescue, the Fourth Earl Fortescue, by Charles Haslewood Shannon. (*Devon County Council*)

Figure 3. Portrait of Sir James Owen. (*Exeter City Council*)

Figure 4. Portrait of Lady J Kirk Owen. (*Exeter City Council*)

THE DEVONS.

Bravo, Devons, you're the sort,
To make poor Bill sit up and snort;
Your "Devon Cream" without a question,
Is giving the Kaiser indigestion!

G.B

Figure 5. The Devons. (*Authors private collection*)

Rifle or Football——Which?

Figure 6. FAB, 'Rifle or Football---Which?', *Devon and Exeter Gazette*, 5 September 1914, p. 4. (*With thanks to The British Newspaper Archive*)

Figure 7. Devon's Recruiting at Ilfracombe. (*Authors Private Collection*)

Figure 8. Recruiting officer swearing in new men; May 3, 1915. (*Authors Private Collection*)

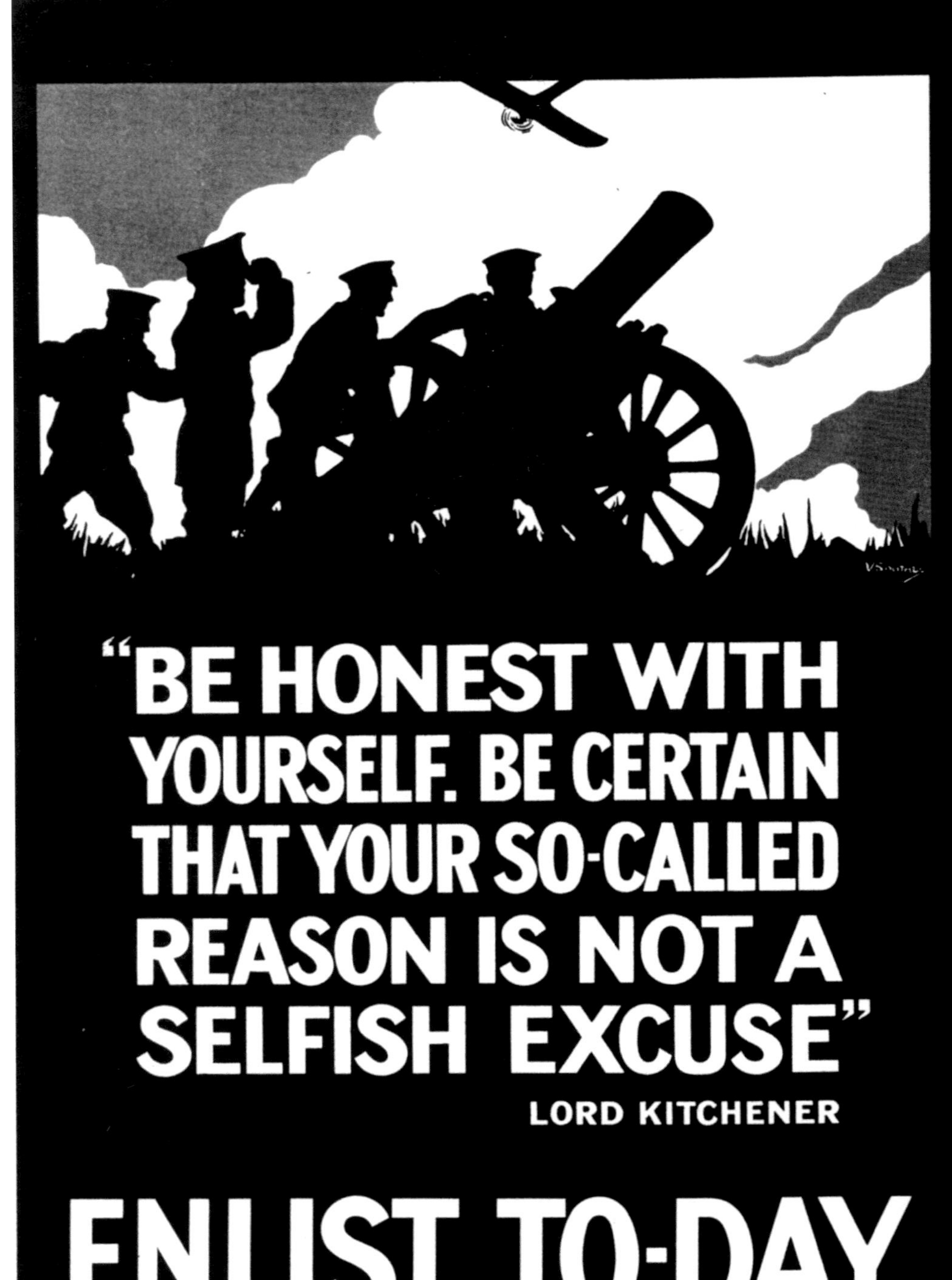

Figure 9. "Be honest with yourself. Be certain that your so-called reason is not a selfish excuse" Lord Kitchener. Enlist to-day; 1915. (*Library of Congress, Prints and Photographs Division, LC-USZC4-11025 POS – WW1 – Gt Brit, no. 99*)

Figure 10. The Recruiting Sergt. Tackling likely recruits. (*Authors Private Collection*)

Figure 11. Photograph of Lady Owen feeding troops at St. Davids Station, 1915, Exeter. (*Image copyright: The Trustees of the Devon and Exeter Institution*)

Figure 12. How I felt before the Tribunal. (*Authors private collection*)

certificates or War service badges. While the police and military authorities inspected the documentation of these men, other policemen, along with the military police, were stationed in positions to guard all the possible exits that a man could use to escape the premises. At the same time, it is likely that unsuspecting eligible men at these 'haunts' were likely to be caught by surprise without their respective documents present since they had come to these venues to unwind or socialise. Once the military officer or policeman was satisfied with the authenticity of the man's documentation, the man was allowed to leave the premises.[86] However, if an eligible man could not produce the necessary evidence of their registration or had left his exemption certificate at home, the police would take down his name and address for further enquiries. The police may even detain him at the police station.

In their reporting of the announcement of these 'round-up' raids for absentees, the *Middlesex Chronicle* used a historical parallel comparing them to Press Gangs used to round up recruits during the Napoleonic wars.[87] However, the 'round-up' raids in Britain during September 1916 more resembled the later 'slacker raids' that took place in 1918 in the United States of America. The men of the APL played a crucial role in assisting Law Enforcement officials to carry out large-scale searches throughout America for suspected slackers and draft dodgers.[88] Like the police forces and military authorities in Britain who co-ordinated individual 'round-up' raids, the American police officers planned the slacker raids to entrap draft dodgers and stop them from escaping. These preparations were evident when law enforcement authorities planned a slacker raid at the Young's and Million Dollar Piers in Atlantic City, New Jersey, on 15 August 1918 since they prepared diagrams of the Piers indicating the positions where each policeman and Department of Justice Agent should be stationed to stop men from escaping.[89] Once they found American military-age men still in civilian clothes, the APL members on the 'slacker raids' challenged them to produce their classification cards or draft registration to prove that they had not avoided the draft.[90] However, if these men did not present these materials when demanded by the men of the APL, they would 'likely be picked up as slackers and detained' until they produced the required documentation to authenticate their credentials.[91] On 7 July 1918, squads of APL officers conducted a 'slacker raid' at the Grand Circuit opening meeting season at the North Randall racecourse near Cleveland, Ohio. These officers searched the people amongst the mammoth crowd for 'men of draft age who had failed to register.'[92] A similar 'slacker raid' occurred in Lexington, Kentucky in September 1918 at the Kentucky Racing Association racetrack. Local agents of the APL in Kentucky supported the County and City police in the raid, and they discovered 12 men at the racecourse who were not carrying their draft cards on them. Officers subsequently brought these men to the courthouse, where they remained in custody until the authorities could verify that they were registered for the draft.[93]

'Round-up' raids occurred in Devon alongside other parts of the United Kingdom. Following complaints from the public that many men of military age were still at large in Exeter who had been overlooked by both the military and the city's police force, a round-up raid occurred in Exeter during the evening of 23 September.[94] Under the direction of Chief Constable Arthur Nicholson, several members of the city's police force visited entertainment venues in Exeter including the Theatre, the Hippodrome and the Picture Palaces. At the Theatre, just after the curtain had come down on a performance of William Shakespeare's *Othello*, the theatre's manager came up to the stage to announce that the police were waiting to examine all the eligible men in the audience. After the ineligible men and women had left the premises, all the remaining men of military age were 'gathered together in the pit' to be questioned.[95] Meanwhile, at the city's Hippodrome, the police took the names and addresses of about thirty eligible men not carrying their exemption certificates. Whilst 318 eligible men produced exemption certificates, 127 did not have the necessary papers on them in Exeter that night. Although the police took the names and addresses of 126 men, the evening's round-up did result in one arrest.[96] The man that the police arrested at the Hippodrome was Harold John Rowe from the mid Devon village of Ide, who claimed that he was waiting for the 'papers to fetch him'.[97]

In Plymouth, the city's police force and military authorities selected the Cosmopolitan Gymnasium as the location for their first 'round-up' raid. They arrived at the Gym on the evening of 15 September 1916 during a boxing match.[98] Although the majority of the men cooperated with the authorities during their search, the police did catch one young man trying to escape through a window and promptly pulled him back inside.[99] Whilst the police made no arrests, they did take the names and addresses of around 200 men who did not produce the necessary documentation.[100] Plymouth police conducted a later 'round-up' raid on 22 September at the city's Theatre Royal and the Promenade Pier. In both locations, the police encountered a few men who, despite wearing their War Service badges, did not think it was necessary to carry their registration cards as well.[101] A correspondent for the *Western Morning News* argued that a reason to explain the lack of arrests on this raid was that the eligible men in the city were now cautious and on their guard due to the earlier 'round-up' at the gym.[102] Later on 27 September, the local police and military authorities raided a music hall in Devonport during an evening performance of *She's a Daisy*. Although the police recorded the names and addresses of several men in the audience, no arrests were made.[103] Three days later, the Torquay police alongside the military authorities launched a 'round-up' at the town's cinema.[104] They discovered a large number of military-age men inside the premises who did not possess the necessary documentation in their pockets. As a result, these men were detained in the cinema's waiting room and questioned by the police. Like the raid at the music hall in Devonport, the police did not arrest any men on the Torquay 'round-up'. Based on this result, a correspondent for the *Western Times* reported that on this occasion, unfortunately, the 'bag' was empty.[105]

On 9 September 1916, Lynton police and military representatives conducted a systematic search for eligible men on Exmoor. One location on the moor they searched was a Gipsy camp.[106] A correspondent for the *Western Morning News* reported that once the police and the military authorities arrived at the camp, many men wearing little clothing bolted from their tents.[107] Despite these fleeing men, the police managed to apprehend two men: brothers William Birch and Robert Birch. When caught by the police, the latter man declared that he was 42 and had grown a beard to give him an older appearance. However, Robert's mother contradicted her son's answer by telling the police that Robert was only 47.[108] The Barnstaple Magistrates fined both men £2 and ordered them to be handed over to the military authorities.[109]

The police and military authorities also decided to target popular events where eligible men from Devon's rural localities would likely travel to meet or socialise. In this case, it was the local autumn fairs. On 15 September, the Barnstaple police and military authorities launched a 'round up' raid at the Barnstaple Fair.[110] Under the direction of Chief Constable R. S. Eddy, the police interrogated between 400 and 500 men who had come to the Fair.[111] Around 30 men had left their exemption certificates at home. In practically all the cases that the police and military authorities encountered, these men had gained exemption but had not brought their certificates with them. Since they did not provide the required documentation, the police detained these men while they made the necessary checks. In one instance, the check lasted two hours, and the man was handed over to the military.[112] On 17 September, the police and Military Authorities launched a 'round-up' raid for military-age men at the Totnes Fair. According to a correspondent for the *Western Times*, the police caught 56 men who were then marched in batches to the police station, where an officer took their names and addresses to make further enquiries.[113]

From the perspective of the police and military authorities, the 'round-up' raids in Devon, like the raids organised for other parts of the United Kingdom, produced very unsatisfactory results.[114] A correspondent for the *Tiverton Gazette* believed that if the authorities launched a 'round-up' raid on Bampton Fair, it would likely have proven fruitless since the men of military age present at the event wore 'conspicuous armlets and were obviously of the type that work on the land, and could not be called up for the Army this year.'[115] Many newspapers criticised the invasive nature of the raids. The *Western Morning News* argued that these hunts for shirkers were counter-productive since they utilised 'Prussian methods', achieved ludicrously small results and caused resentment amongst the general public.[116] The *Taunton Courier and Western Advertiser* expressed similar criticism against the 'press gang policy' after a second 'round-up' raid in Taunton at the Somerset town's Cattle Market on 16 September proved fruitless.[117] Although the *North Wales Weekly News* acknowledged that people held different points of view about the 'round-up' raids, whether they were patriotic or invasive, the tabloid argued that it was utterly unjustifiable on the point of principle 'to arrest men wholesale, and to march them off to the police station, exposed to public ridicule.'[118] One anonymous author from Exeter, writing under the pen name of Citizen, sent a letter to the *Western Morning News* complaining about the efficacy of the 'round-up' raids in the city. According to the writer, it was little wonder that the 'round-up' system was useless because eligible men had found a safe refuge under the navy 'umbrella'. Citizen questioned how many thousands of stalwart eligible men were walking around wearing navy armlets. In their view, these men 'had been "fly" enough' to boast that they had signed up as Navy reservists to 'evade the army in the hope they would not be wanted for the navy for a long time and so save their skins.'[119] One man who sought to find slackers hiding in Bolton was John Kay, an elderly resident, who conducted a 'round-up' raid at the Grand Theatre in the Greater Manchester town. Like the earlier official 'round-up' raids at theatres, Kay demanded that the audience members produce their exemption and registration cards. However, just like the September 'round-up' raids, the people subjected to this search 'resented very much being bothered in this way.'[120] Although Kay claimed he had obtained authorisation from the assistant military representative, Councillor Hargraves, to conduct this search, this was not the case. When Kay stood trial at Bolton Borough police Court on 16 October 1916, Councillor Hargraves said that Kay was troubled with 'an excess of patriotic zeal' for behaving in this fashion.[121] Like other intrusive busybodies motivated by a spirit of patriotism, Kay had taken it upon himself to act because he believed he could supplement the activities of the police to find these shirkers. Indeed, Hargraves proposed that Kay thought he possessed the 'faculty of improving the work of the police in all directions.'[122] Upon review of the case where Kay was prosecuted under the Defence of the Realm Act, the Bench fined him 9s to cover the costs.

Women Workers in Devon

Following the introduction of conscription, the campaign to substitute male labour with women in British industries became a more urgent priority.[123] In the case of agriculture, this ambition was especially acute. Prominent women from Devon's civil society launched a concerted campaign in 1916 to educate the county's farmers about the merits of female labour. One notable figure who attempted to convince Devon's farmers to take on women was Lady Fortescue. At a public meeting in South Molton on 20 January, she declared that Devon's unmarried women were the best alternative source of labour for the county's farmers who required people for farm work. Although the wives of Devon's farmers worked very hard on the land, Lady Fortescue hoped that she could change the perception of the county's farmers towards female labour. One example she used was the women of France who were nobly working the land while their men were fighting in the trenches.[124]

As President of the Devon Women's War Service Committee (DWWSC), Mrs Alice Mildmay was another notable lady who spearheaded efforts to get more women from the county to work on the land. At a meeting on 21 January 1916 in the south Devon town of Totnes, Mildmay revealed that Devon had fallen behind compared to other counties in England.

Northumberland was one such county since it had 56 per cent of women working on the land.[125] Other notable women in Devon also promoted the merits of female labour in agriculture within the discourses of patriotism. Miss Mary Sylvia Calmady-Hamlyn was another prominent local citizen who was instrumental in campaigning for more women to work on the land in Devon.[126] On 4 February, she issued one such appeal during a Women for Service in Agriculture meeting at Barnstaple. To encourage more women to register their interest in agricultural work, Calmady-Hamlyn presented the women's war-work movement in the county as a vital means to restore Devon's patriotic reputation. Since a slur had been 'cast on the patriotism of some parts of Devonshire', Calmady-Hamlyn argued that it rested upon the county's women to 'save the fair name of Devonshire.'[127] Where the men of Devon had faltered by not volunteering and undermining the county's patriotic fame, the county's women had the chance to step forward and restore the county's patriotic prestige by working on the land. She hoped that this challenge to present their patriotism would prompt Devon's women to register their interest in agricultural work and lead the way to self-sacrifice and victory. Indeed, Calmady-Hamlyn claimed it was a slur against the patriotism of parts of Cornwall that spurred Cornish women to register their interest in agricultural work to restore their county's prestige. As a result, Cornwall's register of women was higher than that of other counties in England. Calmady-Hamlyn emphasized this comparison to foster a sense of competition between Devon and Cornwall in the hope that Devon's women would come forward in greater numbers and put Devon ahead of even Cornwall. Fellow speaker Miss Gladys Pott also framed her declaration within the discourses of patriotism when she expressed her confidence that there would be many recruits from the county because 'Devonshire people were highly patriotic.'[128] Calmady-Hamlyn argued that if women of leisure and position demonstrated that they were prepared to undertake agricultural work, they would set a patriotic example to all classes of Devon's women.[129] The sight of these women undertaking agricultural work would provide a more substantial basis upon which they could appeal to Devon's working-class women to work the land. Later in December, the Chairman of the DFU, William Tremlett, also suggested that the example of educated women undertaking work on the land 'would in time stimulate the patriotism of the others.'[130]

One strategy to convince Devon's farmers about women's agricultural capabilities was to demonstrate the achievements of their labour on the county's farms. Francis Acland, the Parliamentary Secretary to the Board of Agriculture and the Liberal MP for Camborne, emphasised an example of their achievements in the House of Commons on 22 May 1916. The anecdote involved a local farmer who had complained to Mrs Mildmay that he could not find a single woman in Devon to spread manure on his farm. Mrs Mildmay accepted the challenge. Accordingly, she organised her house party of ladies, comprising women, rich and poor, to visit the farm and spread the manure. After they had completed the task, the astonished farmer paid them for the work. In turn, they donated their wages to the Red Cross. Acland hoped that the accomplishments of Mildmay's group would make a considerable impression in the county.[131] The secretary for the DWWSC, F. M. Dickinson, also wanted to highlight the achievements of Mrs Mildmay's house party in a letter to *The Times* on 3 June 1916. According to Dickinson, the group's actions had undeniably set a precedent for the county's women. Since the event, these women had worked diligently on the land, engaging in gruelling tasks such as 'pulling turnips, [and] clearing stones off the land.'[132]

Yet some women in the county were sceptical that the campaign initiated by women in Devon's civil society to encourage young unmarried women to undertake agricultural work would be successful. Mrs L. Morgan, a resident of the north Devon village of Newbridge, expressed her misgivings about this campaign in a letter to the editor of the *North Devon Journal*. Although the meetings organised by Lady Fortescue and other notable women appealed to unemployed girls over school age to work on the land, Morgan was pessimistic about their chances of finding these girls. Morgan believed they would have to visit 'houses where domestic servants are kept and appeal to the patriotism of mistress and maids.'[133] Moreover, a wage of three pence per hour to pull turnips alongside other agricultural activities was not, in her view, a worthwhile inducement to convince cooks and housemaids who were earning £20 to £30 a year.[134] Morgan argued that Devon's mothers should focus on their households instead of working on the land. She hoped they possessed enough patriotism to realise that neglecting their families in favour of working on the land would do more harm than good. Morgan added in an ironic tone that Lady Fortescue had achieved what would 'set an excellent example to women of leisure by offering her services to the farmer. No doubt many will follow her lead. They can well afford to do so.'[135] For

Devon's upper-class women, Morgan posited that it would be a 'great pity for any lady to miss this great opportunity (which may never occur again) of showing her patriotism in this way.'[136] The *Western Times* presented a similar critique against the efforts of notable women acting in this way in 1917. The article's author deemed these women as 'female Know-alls' who, after entering rural cottages, ordered women folk to get on the land whilst taking 'good care not to go herself.'[137]

On 4 August 1916, the Devon County War Agricultural Committee reported that there were approximately '2,472 women available for work on the land.'[138] As a point of comparison, 5,000 women had registered with the Women's War Agricultural Committee in Kent by June 1916.[139] Notwithstanding the number of women available to work on the land, DCC concluded in August 1916 that the response from Devon's women and farmers 'was not encouraging.'[140] Despite appeals for farmers to take on female workers, many farmers in Devon were still not convinced that women could undertake agricultural work. Previously, in December 1915, local farmers had informed Sir Ernest Satow about their reservations about women's labour because they were not 'physically strong enough' to cope with farm work.[141] The Men's Committee of Lacehands at the JHC factory in Tiverton expressed comparable gender presumptions against proposals to introduce women to work the factory's lace machines as a temporary wartime measure in 1916.[142] Stephen Reynolds also protested against the possibility of women working on Devon's fishing boats in 1915. Reynolds was adamant that women, whom he derisively described as 'suffragettes', could not adapt to the demanding conditions of working on fishing boats. In light of the unique contribution that fishing made to the nation's food supply, Reynolds argued that fishing vessels needed to be manned by men with irreplaceable fishing experience.[143] By contrast, Liberal politician George Lambert, who came from a farming background, supported the proposals of women working on the land but only in a limited capacity. In an article for the *Sunday Herald*, later reprinted in *The North Devon Journal*, Lambert wrote that whilst 'women could undertake light work at harvest time, weeding, looking after cattle to some extent … they could not drive horses, plough or harrow like skilled men.'[144]

Some contemporaries concluded that farmers' justifications and protests against the prospect of women working in agriculture revealed that these men were ignorant. One woman who encountered such prejudice was

Mrs Easterbrook. Since she undertook agricultural work, she argued that whilst wearing breeches and leggings, she had been 'blackguarded by the farmers around.'[145] Olive Hockin experienced similar ridicule later in January 1917 whilst working on a farm in Dartmoor. The extremely antiquated and 'slow-moving Old farmers of Devon' greeted the prospect of female farm workers 'with sceptical and derisive laughter.'[146] A possible reason for this disdain, Hockin claimed, was that Devon was out of sync with the changes that had occurred in areas closer to London, such as the Home Counties. Accordingly, some Devon farmers were 'motivated by gender presumptions and dictates of tradition, rather than arguments based on rational efficiency.'[147] However, some Devon farmers responded to seeing a woman undertaking specific agricultural tasks, usually completed by a man, with a sense of amazement. WLA member Mary Lees encountered this when she inadvertently gained an audience of four old farmers as she reversed a horse and cart into a shed to unload some swedes. Rather than offer to help her with the task, Lees remembered that the farmers just watched in amazement to see how she would cope.[148]

The county's newspapers were keen to frame the scepticism from agriculturalists towards women's labour within the wartime discourses of patriotism. On 25 May 1916, a *North Devon Journal* correspondent contended that the prejudice shown by Devon's farmers as a class towards women's labour was a significant obstruction. Since these farmers had shown such discrimination against women working in agriculture, the paper concluded that 'this prejudice was unpatriotic.'[149] The *Devon and Exeter Gazette* expressed a similar judgement where the paper argued that 'it was far more patriotic to employ a soldier, a woman or a child to assist in the ingathering of the harvest than it is to complain of shortage of labour.'[150] As a result, Devon's newspapers criticised the choices and patriotism of the county's farmers. Earlier, on 21 January, the Vice-Chairman of the DFU, T. Willing declared that 'he resented the attacks made by a certain newspaper on the patriotism of farmers.'[151] In Willing's view, it was very challenging and 'unjust that farmers as a class should be condemned because of the fault of a few individuals – [who] perhaps [constituted] two or three per cent' of the county's agriculturalists.[152] Indeed, Willing had personally endeavoured through the Labour Exchange at Torquay to obtain the assistance of female labour, but to no avail.[153] Notwithstanding the damning conclusions of Devon's newspapers, the opposition of some Devon farmers towards employing women on the land may not necessarily indicate that they held prejudicial attitudes towards women's capabilities working the land. Instead, these agriculturalists may have been sceptical about accepting prescriptions from individuals who did not possess any experience or familiarity with the farming way of life. On 4 February 1916, Calmady-Hamlyn noted that even before entering the meeting, two farmers were already sceptical about the discussions at the Women for Service in Agriculture event at Barnstaple. One of the farmers suggested to the other that they would not stay long because he declared dismissively that the conversations during the meeting would 'only be twaddle.'[154] Other Devon farmers may have taken similar views towards the prescriptions of speakers at these meetings along with those from women notable figures. Indeed, these agriculturalists may have taken umbrage with these figures' prescriptions since they could dismiss what they had to say and seemed to know how run their farms better than they did.

When faced with these prescriptions from notable figures to accept women workers in agriculture, some agriculturalists were reluctant to cooperate with these requests. Indeed, some Devon dairy farmers complained that it was not practical for women to work in dairy farming. The issue of women working on dairy farms emerged during a session of the Devon Appeal Tribunal at Exeter on 20 October 1916. The military had appealed against the exemption of a farm labourer employed by a local farmer, Mr Rowe. Heathcoat-Amory asked Rowe why he could not get women to undertake some of the tasks involved with dairy farming. Rowe replied that women could not feed and attend to cattle throughout the year. However, Heathcoat-Amory was unconvinced by this explanation and stressed that 'Devonshire women, he felt sure, were not less patriotic than other parts of the country.'[155] Nevertheless, Rowe contended that women could not complete the tasks of working on a dairy farm over the winter. Infuriated with Rowe's obstinate attitude, Heathcoat-Amory replied that it would have to be done. Moreover, he believed it was unacceptable for Devon's farmers to come to tribunal panels and inform them that 'they won't or can't try' to obtain women workers.[156] Hence, the sessions of the Appeal Tribunal provided Tribunalists with an opportunity to prescribe to Devon's farmers the role that the county's women should undertake. He stressed to Rowe that women could undertake farm work in the winter. Heathcoat-Amory used the women of Norfolk as an example to prove this. After visiting the county, he had seen his sister-in-law and niece 'feeding sheep and doing other farm work in the winter[,] and there were 5,000 women up there doing such work all the year round.'[157] However, dairy farmers and dairies in Devon were experiencing difficulties with milk deliveries. During a debate in the House of Commons on 17 October, George Lambert revealed that he had received a letter from one dairy farmer near Plymouth to relay that he was on the verge of giving up since he could not get people to milk the cows or distribute the milk.[158] Based on this letter, Lambert warned the Commons that if more men were taken away from the dairy industry then 'milk would become as dear as port wine.'[159] However, dairies further afield experienced these wartime challenges. Jacob Reynolds, who ran the Heath Farm Dairy in Hertfordshire, also experienced difficulties making milk deliveries in the city of St Albans following the conscription of three of his employees.[160]

Yet Devon's farmers were not alone in baulking about taking on women workers. The farmers of Germany also expressed reluctance to accept women working on their farms. Despite appeals from the German War Office in February 1917 to consider employing women from urban areas to work on their farms, the country's farmers disliked the prospect of 'taking on city women.'[161] However, many German agriculturalists believed that labour reliability was a more overriding priority regardless of gender. They instead called upon women from Germany's rural localities to work on their farms since they possessed relevant agricultural experience.[162] The reluctance to take on inexperienced women labour was also evident in Ireland as one farmer had first-hand experience of this after he employed thirty middle-class girls from urban localities. Most of these women gave up at the finish of their first week since they were unprepared for work on the farm. Although these girls were well-intentioned, the farmer admitted that they ultimately proved to be a hindrance.[163] Lambert advocated that women would have to be taught how to undertake farm work since agriculture was a skilled profession.[164] However, Bonnie White suggests that farmers in Devon, like those in Somerset, were reluctant towards the proposal to establish training farms for women. These farmers probably refused to entertain this proposal because they wanted financial reimbursement in exchange for their services.[165] In a publicity campaign, Devon's newspapers and DCC put forward advertisements that appealed to the county's farmers to take on and train women workers.[166] Nevertheless, despite these appeals, rural women in England may also have been disinclined to take on farm work.[167]

Another factor that played a crucial role in the reluctance of Devon's farmers to take on women workers was their determination to protect their sons from the prospect of military service. In her letter to *The Times* on 28 April 1916, Calmady-Hamlyn relayed what the wife of a Devon smallholder whose son was serving in the armed forces had told her. During their discussion about the prospect of women working on the land, the wife asked her a rhetorical question: Would farmers 'ever employ women so long as they can keep back their sons? Why[,] if they tried women and found they could really help, their sons might have to go!'[168] Indeed, if they took on women labour, they may lose one of their key counter arguments for holding onto their sons. Many Devon agriculturalists claimed they would have to sell their herds or farms if their sons volunteered or were conscripted. Accordingly, they viewed women's labour as a threat to the survival of their farms as family businesses. In September 1916, a report for the Women's County's Committees stated that women in Devon were not ready to work on the land until 'more of the farmers' sons are gone', and the county's agriculturalists were carrying on 'without the help of women.'[169] Farmers seemed to be doing this in Kingston as a local agriculturalist told Edrica de la Pole on 6 November 1916 that they were not employing any women on the local farms because they were not yet short of labour.[170]

Nevertheless, the effects of conscription in the county had become evident in the declining availability of male agricultural labour in some Devon districts. The productivity of Devon's agriculture had weakened to the extent that the county's War Agricultural Committee were resolved on 6 May 1916 to petition the chairman of the local agricultural committees and the Tribunals across Devon to consider the importance of the harvest. Accordingly, due to the serious scarcity of male labour on farms in Devon, the Committee viewed with 'alarm any proposal to take more men from the land; and strongly deprecates the recruiting of any men who are only fit for home service.'[171] To alleviate the situation in east Devon, Honiton RDC put forward a similar request to the surveyor of the district's roads on 21 May 1916 to 'release as many men as possible during the harvest, in order to help the Farmers.'[172]

The experiences of the Buckfast monks during 1916

The declaration of war created a tense atmosphere of fear and suspicion across the British Isles concerning the notion that there existed an enemy from within. In this climate of paranoia, the internal enemy was the German citizen living in Britain. Labelled as 'enemy aliens', the loyalty of these citizens was in doubt since they were suspected to be German secret agents and part of a shadowy, sinister conspiracy orchestrated by Imperial Germany to undermine the British war effort.[173] Although the 'spy fever' against German citizens in Devon was evident in the autumn of 1914, unease continued about the loyalties of the minority community of Benedictine monks at Buckfast Abbey and the presence of forty German and Austrian monks within their order. For the residents of the south Devon towns of Buckfastleigh and Ashburton that surrounded the Abbey, the German and Austrian nationals of military age were not genuine Benedictine monks. Instead, suspicions were rife locally that these men were secret agents operating under the guise of religious holy men.[174] A factor that possibly contributed to this local paranoia was that the Abbey's Abbot, Anscar Vonier, was arrested in Austria in August 1914 because he was a naturalised British subject.[175] Vonier's incarceration prompted Fidelis von Stotzingen, the Abbot Primate of the Benedictine Order of Rome, to communicate with the Austrian ambassador to the Vatican, Prince Johann Schönburg-Hartenstein, to secure Vonier's release. After a brief confinement in the Abbey of St Peter in Salzburg, the Vatican intervened in his detention. Consequently, Vonier was allowed safe passage from Austria to France via Switzerland, and the Abbot returned safely to Buckfast on 15 October 1914.[176]

Yet, the situation worsened for Buckfast Abbey's German Catholic monks when anti-German hysteria flared up locally following the sinking of the passenger ship RMS *Lusitania* by a German U-boat off the coast of Ireland in May 1915.[177] Indeed, this anti-German sentiment was especially true of some members of Buckfastleigh UDC.[178] In June 1915, the UDC members started a campaign appealing to the Home Office to have the German and Austrian monks removed from Buckfast Abbey. The Council hoped the Home Office would understand their concerns, remove the 'enemy alien' monks from the Abbey and send them to an internment camp. During the First World War, German citizens in Britain were sent and detained in internment camps across the British Isles in locations such as Dorchester, Islington and Douglas on the Isle of Man.[179] However, a Committee of the Home Office in 1915 dashed the Council's hopes to send the German monks to one of these internment camps. The Committee concluded that the German monks presented no danger to the communities surrounding the Abbey and exempted them from internment.[180] Under the terms of a special agreement, the Home Office allowed the monks to continue their religious activities uninterrupted alongside their efforts to rebuild the Abbey, gardening, farming and bee-keeping. Moreover, whilst the German monks retained their residence at Buckfast, Vonier had to notify the police if any monk left the Abbey grounds.[181]

The internment of enemy civilians like the German and Austrian monks at Buckfast Abbey was problematic because it exposed the ambiguity of the civil/military divide, blurring the boundaries between civilian and combatant, which created 'categories of people who did not fit neatly in either.'[182] This ambiguity and the Home Office's decision to grant special dispensation to these German monks contributed to the prolonged local uneasiness towards the monks and the Abbey. After visiting the areas neighbouring the Abbey and making enquiries amongst residents about the German monks in January 1916, a representative from the *Western Morning News* reported that feelings amongst the locals were still running high against the monks.[183] An editorial in the *Devon and Exeter Gazette* on 13 January went so far as to advocate for removing the German monks from Buckfast Abbey. Transferring these monks to a genuine internment camp would allow them to be kept under close supervision and address the local concerns about public safety. Regardless of whether they were holy men, the newspaper stressed that the German monks were still subjects of Kaiser Wilhelm II and belonged 'to an enemy race.'[184] Other figures also argued strongly for sending the German and Austrian monks to a genuine internment camp for enemy aliens. The anti-Catholic campaigner John Alfred Kensit was one such advocate who launched a sensational tirade against the monks during a lantern lecture at Plymouth's guildhall on 15 February. Kensit was primarily aggrieved that the Home Office had given a special dispensation to the German monks. Whilst the British Government had deemed it necessary to intern German protestant missionaries in India, Kensit questioned why they did not apply the same treatment to the German monks at Buckfast. A *Western Morning News* correspondent who attended the lecture noticed that the audience members reacted angrily towards this news. Whilst many spectators shouted that it was a 'shame', some yelled 'Let's go and do it' acting as a rallying cry for support amongst their fellow attendees to instigate a form of mob justice.[185]

On 8 February 1916, the *Western Morning News* suggested that one of the main reasons for local suspicion against the monks was that the community had made no public expression of regret at the sinking of the *Lusitania*.[186]

The fact that the monks had made no attempt to disassociate themselves from the action had 'rankled local folk.'[187] The absence of any statement from the monks condemning the sinking produced a vacuum later filled by local hearsay and rumour regarding the monks' views on the tragedy and their loyalties. Teignmouth resident S. John Thorpe tapped upon anti-Catholic fears when he expressed his doubts about the monks' allegiance in a letter to the *Western Morning News*. He suggested that they were 'still under "obedience" to the Papal Court, which certainly at times conflicts with our own.'[188] Professor George T. Ragsdale, the Chief of the Louisville Division of the APL in Louisville, Kentucky, evoked similar suspicions about the sympathies of the German population in the city.[189] At a luncheon meeting of Louisville's Advertising Club on 1 March 1918, Ragsdale made the unsubstantiated claim that the city's German population had celebrated the sinking of the passenger ship SS *Tuscania* with the loss of American soldiers.[190] He also put forward a more sensational allegation to reinforce the perception that the Germans at large in the city were the enemy within and part of an even greater conspiracy, scheming behind closed doors. Ragsdale claimed that there was 'a large force of German reservists' who conducted secret drills in the basement of a large unspecified building in Louisville in April and May 1917.[191] Amongst the local populations surrounding Buckfast Abbey, conspiratorial views also manifested as far-fetched rumours about what the monks were up to within the Abbey's walls. One such implausible tale was that a Father of Buckfast had stowed petrol specially reserved for use by German Zeppelins and he had enough to last five years. However, after inspection of the petrol store, it was discovered that the store only had one can of petrol.[192] Distressed that people believed such fearful rumours, William Leighton from Blackburn wrote to the *Western Morning News* to recommend that these people should visit the monks in the hope that such hallucinations would disappear.[193]

Following consultations with figures from the military and the police, the conditions of the monks' non-internment were tightened. These stricter measures included each monk being 'entirely confined to the Abbey grounds except for three [of them] who were allowed to go to work on the farm, accompanied by a British or allied citizen.'[194] Although the Abbey was designated a prohibited area and more significant restrictions imposed on the monks, some members of Buckfastleigh UDC remained unsatisfied and wanted the Home Office to pursue an inquiry to address the matter. One of the strategies that the Council employed to pressurise the Home Office to do this was to request local MPs, such as Sir John Spear and George Lambert, to put forward questions to the Home Secretary, Herbert Samuel, in the House of Commons.[195] On 16 August 1916, George Lambert asked Samuel about the status of the Buckfast monks during a Parliamentary debate. However, Lambert presented his enquiry along the lines of public safety. Lambert asked the Home Secretary whether he was satisfied that national security was not in any way 'jeopardised by the residence of these alien enemies under the conditions now imposed?.'[196] In his reply, Samuel declared that only a few of the Buckfast monks were enemy nationals, and following consultations with Captain Herbert Reginald Vyvyan, the Chief Constable of Devonshire, removing them from the Abbey was deemed unnecessary.[197]

Although high-profile local figures complained about how Buckfastleigh's UDC treated the German and Austrian monks, local and national newspapers supported the Council's campaign to remove them from the Abbey and place them into an internment camp.[198] One national tabloid that agreed with and supported the stance of Buckfastleigh's UDC was *John Bull.* Edited by former politician Horatio Bottomley, *John Bull* was a weekly tabloid that vigorously warned its readers about German nationals in Britain and the threat they posed as the enemy within. In the case of the German monks at Buckfast, the magazine argued that whilst these men wore the robes of the Benedictine order, they were still cruel Huns underneath their religious garments.[199] Accordingly, *John Bull* described the German monks of Buckfast in jingoistic terms as 'Holy Huns', similar to the label that the publication used to describe German nationals as 'Germhuns.'[200] The magazine concluded that the Home Office's existing safeguards were inadequate and ridiculous since these 'Holy Huns' could freely meet members of the general public who visited the Abbey. *John Bull* was also unsatisfied that the monitoring of the German monks' letters rested with Abbot Vonier, arguing that no 'proper' censorship system was in place to handle these monks' correspondence.[201] The *Times* also later reported that the restrictions against the monks were insufficient because no one living surrounding the Abbey 'knew which of the monks were German.'[202] Indeed, feelings amongst the local populations still ran high because of a 'statement that the authorities had allowed three of the monks to return to Germany.'[203] When considering Buckfast Abbey's proximity to Plymouth and the strategically significant Royal Naval bases, *John Bull* claimed it was an outrageous scandal that these 'Holy Huns' were allowed to remain in the Abbey despite the grave threat that they posed to national security.[204]

Still unhappy with the measures introduced by the authorities to safeguard the local community, the UDC sent a memorandum to the Prime Minister, the Home Secretary and other Parliamentarians in early July 1916. The document appealed for imposing more significant restrictions on the monks and anyone visiting the Abbey.[205] The Council did not wait long to have their grievances addressed since Second Lieutenant L. A. Wilde, a practising Roman Catholic from the Sherwood Foresters, called for a special meeting between members of the UDC and the Abbey representatives. When this conference occurred on 12 July, Wilde argued that he wanted to defend the Catholic community at Buckfast rather than just the enemy aliens in the Abbey. He felt compelled to do so because of the attacks against the monks since they were Roman Catholics.[206] Nonetheless, Buckfastleigh Councillor J. Willcocks contended that national security motivated their concerns rather than religion because allowing forty Germans to remain in the Abbey was, in his view, 'absolutely dangerous.'[207] Indeed, Willcocks suspected that there may be one or two amongst the forty Germans who were 'in the pay of the German or Austrian government.'[208]

Alongside Wilde, the Abbey's Lord Abbot was present during the special meeting to represent the monks. Vonier explained to the Council members that the community had correctly carried out the regulations stipulated by the Home Secretary, Captain Vyvyan and the General Commanding the Plymouth Defences, General Penton. Moreover, Wilde wanted to clarify that he acted on behalf of the Catholic body at Buckfast. In his view, the religious community should not be considered in the same way as enemy aliens were but instead considered on their own terms.[209] Nevertheless, in their coverage of the special meeting, *John Bull* claimed that it was disgusting that a serving British Army Lieutenant would defend the 'Germhun' monks. Indeed, it was downright shameful that Wilde's religious predilections had 'warped his sense of patriotism.'[210]

On 16 August 1916, the Home Secretary announced in the House of Commons that he had appointed the veteran civil servant Sir Louis Dane and Colonel A. J. Sykes, the Conservative MP for Knutsford, to head a Special Commission to consider the cases of enemy aliens, including the German monks of Buckfast Abbey, and whether they should be allowed to remain in prohibited areas.[211] At a special meeting held at the Abbey on

7 October, Dane and Sykes met representatives from the UDC and the Abbey representatives alongside Captain Vyvyan to discuss the matter.[212] The Council made their case to Dane and Sykes that they had faced the question of the forty 'enemy aliens' resident in the Abbey before them several times, and their representations to the Home Secretary had been unsuccessful. The UDC also remained unsatisfied that the censorship of the monks' correspondence remained with the Abbot. The most grave point the Council raised was that three 'alien enemies', all young men in their teens, had been allowed to return to Germany, and they may 'take [back] valuable information to the enemy.'[213] The special meeting also allowed the monks to engage with the Council's concerns. They stressed that the community's loyalty was not in question as they had no connection with any German house, three members were serving with the forces in France, and they had complied with the conditions set down by the Home Secretary. In addressing the Council's complaint against the Abbot handling the censorship of the monks' correspondence, the Abbey's representatives argued that all the letters delivered to the Abbey had to pass through the existing official censorship system.[214] Moreover, the three youths who had returned to Germany had obtained permits from the Home Office and it was difficult to imagine that they could pass on valuable information to Germany considering the restrictions on their movements in the Abbey.

Following their visit to Buckfast Abbey, the Home Office Special Commission concluded that it was not advisable to disturb the Benedictine community. Rather than remove the monks from Buckfast and send them to an internment camp, the Special Commission recommended that the Abbey should now be treated on the same lines as an internment camp, and special Constables monitor the Abbey.[215] When the Buckfast UDC convened for their meeting on 4 December 1916, the Council's Clerk, Edward Windeatt, revealed that the Chief Constable of Devonshire had written to Superintendent Carey, requesting him to consult with the Council about obtaining special constables. However, Carey informed the Council that he could not find men willing to act as special constables to watch the Abbey because he discovered that no one locally wanted to 'have anything to do with the work.'[216] The Council's chairman believed that the Chief Constable should be informed that it was not their place to appoint special constables to monitor the Abbey. The discussion about obtaining the special constables revealed how aggrieved the Council was about the findings of the Special

Commission. Fellow Council member George West acknowledged that it was a farce. Whilst the Council were the ones who had made the complaint against the forty 'enemy alien' monks and wanted them removed from the Abbey, they ended up in a worse predicament since the Home Office had decided it was up to the Council to look after the monks.[217] During the previous two years, the Council acknowledged that they had encountered a 'good deal of criticism' in their campaign to have the 'enemy aliens' evicted from the Abbey.[218] Nevertheless, they still believed that they were in the right. Despite questions in Devon's newspapers about the result of the inquiry, the Special Commission's report appeared in the press later that month, informing the public that Buckfast Abbey was 'now [to be] treated on the lines of internment camps.'[219] At first glance, these measures by the Home Office indicate that the monks were now under a form of house arrest due to the restriction on their movements solely within the Abbey and its grounds, and that special constables conducted surveillance of Buckfast Abbey. However, a Home Office representative clarified that technically, under the Special Commission's scheme, the German and Austrian monks resident at Buckfast Abbey were interred as prisoners of war.[220]

Yet it was not just the monks of Buckfast who were suspected to be the enemy within. In January 1915, Stephen Reynolds discovered he had been the subject of local gossip and speculation that he was a German agent. Reynolds was informed of this by the niece of the local newsagent who had just returned from Cullompton. She told Reynolds it was a 'fact' that the man who wrote books and lived in Sidmouth was 'a German spy.'[221] Like the German monks of Buckfast Abbey, some suspicious Devon residents probably questioned and speculated about what Reynolds was doing behind closed doors. Indeed, Scoble suggests it was the writing of books that 'merited the most suspicion' against Reynolds.[222] According to the newsagent's niece, the people she had spoken to in Cullompton had become convinced that these rumours about Reynolds were genuine because he had a house on the cliffs near Sidmouth. They concluded that the house was an ideal location for Reynolds to conduct spy-related activities because he went up to the property under cover of night to send signals out to sea.[223] Previously, in 1913, Reynolds had bought a small plot of land on the cliffs and built a cottage on his land in 1914.[224] Alongside his preoccupation with writing books, the fact that Reynolds had a property on the cliffs near the sea was evidence enough to confirm to some people that Reynolds was a German secret agent. Reynolds did not take these rumours to heart, describing them as a yarn because he had only been up to the cottage on three occasions since 4 August 1914 and the property had stood empty. Yet Reynolds still believed that this matter should be brought to the attention of Earl Fortescue as Lord Lieutenant or another authority in Devon so that he could use 'his influence to curb the reckless mendacity of his county.'[225] Like the far-fetched conspiracies about the Buckfast monks, Reynolds claimed it had become challenging to disentangle fact from fiction due to an 'enormous mass of lying reports circulating in the county.'[226] In his view, the sheer quantity of devastating rumours and baseless accusations would distract local authorities. As a result, pursuing these false leads would inevitably lead to valid evidence of spy activities becoming obscured or, even worse, overlooked entirely. Another writer who faced suspicion since he wrote books was the novelist D. H. Lawrence when he and his German wife Frieda moved to Cornwall in 1916. During 1916 and 1917, the local police monitored the behaviour of Lawrence and his wife.[227]

Conclusion

Although the patriotism of Devon's men was not always self-evident under conscription, there were still opportunities to judge an individual's patriotism during the sessions of Devon's local tribunals or those of the county's Appeal Tribunal. Within the semi-judicial proceedings of arbitrating upon the appeals against conscription, Devon's tribunalists attempted to police the discourses of patriotism by labelling what behaviour was patriotic and what was not. Based on the merit of individual claims against conscription, along with the behaviour of those appealing against military service, the county's tribunalists made value judgements about the patriotism of Devon's men or those representing them. The fact that some Devonians were more absorbed with the survival of their livelihoods and local priorities, despite the tribunal panel's prescriptions to consider the national interest, led some of Devon's elite to deem their behaviour unpatriotic. Whilst the tribunal panels applied the criteria of the MSA when considering the appeals for exemption from military service, contemporaries did not view these proceedings in this way. Devon's tribunalists also took on an explicit exhortative role where they attempted to extend their influence over local wartime politics and adjudicate upon the wartime behaviour of Devonians. Like in other parts of the United Kingdom, the 'round-up raids' in Devon did not succeed in bringing men who had avoided military service to justice.

Despite attempts to convince Devon's farmers of the patriotic necessity and the benefits of female labour, many remained reluctant to accept inexperienced women. However, the county's agriculturalists took umbrage with the prescriptions from these figures. Nevertheless, the ladies from the county's civil society dismissed the justifications from farmers against women working on their farms, and Devon's newspapers sought to frame such validations as unpatriotic. Some farmers in the county were reluctant to take on women as they sought to keep their sons on the farm to try to preserve the future of their family businesses. Meanwhile, members of Buckfastleigh's UDC were concerned about the German and Austrian monks of Buckfast Abbey, and these figures started a campaign for the Home Office to remove the monks from the Abbey and have them relocated to an internment camp. Despite their continual attempts, the Home Office disagreed with the Council that the monks were a threat to national security and granted them a special exemption from internment.

Chapter 5

The Effects of Remobilisation, 1917 and 1918

During the autumn of 1916, it became clear to contemporaries that the Asquith Coalition Government was in a dreadful state.[1] Amidst escalating tensions in the Cabinet, there was increasing speculation that Asquith's authority was waning and he was no longer fit to serve as Prime Minister.[2] The crisis that had engulfed the Coalition reached a critical point in early December 1916.[3] Following the political intrigue in Westminster was Plymouth resident and newspaperman Robert Alfred John Walling. In a private note on 1 December, Walling launched a scathing critique of Asquith's Coalition Government, deeming it to be frail 'in its joints' and foolish 'in its doings.'[4] Although the Government was in a terrible state and appeared to be teetering, Walling believed it would not collapse since there was 'nothing to stand up in its place.'[5] Nevertheless, after Lloyd George resigned from the Government on 5 December, Asquith lost the support of senior Conservative figures in his Cabinet and the Coalition Government fell the following day. After Andrew Bonar Law, the Conservative party's leader, informed King George V that he could not form a government, Lloyd George was sent for in the hope that he could establish one.[6] On 7 December, Lloyd George became Prime Minister.[7]

Upon hearing that Lloyd George was now Premier, Edrica de la Pole could not contain her delight with the news. It had also given her a sense of cautious optimism. De la Pole recorded in her diary that under Lloyd George's premiership, she believed there was now the chance that 'perhaps we shall "get a move on" with the War.'[8] Going into the third year of the war, the ambition to "get a move on" with the conflict entailed recognising that new sacrifices and measures, previously deemed unacceptable, would need to be made or introduced to secure the prospect of victory. A *Western Times* editorial published on 23 December 1916 advocated a prescription of determination because the only thing left for the Allies to do was to pursue the War with redoubled vigour. The new Lloyd George Coalition Government created a new War Cabinet and new Ministries to work towards re-engaging with the War. Like the introduction of conscription, these new measures also saw the recognition of civil society managing new Committees to oversee these responsibilities on a local level. However, unlike de la Pole, many Devon residents did not accept the measures introduced to "get a move on" with the war and pushed back against these measures. Looking locally to Devon, the *Western Times* editorial argued that it was 'useless to cloak the fact that we have had a great deal of unpatriotic action in the [county's] rural districts – that the safety and honour of the country have been made to play seconds to self-interest and even cupidity.'[9] Whilst it was significant to recognise what the remobilisation of the British war effort entailed, achieving it over the last two years of the war was an uphill struggle. One vital project of remobilising the British war effort in agricultural counties like Devon was to increase domestic food production.

Food supplies and war-weariness

On 1 February 1917, Imperial Germany restarted the campaign of unrestricted submarine warfare against merchant ships in the Atlantic Ocean, hampering the transport of food supplies to Britain.[10] Alongside the sinking of merchant shipping by German U-boats, the bad harvest of 1916 meant that the British population faced the genuine prospect of food shortages in 1917.[11] The nation's predicament was evident to Earl Fortescue after attending a Board of Agriculture conference in London on 18 April 1917, where he noted in his diary that: 'We are eating corn faster than we can import it.'[12] It was clear to Fortescue that a large amount of grassland needed to be tilled to grow more wheat for the harvest of 1918.[13] In Devon, the county's War Agricultural Committee sought to encourage the county's landowners to increase domestic food production.[14] However, not all of Devon's landowners and farmers were prepared to cooperate with this directive. On 15 May 1917, the *Devon and Exeter Gazette* suspected that the government's request to plough up 150,000 acres for arable crops would constitute a further test of the 'patriotism of the Devonshire farmer.'[15] Previously, George Lambert informed the House of Commons during a debate on Food Production in February 1917 that Devon's farmers had sown less wheat. He relayed information that he had received in a letter from a Devon War Agricultural Committee member who confessed from conversations he had had that this was 'the case generally in the county.'[16] Lambert stressed that Devon's farmers had been hampered by the lingering uncertainty about whether they could be conscripted and withdrawn from the land. Accordingly, Lambert reinforced his defence of Devon's farmers in that they 'cannot expect any man to plant or till crops if he has not a reasonable opportunity to be able to harvest them.'[17] At the same time, just as some Devon farmers dismissed the prescriptions from people without agricultural experience, other farmers were not keen to accept prescriptions on how to use their land. In January 1917, the *South Devon Weekly Express* reprinted the comments that a well-known but anonymous public official had made about three uncooperative Devon farmers. Based on his encounters with these stubborn agriculturalists, the official concluded that they possessed 'unfortunate and unpatriotic ideas.'[18] The first farmer he met declared to the official that he would not plant a single potato more than he did in 1916 since the Government had 'fixed the price [of potatoes] so low.'[19] The second was equally obstinate. Despite having a large stock of wheat, the second farmer declared to the official that unless he could get 10s a bushel for it, he threatened to grind the grain 'down for his pigs.'[20] The third agriculturalist, however, was the most defiant when he expressed his opposition to undertaking any additional farming for the war effort. When asked what he planned to do with one of his large fields, the farmer replied that he would do nothing with it. The official was stunned, replying that he could put the field to wheat, which would lead to a 'splendid financial result' for the farmer.[21] However, the farmer retorted that this did not concern him, and he justified his refusal to cooperate because the Government had taken his son. Deprived of his son, the vindictive farmer declared that the Government would have to come and till his field because "'I shan't.'[22] However, some Devon farmers who dedicated more of their permanent grass to growing arable crops promoted their decision within the discourses of patriotism. During a Crediton War Agricultural Committee meeting on 11 August 1917, local farmer Mr Batting launched a protest against 'Crediton farmers being called unpatriotic and Axminster people praised up.'[23] He pointed out that this was uncalled for since Axminster had only promised 6,000 acres out of 54,000 whilst Crediton promised 21,000 out of 94,000 acres.

The Lloyd George Coalition government introduced the Corn Production Act to encourage farmers in Devon and across the United Kingdom to grow more arable crops. After Parliament ratified the Act in August 1917, the legislation set guaranteed prices for oat yields and wheat as financial incentives for farmers to grow more cereals.[24] However, despite these inducements, Devon's agriculturalists, like many of Britain's farmers, resented the 'government's efforts to increase the arable acreage.'[25] On 18 September 1917, the DFU received several complaints from farmers in the county against the Act's implementation. DFU representative, Mr Willing, stressed that Devon's farmers did not universally support the legislation because Devon was not a corn-growing county. Due to the strength of pastoral and dairy farming practices in Devon, Willing was sceptical that they would comply with the order. Willing's doubts were evident in the response from the county's agriculturalists towards a circular that appealed to them to plough up 30 per cent of their grassland acreage for the production of corn or potatoes. Many Devon farmers believed that this request was a 'drastic measure.'[26] However, Willing also revealed during the meeting that he had received two replies from other National Farmers Union Executive Committee members who stressed that Devon's War Agricultural Committee had no authority to ensure the total compliance of the county's farmers with the order.[27] Other contemporaries believed that Devon's War Agricultural Committee had a limited influence in ensuring the involvement and conformity of the county's farmers with wartime directives. Although it was as patriotic, 'well-intentioned, and earnest as any War Committee', Lambert told the House of Commons on 8 February 1917 there were doubts about its effectiveness.[28] A very active member of the Committee had conveyed his serious doubts to Lambert that the county's war agricultural committee would achieve very little.[29] Lambert confessed that the Devon War Agricultural Committee's efforts were only small actions that would not lead to the substantive changes required since 'plants do not spring up by walking round fields or [by] placing advertisements on walls.'[30]

Yet, some farmers declared that they were prepared to defy this drive to increase the acreage of arable food. On 28 December 1917, the chairman of the Dulverton War Agricultural Committee, J. Tapp, informed the committee members there was a feeling of discontent among patriotic farmers in the area. According to Tapp, these farmers were aggrieved that some of their neighbouring agriculturalists refused to 'break their land for corn.'[31] These neighbouring farmers held such firm objections against this that they declared they were prepared to 'go to prison rather than plough their land.'[32] Colonel Harry William Heathcoat-Amory warned that the members of the Committee 'must watch out for unpatriotic farmers who would not break their land for corn.'[33] The Committee's Chairman, Tapp, expressed his belief that on the whole farmers would be 'patriotic and plant all the corn they can.'[34] Alongside those who declared that they would not dedicate their pasture land to grow more corn, some Devon farmers devised cunning strategies to try to get around ploughing up their fields. At a meeting of the Tiverton District War Agricultural Committee on 4 December 1917, a Culmstock farmer brought to the attention of Sir Ian Heathcoat-Amory that 'many unpatriotic farmers were displacing their young stock by cows to escape the tillage obligation.'[35] In reply to this, the Committee's chairman H. G. New, argued that the cows should be ignored and the farms would still be 'made to give their quota of tillage.'[36] Although Lambert was concerned that less wheat was being grown in Devon, Fortescue later recorded in June 1918 that Devon's farmers had achieved and went beyond the original quota of 130,000 acres of additional land to be tilled to corn in 1917.[37]

Nevertheless, some Devon landlords wanted their tenants to refrain from complying with wartime directives. In February 1918, it came to Fortescue's attention that some landlords who had disapproved of the order by the Devon War Agricultural Executive Committee to break up permanent grass, had 'given notice to quit to the tenants who have received such orders.'[38] This refusal was also evident amongst some local landowners in Ottery St Mary. Although the majority of those who owned land locally had 'complied with the requirements of the War Agricultural Committee', Sir Ernest Satow learned from local resident Mrs Whetham that local landowners, Lord Coleridge, Mrs Weldon and Colonel Mackintosh had refused 'to do their duty in sowing corn or planting potatoes' on their land.[39] However, due to the crisis in food supplies, farmers were criticised for their choices. Richard Coles, another local tenant farmer was later prosecuted for not 'sowing the amount of cereals [that] he was ordered [to sow] by the War Agricultural Committee.'[40] However, Coles revealed that he had put in dredge corn in ignorance and was unsuccessful in his attempts to get labour. He was fined £20 inclusive along with £5 for solicitors costs.[41]

To help Devon's agriculturalists break up more of their pasture land to grow more arable crops, they were encouraged to accept the introduction of tractors on their land to offset the loss of their horses. Whilst tractors did render material difference, the tractor was an unsuitable piece of equipment for the geography of some parts of the county. Earl Fortescue recalled that numerous fields in north Devon, especially, were either 'too small or hilly to be ploughed or cultivated by anything but horses.'[42] Consequently, Fortescue noted that tractors had barely ploughed 3,000 acres in north Devon out of a total cereal area of 89,000 acres in June 1918.[43] The tractor also experienced problems in South Devon. In November 1918, Edrica de la Pole wanted two acres of her land tilled by a tractor and applied to have this done. However, a tractor driver informed de la Pole that ploughing her two acres would not be cost-effective since having the tractor work her small patch of ground would not cover the tractor's oil costs. He also told de la Pole that there was another reason why he was reluctant to use the tractor on small parcels of land. As a piece of agricultural machinery, he confessed that the Titan tractor did more harm than good since it messed up so much ground that it was practically 'useless except on large fields.'[44] Indeed, the *North Devon Journal* revealed on 25 October 1917 that reports of the work done by motor ploughs in Devon compared unfavourably with other counties due to the rough nature of land leading to excessive costs.[45]

Fortescue later recalled that the county's farmers were reluctant to use the tractor ploughs because they were challenging machines that caused 'no end of trouble.'[46] Catherine Durning Whetham, a poet and resident of Ottery St Mary, encapsulated the trouble evident with these tractors in her poem 'The Tractor'. The tractor was such a troublesome piece of machinery in Devon, Whetham contended, that even its own technical experts would like to ban it. Whetham centred the blame on all these problems on Rowland Prothero, the President of the Board of Agriculture and Fisheries from 1916 to 1919. She believed that Prothero was vain and deluded in his attempts to introduce the tractor in Devon.[47] One agriculturalist who was deeply sceptical about introducing tractors onto Devon's farms was Henry Pearse, who complained about them in a letter published in the *Western Morning News* in December 1917. Since he had seen several tractors lying dormant and 'rusting not far from Plympton station', Pearce was convinced that the tractor was an expensive and useless experiment just as introducing inexperienced soldiers and untrained women labour onto farms had been.[48] Since the negatives of the tractor appeared to outweigh the benefits, some farmers in the county remained unconvinced about accepting the introduction of this novel but impractical contraption. However, some of the county's agriculturalists may have viewed the tractor as a potential threat and did not intend to use it since they did not want to replace the labour, they had fought so hard to keep. When Earl Fortescue reflected on the introduction of tractors in the county, he concluded that tractors were a 'doubtful success' due to their novelty and the costs involved.[49]

At the same time, the county's civilian population participated in this campaign to increase domestic food production. On 8 January 1917, the Devon War Agricultural Committee saw an opportunity to encourage villagers in Devon's more remote areas to grow potatoes and keep pigs.[50] Local government bodies in Devon responded to the calls for increased potato production with campaigns to increase the cultivation of potatoes in allotments and private gardens.[51] However, some Devonians did not see the imperative of transforming land for food production. On 20 April 1917, the *Western Morning News* printed an anonymous letter, signed under the initial 'S.', complaining about four men who had recently constructed a pleasure garden in Okehampton. In the author's view, utilising the land for a frivolous activity was simply inexcusable. By building a pleasure garden, these unpatriotic men squandered the land's potential because other '"patriotically minded"' people had dug up their gardens the previous summer to increase domestic food production.[52] However, the letter's author revealed that the pleasure garden was not the only land in Okehampton wasted on frivolous pursuits since a group of selfish people had decided to build a new tennis court. Complaints such as this letter acted as denunciations that highlighted such outrageous waste and served an essential function in the discourses of patriotism. By using the social morality of wartime, contemporaries had slated those who carelessly wasted food as unpatriotic, but the idea of unpatriotic waste also applied to land use. In the context of food production, the letter's author sought to publicly shame those people in Okehampton who had made selfish and unpatriotic choices with their land.

Meanwhile in Ottery St Mary, the UDC had received many requests by February 1918 from persons who wanted allotments. However, the Council faced a problem: there was no land available to cater for this great demand.[53] The following month, the Council's Allotments Committee decided that Rag Field, known locally as Rag, should be utilised for domestic food production and the land converted into allotments. Accordingly, they approached Lord Coleridge, the field's owner, and local farmer H. D. Willock, the land's occupier, to inform them of the Committee's proposal. If the Committee received an unfavourable response, the Council would use compulsory powers to obtain Rag Field.[54] At a special meeting of the Council scheduled to discuss this option for the land, the Council had received Willock's reply stating that if the Council took the land with compulsory powers, he would then claim £50 as compensation. According to Satow, Edwin Vinnicombe, the UDC's chairman, reacted quite violently to Willock's '"ungentlemanly"' letter since Willock had protested it would be a '"crime"' to take away a field that was, as pasture land, producing milk and butter.[55] Willock's demand for compensation was a checkmate-style move intended to end the discussion about taking one of his fields away from him. By contrast, one of Coleridge's other tenants, William Salter, did not hesitate to offer the Council the use of his field for allotments.[56] Although the Council accepted Salter's offer, they still wanted to acquire Rag Field for allotments. As a result, the Council agreed to deputise Vinnicombe and fellow Council member Manning to ask Willock if he would reconsider and 'give way' on the Rag.[57]

On 3 April, the matter came to a head at the UDC's meeting where, despite Vinnicombe and Manning's efforts, Willock was determined not to surrender 'Rag Field' to the Council. After hearing this, Vinnicombe sought to chastise Willock and moved for the Council to pass a resolution condemning Willock's action as 'selfish and unpatriotic.'[58] Whilst no member of the UDC seconded the motion, Vinnicombe presented Willock's refusal within the discourses of patriotism. Since he refused to allow others to convert the land into allotments to grow potatoes and vegetables for the benefit of the wider community, Vinnicombe presented Willock as a selfish man who lacked patriotism. On the other hand, for Willock, it may not have been a question of food supplies. He may have felt compelled not to release the land since he did not want to yield to the pressure from the Council. As a result, Willock sought to retain 'Rag Field' as pasture land under his tenancy rather than lose it under the pretext of food allotments. Indeed, he may have feared that he could lose the land permanently.

Devonians suspected the county's farmers sought to exploit the crisis of food supplies since they believed that these agriculturalists were motivated by their wallets rather than their patriotism. In the case of potatoes, these farmers in Devon faced accusations that they were profiteers, hoarding potatoes until the price of potatoes increased. During a meeting of Northam UDC on 4 January 1917, Councillor Frederick Wilkey claimed that he knew of one man who lived within two miles of the north Devon town who possessed a large quantity of potatoes. However, the man was holding onto these potatoes and was simply biding his time, waiting for higher prices. Accordingly, Wilkey believed that something should be done.[59] However, the

North Devon Herald on 11 January 1917 demanded to know who this man was since to hold up supplies of potatoes in the paper's view was 'distinctly unpatriotic' and constituted an offence under Defence of the Realm Act.[60] Since many innocent people could be suspected, the paper believed that Wilkey should give the name of this man, 'if he feels himself on sure ground as to his facts.'[61] However, Hockin revealed that if 'all farms were like ours, and had, owing to the shortage of labour, reduced their potato acreage to less than half, and with disease rampant in addition, it is little wonder there was a scarcity.'[62] The introduction of the Potato Order in September 1917 did increase potato production across Great Britain since the supply of potatoes expanded considerably between 1917 and 1918.[63] The dire situation regarding potatoes led Mrs Symons, a resident of Totnes, to propose an unorthodox solution to help with the crisis. She advocated that potatoes should be grown in unused plots of consecrated ground in the cemetery of the south Devon town. Although Totnes Town Council and the LGB supported her proposal to till the cemetery's consecrated ground for this purpose, the Diocese of Exeter held firm objections.[64] However, Mrs Symons did not give up and wrote to the Bishop of Exeter, Lord William Cecil, asking him to reconsider. In his reply, Cecil reluctantly conceded to Mrs Symons's request, making the exception on the basis that 'David ate the shrew-bread.'[65] Moreover, he emphasized that all the food grown in these plots 'must be given away to the poor.'[66]

In early 1917, the residents of Plymouth and Exeter, like the populations of London, Paris and Berlin, encountered difficulties acquiring food.[67] On 27 February 1917, Mabel Hammond acknowledged similar awful problems to get hold of food, particularly meat, in Exeter.[68] Meanwhile, the situation surrounding food supplies was rather severe in Plymouth. F. Ashe Lincoln remembered that his family were fortunate enough to obtain sufficient food supplies, including dairy products because Lincoln's grandfather owned farms on Dartmoor.[69] Like Lincoln's family, many urban populations used family connections with rural relatives to try to obtain food. In Prague, the city's residents from 1916 onwards travelled to the countryside to buy directly from food producers since there were unable to acquire all the food they needed by queuing. Although peasants accepted money to purchase food, a system of bartering existed where items from the city could be used in exchange for food items.[70] However, Devonians suspected that urban populations travelled to the county because they were trying to plunder the food resources of the Devon countryside. On 7 April 1917, Colonel E. H. Holley, Okehampton's Mayor, informed the Town Council that the town's market had become swamped with an increased number of 'unscrupulous dealers' and traders who 'pounced' upon the local food items at the market.[71] However, these traders took their purchases to Britain's urban centres to take advantage of the higher prices and increased demand for food in these locations. According to Holley, it was the wealth and war bonuses present in Britain's cities that had enticed and enabled these traders to buy goods and reap the benefits of selling this local produce at higher prices, making enormous profits. The comments made by Okehampton's Mayor tapped into the representations of the profiteer, which stressed a critical and ethical opposition between the profiteer and the consumer that tapped into the cultural codes of the social morality of wartime.[72] Holley was adamant that these traders' actions had meant that the town's population faced the decision to either go without food or 'pay through the nose [for it].'[73]

Although the introduction of fixed food prices intended to stop instances of profiteering, some food producers and traders in the county resented this measure, deeming these prices as intrusive. On 17 October 1917, at the pannier market in the North Devon town of Holsworthy the local police informed the sellers of butter that the maximum price they could sell a pound of butter was 2s 2d under the Food Control Order. However, some farmers' wives were reluctant to sell the butter at this price. One farmer's wife had brought a basket of nearly 50 lbs of butter to the market. After being informed of the fixed charge for the dairy product, she refused to sell her supplies and took her produce home with her.[74] When the *Western Times* reported on the incident, they deemed the refusal of the farmer's wife to sell her butter as an 'unpatriotic action.'[75] Based on the experiences of farmers selling butter to the highest bidder, Dr G. M. Winter, the Chairman of the Torquay Food Control Committee suggested on 22 October 1917 that: 'We are beginning to doubt whether there is much patriotism about the British farmer.'[76] Local Food Control Committees, like those in Torquay and other parts of Devon, acted as the 'intermediary between the Food Controller and the public on the one hand, and the retailer and the public on the other.'[77] Like the military service tribunals, civic figures from local government sat on the Food Control Committees. Local government entities also appointed local food inspectors who sought to ensure that shopkeepers and traders sold food at the correct weights and prices. However, these figures who sought to superintend the business affairs of local food retailers were not well received. When two food inspectors visited Pannier market at Bideford in July 1918, their activities caused umbrage in some quarters. Some traders were so appalled by the interference of these Inspectors that they threatened to 'not bring their butter to market at all.'[78] Traders viewed these food inspectors as interfering, meddling busybodies who monitored their business practices and intervened to control their behaviour. Hence, the introduction of food prices gave these food inspectors, alongside patriotically minded citizens, the opportunity to police the activities of food sellers in the name of the war effort.

In the neighbouring county of Dorset, novelist and local notable Thomas Hardy undertook a more active role in bringing wartime profiteers to account. Alongside Major William Burrough Cosens, Hardy adjudicated upon several food-profiteering cases at the Borough Petty Sessions from 1917 to 1919.[79] Hardy probably viewed his wartime role within a judicial framework because he had since 1894 served as a JP for Dorset. Although Hardy justified his actions in the interest of clamping down on profiteering, his attempts to police the business activities of Dorchester's shopkeepers had made him an unpopular figure in the town.[80] These shop proprietors undoubtedly regarded Hardy as a do-gooder or an interfering busybody intruding upon their business affairs. Florence Hardy, Thomas Hardy's wife, touched upon how the shopkeepers felt aggrieved by her husband's unwelcome activities in a letter she wrote to Louise Yearsley on 10 November 1918. Florence Hardy feared that she would soon not be allowed to enter any shop in the town due to the unpopularity of her husband's actions amongst the shopkeepers of Dorchester.[81] Since her husband wielded such power, these shopkeepers may have suspected that she was a scout for Hardy who could likely inform him of any underhanded business practices. The suspicions of these retailers were not unjustified as food inspectors used individuals to act as undercover scouts to conduct reconnaissance visiting traders on their behalf. On 20 October 1917, Atkin S. Carter, the acting local food inspector for Chesterfield, used his wife, Florence Mary Carter, to discreetly check the weights and prices of meat from traders in the Market Place of the Derbyshire town.[82] Some food inspectors sent young girls into shops as inconspicuous proxies to make purchases, hoping that they would more likely catch shopkeepers not adhering to the regulations.[83] Florence Hardy's fears that some traders could refuse her entry to their premises were not unwarranted since Hardy made no exceptions towards any shopkeeper in Dorchester engaged in profiteering. Even the family's grocer did not escape being penalised because Hardy and Cousins imposed a fine of £15 on Charles Henry Smith for over-charging his customers for ground rice.[84] Moreover, the fact that Smith was a Town Councillor and member of Dorchester's Food Control Committee added to the scandalous nature of the case.[85]

Another shopkeeper caught over-charging his customers was grocer Lewis Kauffman in Stepney, London on 2 February 1918. Whilst on duty watching the line of customers outside Kauffman's shop, a local Constable received a complaint from Mrs McCarthy that the grocer was charging 7d for half a pound of margarine. However, the maximum price retailers were allowed to charge for half a pound of margarine at this time was 6d. Upon entering the shop, the policeman challenged Kauffman over McCarthy's complaint about overcharging for margarine. However, in the face of the Constable's enquiry and the complaints from his other customers about the price he was charging for margarine, Kauffman boldly declared: 'It is my shop and my margarine, and I shall do what I like with it.'[86] Kauffman also had two assistants working in his shop: Mrs Golda Cash and her daughter Rebecca. While Mrs Cash handed the margarine packets to the customers, Rebecca took the payments. During this heated quarrel in the shop, Rebecca leapt to Kauffman's defence and confronted the Constable: 'You dirty ------- dog; what has it got to do with you?.'[87] After an inspection of the basement of Kauffman's business premises, the police discovered that he had stockpiled margarine as there were twenty-eight cases of the dairy product weighing 28 lbs each.[88] At Thames Court police Station on 9 March 1918, Kauffman received a Prison sentence of six weeks for selling margarine above the maximum price, along with a £10 fine and £1 1s. in costs. The Magistrate involved with the proceedings also used this profiteering case as an example to warn other shopkeepers: '"It was time the minds of certain tradesmen were disabused of the idea that they could do as they liked".'[89] Indeed, he stressed that these tradesmen needed to put the profit motive to one side and realise that: '"At the present time they are simply trustees of public property".'[90]

Yet, the increased prices for specific food items in Devon contributed towards some of the county's population expressing disillusionment about the conflict by 1917. An elderly resident in the Dartmoor village of Lustleigh complained to local writer Cecil Torr that the war was terrible because bacon had become so expensive. Another old-age villager nearby overheard the man's gripe and joined the conversation between the two men to add his grievance about the conflict. However, he expressed his objection against the war using a hypothetical comparison. He questioned why the nations were fighting each other because the war was, in his view, as pointless as the people of Lustleigh waging war against the population of the neighbouring town of Bovey Tracey.[91] Olive Hockin witnessed a similar exhibition of war weariness when four local men took a break from haymaking on Dartmoor in June 1917. Over tea, the men discussed the topic of the war, and they revealed that they were not prepared to endure the war's burdens any longer. Local carpenter Arry 'Ickey (sic) had lost his patience with the conflict after hearing that German submarines were sinking all British shipping. He declared to the other men that it was time that the war should stop. Rather than send men off to war, 'Ickey asserted that the men who made the conflict should go out and fight because it was not a working man's war.[92] Local rabbit trapper Billy Withecombe also objected to the conflict carrying on due to a wartime ban prohibiting farmers from selling their wool. In his view, this severe measure confirmed that the war was an unacceptable intrusion that must cease since it interfered with a '"man's own farm".'[93] Ultimately, Withecombe viewed the war as an annoyance that hindered the working practices of local farmers since he was more concerned with the survival of these local farms rather than the national interest.

In Devon, like other parts of the United Kingdom, public opinion towards the war was complex. Other instances of disillusionment with the war do not necessarily indicate outright anger against the conflict. Instead, many Devonians had become tired of it. On 10 February 1917, Edrica de la Pole pondered in her diary how endless the conflict seemed to be in that it was beginning to feel 'as if neither the Winter nor the War will ever end.'[94] Later in Plymouth, James Thomas Rogers experienced a more profound sense of bafflement about the war on 13 June 1917. After reading in the newspapers about the devastation caused by the latest air raid on London, he struggled to come to terms with the terrible nature of the conflict. Reflecting upon the event in his journal, Rogers decided to evoke the words of the 13th Psalm, where he questioned in a tone of disbelief and exhaustion as to how long the war could carry on: 'How long O Lord? How long!.'[95] Albert Best, a plumber and resident of Teignmouth, experienced a similar pause for reflection about the war on 4 August 1917. Looking back on the three years since the outbreak of war, Best acknowledged in his diary that no one expected the war Britain entered on 4 August 1914 would develop and transform into 'such a big thing[,] lasting so long.'[96] Now, on the third anniversary of the conflict's declaration, Best recorded that he felt a sense of disorientation about the conflict because it appeared to him that the war's end was not yet on the horizon.

NWAC and economic remobilisation

For many civilians across the belligerent nations, 1917 was a breaking point. Tired of the conflict, many citizens felt uncertain about the war and questioned how much longer they could tolerate the war carrying on.[97] The British and French governments viewed the disregard and disillusionment expressed by civilians and combatants towards the war, otherwise described as war-weariness, as the most pressing danger for their respective war efforts during 1917 and 1918.[98] Politicians in Britain and France were worried that disillusionment towards the war might translate into internal upheaval. As a result, the state in both nations discreetly intervened to preserve and galvanise the morale of their exhausted civilian populations by creating two nominally independent umbrella organisations to pursue these aims. In Britain, Lloyd George's War Cabinet created the National War Aims Committee (NWAC) in July 1917, whilst the French state established the umbrella organisation of *Union des Grandes Associations contre la Propagande Ennemmie* (UGAPCE).[99] On the British home front, the government-backed advocacy of the NWAC to combat weariness towards the war and remobilise civilian morale was extensive. During the last fifteen months of the conflict, local notables and civic dignitaries across Britain promoted and assisted the efforts of the NWAC on a local level. Like other parts of England and Wales, various speakers at NWAC meetings in Devon often dwelt on a locality's unique qualities or war-related achievements in the hope that this would inspire communities to continue to support the conflict.[100] An example of how speakers tailored their message to match the specific localities was at a meeting in the mid-Devon town of Crediton on 29 November 1917. During his address, Harry Elston, the Chairman of Crediton's UDC, championed the town's accomplishments for the war effort, such as recruitment and the war savings movement.[101] Speakers at other NWAC meetings also sought to remind their audiences about the moral imperative of Britain's righteous stance against German might. One speaker who invoked the morality of Britain's position when going to war in August 1914 was Plymouth City Council member Isaac Foot at a NWAC conference in Plymouth on 21 February 1918. Foot professed that notwithstanding 'all the irritation and bitter outbursts[,] there remained the full recognition that we went to war in a just cause and with clean hands.'[102] Liberal MP George Lambert proclaimed a similar message of firm determination in Okehampton on 5 January 1918. He urged the audience to realise the seriousness of the crisis they were going through, and everyone must put aside their own personal grievances for the sake of the war.[103]

At a NWAC meeting in Exeter on 14 December 1917, James George Owen also referred to this sense of duty when he asserted that the city was firmly behind the war and would continue to support it.[104] During the same meeting, Exeter's Conservative MP, Henry Duke, encouraged Exonians to remain steadfast and be prepared to make more sacrifices to support the war effort. The German people, he asserted, had deliberately raised a 'Frankenstein' whereby they either 'must be delivered from it, or the Allies must come under its heel.'[105] By referring to Mary Shelley's gothic novel *Frankenstein*, Duke portrayed the German military machine as a monstrous creature that would bring uncontainable and rampant destruction like Victor Frankenstein's creation. The fact that Duke had characterised the military machine of Germany in this manner strengthened the idea that it was an aberration of nature that needed to be vanquished.

Whilst Duke used literature as a point of reference in his address in Exeter, Earl Fortescue turned to history in his speech at a NWAC meeting in Newton Abbot on 19 December 1917. Earl Fortescue quoted one of the war speeches by William Pitt the Younger, who served as Prime Minister when Britain was fighting against Napoleon Bonaparte.[106] By quoting from Pitt the Younger, Fortescue's sought to stir the patriotism of those present by evoking a past figure whom contemporaries held in high esteem. Indeed, after hearing Fortescue's speech, the *North Devon Herald* argued that he had cited Pitt 'as an example of self-sacrificing patriotism.'[107] A columnist for the *North Devon Journal* was equally impressed by the message from the speakers at the first meeting of the NWAC in Barnstaple. After listening to Earl Fortescue and other speakers at the event, the columnist suggested: 'No true patriot would dream of ceasing hostilities until Prussian militarism had been crushed and a world-peril thereby removed.'[108]

Yet, on 27 October 1917, an audience member challenged and disrupted the speaker at one evening meeting of the NWAC in Newton Abbot. After the speaker, T. Enfield, launched a scathing attack against the Labour politician Ramsay Macdonald, since he had previously opposed the war, one man in the audience heckled Enfield and said he was talking 'Rot.'[109] He also challenged Enfield directly, by shouting at him: 'Why don't you go to fight yourself?.'[110] Enfield replied that he was ineligible for military service since he was born in 1861. He also revealed that he had tried unsuccessfully to enlist on three occasions. However, the audience member countered Enfield by saying he could have put his age back, thus rendering himself available for military service. Enfield shouted back that the man had gone to great lengths to ensure he did not go. The man replied that he was a pacifist and did not agree with the conflict. At this point, Enfield seized upon this opportunity to try to turn the tables against the pacifist heckler. Enfield highlighted the contradictions of the pacifist's earlier declaration in his retort. Although the pacifist opposed the war, he still wanted Enfield to go off to war and fight despite his age. According to a correspondent for the *Western Times*, the retort from Enfield cut right through the heckler's protestations.[111]

At the same time, NWAC events in Devon allowed the county's local elite to prescribe certain acceptable behaviours. Like fellow speakers at meetings of the NWAC across the United Kingdom, Devon's local elite used these events to try to bolster War Loan campaigns.[112] During his address at a NWAC meeting in Okehampton on 5 January 1917, Sir John Spear appealed for the town's residents to donate money to support the government. Since there was allegedly a lot of money in the locality, Spear proclaimed that he was confident that the 'people of the Okehampton district were patriotic enough to supply it.'[113] Charles Sandbach Parker, the Unionist Candidate for the Barnstaple Division, delivered a similar message during an NWAC meeting in Bideford on 29 October 1917. Although Parker acknowledged that taxation had tripled, he stressed that the audience needed to remain steadfast in supporting the war effort: 'We must stiffen our backs, tighten our purse strings, lend all we can to the Government, and see the thing through.'[114]

As a practical contribution towards the war effort, investments in War Loans were a popular form of economic mobilisation in Devon. An example of the success of these loans in Devon was the Third War Loan. Launched in February 1917, the Third War Loan was also known as the 5 per cent War Loan. Although he was not present at a meeting in Newton Abbot on 31 January 1917 to promote the War Loan, the Conservative MP for Honiton, Major Morrison Bell, sent a telegram to relay that he endorsed it. In his message, he expressed his confidence that Devon's patriotic men would support the Loan.[115] According to the Town Clerk of Exeter, Hugh Lloyd Parry, support for the Third War Loan in the city 'exceeded all expectations.'[116] He believed that the citizens of Exeter enthusiastically supported the Third War Loan because of a coordinated campaign to raise awareness about it across the city. Alongside information bureaus set up in the city to promote the loan, influential citizens from Exeter's civil society endorsed the 5 per cent War Loan. The city's Mayor was one civic figure who helped with this concerted drive by addressing several public meetings to promote the War Loan. Owen also provided a personal appeal that Boy Scouts and pupils from elementary schools distributed to the homes of around 1,000 residents across the city.[117] Moreover, the Exeter branch of the National Provincial and Union Bank of England addressed a joint appeal to their customers to invest in the War Loan. On the last day of the War Loan, 16 February 1917, there was a great rush to promote the Loan. Owen dispatched a final appeal for people to lend money to the War Loan: 'Do not be compelled. Be a patriot. Come forward freely.'[118] In total, the city of Exeter subscribed around £1,250,000 towards the Third War Loan.[119]

Local authorities in Devon also sought to promote the 5 per cent War Loan. In Ottery St Mary, M. W. Ellis, the UDC's chairman, on 6 February 1917 stated to those present at a public meeting in the town hall that he was not on a mission to beg them for money. Instead, he asked them to make a little sacrifice by lending some money to help their country: 'What was wanted was for each individual to show patriotism. Every penny that could be got was wanted to be put into this Loan.'[120] Alongside these appeals, local authorities also sought to demonstrate their patriotism towards the 5 per cent War Loan by investing money into the War Loan from their finances. In Barnstaple, Alderman and Chairman of Barnstaple Town Council's Finance Committee, Arthur J. Reavell, suggested that Barnstaple would follow the 'patriotic lead set by the larger municipalities' by purchasing a block of £10,000 worth of the War Loan.[121] On 2 February 1917, the UDC of the east Devon seaside town of Seaton decided to invest £1,000 towards the 5 per cent War Loan from their finances.[122] By contrast, Tavistock's RDC decided to invest £3,000 in War Loan stock.[123] Meanwhile, the *Devon and Exeter Gazette* reported that DCC had invested £40,216 0s 11d in the 5 per cent

War Loan.[124] A reason to explain the success of War Loans in Devon is that, alongside their appeal as a financial investment, they provided individuals and local authorities a crucial means to demonstrate their patriotism and commitment to the war effort in a practical manner. Indeed, Earl Fortescue wrote to the editor of the *Devon and Exeter Gazette* to commend the men and women of the county who had 'patriotically made it their business to go round with bundles of application forms and canvass their neighbours for subscriptions to the War Loan.'[125]

Alongside War Loans, the War Savings movement achieved similar success in Devon. The Devon County War Savings Committee was formed in July 1916. According to the Committee's Secretary, J. E. Holden, they had achieved remarkable results in their first year of work. War savings certificates were significantly popular amongst the county's population. According to Holden's statistics comparing Devon with the rest of the country, Devon stood 19th out of a list of 55 county areas that included London and other large industrial centres.[126] The following year, the Devon County Central War Savings Committee report revealed that by 31 July 1918, Devon had local committees in 41 centres 'to which were affiliated 577 War Savings Associations with a total membership of 39,499 people.'[127] The War Savings Movement was particularly successful in Exeter. Through the banks and local post offices in the city, the population of Exeter had purchased 850,000 War Certificates up to the end of 1919. Based on a population figure of 60,000, the Town Clerk estimated that each person in the city had purchased over 14 certificates, which was extraordinary when compared to the national average of around '8 certificates per head.'[128] As a result, the citizens of Exeter had 'purchased more than 75 per cent more War Savings Certificates than the average purchases of the whole country.'[129] The residents of the mid-Devon village of Exwick demonstrated similar dedication to support the War Savings Movement. According to the Secretary of the village's War Savings Association, A. H. Rousham, the organisation achieved great success. The Association had 128 members, including adults and children and 1,327 certificates had been purchased and £1,028 had been subscribed by the end of 1918.[130] The Crediton Urban and Rural War Savings Associations attained similar feat as they had collectively raised a total of £3,099 8s 10d by 15 February 1918.[131]

Another instance where the War Savings movement succeeded in Exeter was the 'Tank Week' in December 1917. Like other towns and cities across the United Kingdom, Exeter sought to raise money for the war effort by utilising a model Tank as a centrepiece for this fund-raising campaign.[132] Starting on 10 December and ending on 15 December 1917, this model Tank was paraded through the streets of Exeter to raise awareness of the 'Tank Week' and encourage the city's citizens to apply for War Bonds.[133] After this procession, the Tank was 'placed in Bedford Street, and became a centre of attraction where subscribers could make application for War Bonds.'[134] Like the Victory War Loan, the city's citizens were encouraged to invest on the basis of demonstrating their patriotism. During the week, a total of £40,400 was subscripted.[135] Based on the success of the 'Tank Week', the *Devon and Exeter Gazette* suggested that many people had shown 'their patriotism by investing money in War Bonds or War Certificates.'[136] In the United States, similar campaigns encouraged American citizens to subscribe money to Liberty Bonds. However, Adam J. Hodges reveals that businesses in Portland, Oregon applied pressure to their workforces to purchase these Liberty Bonds since these firms were 'eager to trumpet their patriotism' to the public.[137]

The county's newspapers also played a critical role in promoting the War Bond and War Saving Certificate campaigns through advertising. These advertisements encouraged individuals to support these forms of economic mobilisation through distinctly local ties. On 5 July 1918, the *Western Morning News* ran one promotion for War Loans and War Savings Certificates. At the top of the page was a picture of the badge for the Devonshire Regiment with the title 'Back up the Devons!.'[138] Alongside this evocation of the county's Regiment, the item directed its appeal to the residents of the south Hams town of Ivybridge and the south Devon village of Ermington. The item stressed that they should remember that every pound and shilling that they gave to either War Bonds and War Savings Certificates helped 'the cause for which *they* are fighting – our own Devon lads.'[139] Therefore, war-related savings marketing campaigns on the British home front integrated local identities as a critical feature to encourage local populations to invest.

Tribunals authority contested and the 'Clean Cut'

Despite the urgent need for recruits during 1917 and 1918, the figures who sat on the county's tribunals still encountered Devonians whose behaviour they judged unpatriotic. An example of this was the appeal of Leopold Blackmore, a slaughterman from Bere Alston, on 9 April 1917. The Plymouth panel of the Devon Appeal Tribunal told Leopold and his father that they would uphold the Military's appeal against his son's exemption. After hearing this, Leopold's father reacted angrily to the news and defiantly declared his hope that 'England would starve.'[140] Although Leopold's father wanted to shock the members of the Tribunal, Carlile Davis, the Clerk of the Tribunal, was unflustered by his provocative statement and sought to remind him that they were all in the same situation. Accordingly, Davis retorted on behalf of the Tribunal that they hoped he would 'be here to starve with us.'[141] Another incident that constituted unpatriotic behaviour in the eyes of Tribunalists occurred during the Military's appeal against the exemption of Frederick Thomas Waye, a wheelwright from Bishops Nympton, when the Devon Appeal Tribunal met in Barnstaple on 5 July 1917. Despite the Tribunal deciding to uphold the Military's appeal, J. M. Metherell, the Tribunal's representative for the Board of Agriculture and Fisheries, declared that men such as Waye were essential in rendering support to farmers. In his view, the Army should not take them because of the Government's request for three million additional acres to be ploughed for food production. Metherell's remarks prompted someone present in the court to applause. This reaction caused Lieutenant Stirling to snap back:

> 'That's a very popular decision in north Devon – it's far away from the firing line! I think when a man who should be doing his duty is at home, the person who claps is not a patriotic citizen. When words are spoken to the effect that young men should be left at home they are clapped.'[142]

Lieutenant Stirling believed that it was shameful that some people in North Devon still did not understand the urgent need for men for the Army. After hearing Stirling's response, Metherell countered that North Devon was as 'patriotic as any part of the country.'[143] However, Lieutenant Stirling reprimanded Metherell by arguing that he should associate himself with the Lieutenant's remarks and ask people who came to tribunals not to clap.

On 9 March 1917, Sir Ian Heathcoat-Amory advocated that the people of Devon could no longer prioritise the 'need of any individual business' because the national interest had to come first.[144] However, despite these requests to reconsider their priorities, some Devonians remained more concerned about the plight of their businesses than the war. This concern was evident in the appeal of Harold B. Tucker, a director and secretary of the Totnes jam manufacturing business, Tucker and Sons Limited. After a review of his application for exemption against conscription, the Totnes Tribunal granted Tucker a temporary exemption until 1 July 1917 to provide adequate time for the business to train a substitute. However, the Military appealed against the decision of the Totnes Tribunal. When the Plymouth Panel of the Devon Appeal Tribunal reviewed the Military's appeal on 7 May 1917, they reduced Tucker's temporary exemption to 1 June 1917. Upon hearing that he had lost a month from his exemption, Tucker felt compelled to respond. He complained that the Panel's decision was inconvenient for their business since they were in the middle of their annual stock taking.[145] Like other people employed in family-run businesses, Tucker realised the ramifications of the Tribunal's decision upon their business. By raising this complaint, Tucker was probably concerned about how this reduced temporary exemption would interfere with a crucial time for the company. Principally, Tucker would have less time to find a replacement alongside the annual stock-taking. However, Sir Trehawke Kekewich was not sympathetic towards Tucker's protestation. To Kekewich, it seemed to indicate that Tucker selfishly prioritised the preservation of the business in wartime over the needs of the conflict. In his reply, Kekewich utilised Tucker's words to criticise him instead. He stressed that Tucker should set aside his business concerns since 'we are in the middle of the biggest war ever known.'[146] In their coverage of the proceedings, the *Western Morning News* highlighted these competing priorities to the extent that it seemed to be jam-making versus the war.[147]

A similar businessman who resented the interference of the tribunals was W. B. Hook, slaughterman and butcher. The military had applied for the exemption of Brook's son, Leonard, to be withdrawn as they believed that a man over military age could help run the business rather than have the help of his son. At the Honiton Borough Tribunal, one tribunal panel member, Mr Lawson, stated that Hook could get a woman to take on the meat deliveries rather than the undertake them himself. Indeed, he claimed that 'Honiton had done well and responded patriotically in all things.'[148] However, W. B. Hook abruptly declared to the tribunal that if they were to 'take away' his son, he would 'put up the shutters.'[149] Although the Tribunalists may have interpreted Hook's statement as a threat, it reveals how Hook felt powerless as the tribunal was 'taking' his son away from him. Lawson retorted that it was not patriotic of Hook to speak this way. Indeed, Lawson said Hook would 'not receive any sympathy from that Tribunal or any other Tribunal if he told them he would put his shutters up.'[150] The tribunal adjourned for two months for Hook to find a substitute for his son.

Yet there were Devonians who evaded the tribunal proceedings. Sidney Linscott was one man who failed to attend the Exeter Panel of the county's Appeal Tribunal. Rather than defend his appeal on the grounds of conscientious objection, he submitted a letter to the Panel in his absence. However, Linscott used his letter to criticise the Exeter County Tribunal and how he believed the body could not provide impartial assessments concerning the appeals of conscientious objectors. For Linscott, local men were 'more competent to deal with local applicants and their affairs than a conglomeration of agrarian gentlemen.'[151] Some contemporaries may have interpreted Linscott's refusal to face the tribunal panel and sending a letter to cover his absence as a cowardly way to express his criticisms against the tribunal panel. As a result, Linscott's letter functioned as a strategy where he vented his criticisms without personally facing admonishment from a tribunal panel. However, a correspondent for the *Western Morning News* judged Linscott's accusation in his letter to be a slur against the Exeter Tribunal.[152]

Tribunal panels received other letters from Devonians who believed that some men had unfairly gained exemption because they had not been entirely sincere in the information they provided in their applications for exemption. However, while the authors of these letters felt compelled to write to the county's Appeal Tribunal and their local tribunals about such cases, they would only submit this information anonymously. On 31 March 1917, G. H. Fairbrother, the military representative for the Bideford Borough Tribunal, received an anonymous letter from an individual writing under the pen name of 'Fairplay'. The author demanded that unless certain action was completed, he threatened to refer the matter to Lieutenant Stirling or the War Office. According to a correspondent for the *North Devon Journal*, using 'Fair play' as a pen name was a regrettable choice of signature for 'a person trying to stab another in the back.'[153] The Tribunal's chairman, T. Pollard, admitted receiving one or two anonymous letters. However, he was not prepared to accept the information of these letters and disregarded them, throwing them into the fire.[154] Previously, tribunal panel members had advocated ignoring such testimonies even though these documents probably disclosed the truth.[155] Sir Ian Heathcoat-Amory had also received many anonymous letters and while they often contained 'startling and often interesting information', he wished the writers included their names.[156] In Louisville, Kentucky, APL member and attorney, J. Van Norman, was also wary of accepting anonymous letters reporting instances of disloyalty or cases of slackers. In a statement to the press, he argued that nameless letters should be ignored because he believed that 'all true Americans will give their names in order to aid their government.'[157] However, other APL members were not as reticent as Van Norman as they relied upon rumours, hearsay and undocumented accusations as the basis to question individuals they suspected of unpatriotic activities.[158]

On 1 August, the Barnstaple Borough Tribunal reviewed the case of William Smoldon, who worked as a wheelwright, ironmonger, and undertaker. Although the military had applied for his certificate of exemption to be withdrawn, Smoldon had written a letter to the Munition Area Recruiting Officer (MARO) offering to go into munition work. Smoldon told the tribunal that 'he [previously] had a spark of patriotism left in him, but that vanished when he saw so many single general service men about the town.'[159] Whilst he stated that he would undertake work of national importance, Mr Woodcock, the Tribunal's military representative, was not impressed by Smoldon's melodramatic declaration. He offered a description of Smoldon's attitude in that it was: 'For God's sake put me anywhere, but don't put me in the Army.'[160] Alongside the coverage of Smoldon's appeal in the *North Devon Herald* and *North Devon Journal*, the *Devon and Exeter Gazette* commented on Smoldon's statement about his sense of patriotism. The latter paper argued that Smoldon's declaration was not equivalent to the patriotism of a Bideford mother who 'did not oppose the taking of her last son to war, but sends him to do his duty.'[161] Neither did it correspond to the Strentiford family from the mid Devon village of Morchard Bishop, who had nine men in the Army. When framed alongside such examples of families who had stoically demonstrated their patriotism, the paper mocked Smoldon's ostentatious announcement: 'As I say, there are varying degrees of patriotism, and, unhappily, there are instances where the spirit does not only appear dormant, but stone dead.'[162]

During the one-hundredth meeting of the Exeter city tribunal, the tribunal's Chairman said that he hoped that the 'members were satisfied with the patriotism shown and the hours they had put in during the past eighteen months. He did not think any tribunal in the country had better attended to their work.'[163] Later, the tribunal chairman commended the work of its military representative, Mr Ross, on 9 May 1917. In his tribute, Stocker asked if the meeting's minutes would record their appreciation of Ross's time devoted to his work. Such a tribute would, he hoped, inspire other people to emulate Ross's patriotism and zeal.[164] However, like the otherness that some Devonians felt about the tribunals, some may have viewed such commendations from those involved in the county's tribunals as self-congratulatory. As the tribunal's military representative, Ross primarily sought to make the case to secure men for the Army.

Although many on the tribunals considered themselves as dispensers of justice, this sense of self-congratulation from Devon's tribunalists about their work may have seemed odd to some contemporaries when compared to the men that they sent off to fight. Written under the synonym of 'Plymothian', the author criticised the exemptions granted by the Plymouth tribunal. The author suggested that the tribunals provided Devon's notable elite with a means to extend their status as eminent dignitaries in the county. The war was, he argued, an exceptional opportunity that 'afforded to so-called public men to conclusively show their claim to such a title by simple example, which in these days is worth so much more than any precept, of which we hear far too much.'[165] Pacifist writer Caroline Elizabeth Playne would later write about the tribunals in similarly negative terms when she described that 'a great deal of patriotism was displayed at the expense of other men's sons.'[166] Some contemporaries in Devon may have viewed the tribunal panels as sending off other men to war, and it was a false equivalence to claim that they were undertaking a patriotic duty. Instead, they were undertaking a desk job and sending young men off to fight rather than undertake military service themselves. Maureen Healy suggests that the residents of wartime Vienna disparaged the men at home who undertook administrative work in comfort from a desk as 'unworthy' compared to the men fighting on the frontline.[167] There were instances where Devon's tribunalists experienced abusive behaviour from local populations. On 31 January 1918, the *North Devon Herald* reported on Councillor Frederick Wilkey's claim that he had been publicly insulted by persons from Appledore in regard to his activities on the Northam Tribunal.[168] Although he said he was unfazed by these insults directed against him, he was concerned that the same persons had also targeted his wife and subjected her to frequent abuse in the market.

Following Russia's withdrawal from the war after the Bolsheviks signed the treaty of Brest-Litovsk on 3 March 1918, Imperial Germany transferred troops and material from the Eastern front to the Western front. With the transfer of these resources to the Western Front, the German Army launched a new offensive on 21 March 1918. Alternatively described as *Kaiserschlacht* (Kaiser's Battle), General Erich Ludendorff coordinated the German Spring Offensive to achieve a strategic breakthrough against the British and French Armies. Initially, these surprise offensives achieved limited success but not the decisive victory that Ludendorff had envisaged. Nevertheless, the German Spring Offensive provoked alarm in Britain and led to an emergency situation and a greater requirement for more men for the Army.[169] The development placed the War Agricultural Executive Committees for specific counties across the United Kingdom under increased pressure with designated quotas to provide additional men for the Army. The task became known as the 'clean-cut'.

Across the United Kingdom, county War Agricultural Executive Committees, like the one in Staffordshire, pressured rural areas to release men in June 1918.[170] Devon's War Agricultural Executive Committee had to source 1,000 men for the Army from the county's agricultural sector. This quota was split between the Committee's four divisions to achieve this target. The Northern Division, chaired by Fortescue, had to supply 250 men.[171] Although the Eastern Division had found its quota of men by 16 June 1918, Heathcoat-Amory expressed doubts whether the Western Division would achieve their share. Based on his experiences reviewing 100 cases from the Western Division before the county's Appeal Tribunal, he believed that for the Western Division to find their quota of men must have been a 'more difficult [task] even than the finding of ours has been.'[172] R. F. Woodcock, the secretary of Devon's War Agricultural Executive Committee, also came to this conclusion when he suggested in a letter to Earl Fortescue dated 20 June 1918 that the Western Division was the weakest link.[173] It was a demanding and painful task for the Devon War Agricultural Executive Committee members to go through the list of the 2,500 men employed on the county's farms, many of whom had received exemptions for farm work, to achieve Devon's quota. Fortescue remembered this was the worst challenge the Devon War Agricultural Executive Committee faced throughout the war. Moreover, the Committee had a very small margin of men to select from. Earl Fortescue ascribed the reason behind this was that there had been more active recruiting in South and East Devon.[174] These areas experienced less dissent and were more conservative compared to the North and West districts of the county. These factors, 'though no party or creed is more patriotic than another', had unquestionably affected recruiting.[175]

Nevertheless, nearly all of the members of the Committee who were farmers played up well to the task.[176] Fortescue believed that these agriculturalists cooperated with this task because he had accidentally insisted early on that the son of one of these men should join up. However, the father of the chosen man did not respond well to being placed in this predicament. Since his son had to go off to war, he was determined that other farmers should not be exempt 'on the principle of the Fox who had lost his tail [and] was thereafter all for drastic measures with other people.'[177] Although the Committee reached their quota, some agriculturalists in Devon did not support this combing-out process. In a letter to the *Devon and Exeter Gazette* on 10 May 1918, one farmer advocated that the authorities could take the many men who had flocked to Devonport Dockyard to avoid military service instead of agriculture bearing the brunt of losing yet more men before the harvest.[178] As a protest against taking men away from their farms, some Devon farmers had threatened to put cattle into the fields that they originally wanted to harvest for hay. Upon hearing these rumours, Fortescue stressed that if any farmer decided to do this, he sought to remind them about the Defence of the Realm Act powers entrusted to the Agricultural Executive Committee. These farmers could be 'compelled to farm as directed, and are liable to £100 fine and (or) imprisonment if they fail to do so.'[179]

Surveillance of the Buckfast monks

On 1 January 1917, the members of Buckfastleigh UDC met to discuss the letter they had received from the Home Office that clarified the arrangement of designating Buckfast Abbey and its grounds as an internment camp. The Home Office stressed that as an internment camp, the Abbey and grounds would need to be monitored by local special constables or local volunteers under the jurisdiction of Captain Herbert Reginald Vyvyan, who was responsible for obtaining special constables to undertake this duty. Moreover, the letter stressed that it was never the case that the UDC had to 'appoint special constables or give any directions to them.'[180] After hearing the letter's contents, the Council's Chairman, J. Willcocks, argued that these arrangements were unsatisfactory because there was no one to guard the Abbey.[181] Since the UDC members still viewed the German monks as a danger, they did not abandon their efforts to have the 'enemy aliens' removed from the Abbey and sent to an internment camp. In their meetings during the spring of 1917, the Council continued to correspond with Devon MPs, such as Sir John Spear and George Lambert, about the matter.[182]

On 12 February 1917, Captain Vyvyan met the Bench of Totnes Divisional Petty Sessions to request the services of special constables to watch the Abbey. Vyvyan informed the Magistrates that he had endeavoured without success to obtain special constables from the neighbourhood and from as far away as Torquay and Newton Abbot. Accordingly, he appealed to the Bench for the services of fifteen special constables who would take regular shifts individually and in pairs to monitor and patrol the Abbey. Although the work would not be difficult, Vyvyan stressed that it would be unpaid. Another critical duty of these special constables was to ensure that three of the monks authorised to undertake farm work were 'accompanied by a British subject or a friendly alien' on their way to the farm.[183] Vyvyan revealed that the Abbot had also promised to provide accommodation for any special constable required to reside in the Abbey overnight.[184] On 19 February 1917, the Magistrates held a second meeting with Vyvyan, asking him further questions about his request. Whilst Vyvyan had approached the Military for men to undertake the work, no soldiers from the Royal Defence Corps were available. Moreover, he revealed that thirty-six 'alien' monks still resided at the Abbey as four of the 'aliens' 'had been interned at their own request.'[185] After these questions were answered, the Chairman asked 'Why can't the lot be interned?', Vyvyan replied that the Secretary of State had informed him that 'it can't be done.'[186] Upon the Bench's return from their deliberations, they concluded that the Abbey and its grounds were unsuitable for an internment camp. Treating Buckfast Abbey on the same lines as other internment camps was impractical because the premises were inadequately fenced. The Magistrates believed that a large number of men would be required to monitor the large areas of the Abbey estate. In their view, local authorities should not be responsible for monitoring the 'enemy aliens' at the Abbey. Instead, it was a national duty that was too important to be overseen by 'untrained men.'[187] Accordingly, the Bench agreed that the Government should relocate the German and Austrian monks of the Abbey to an internment camp.

In their reporting of the meeting of the Totnes Divisional Sessions, the *Western Times* described the session as the 'Buckfast fiasco.'[188] By contrast, *John*

Bull ran an article on 10 March 1917 that commended the assessment of the Totnes Magistrates and advocated that the German and Austrian residents should be removed from the Abbey to be 'snugly and safely interned.'[189] Sir Clement Kinloch-Cooke, the Conservative MP for Devonport, used the comments of the Totnes Magistrates to reinforce the case for the monks' internment during a House of Commons debate on 27 February 1917. Given the proximity of the Abbey to the coast and a town undertaking government work, Kinloch-Cooke suggested that local authorities should not guard the Abbey and grounds since 'watching alien enemies was not a local [duty] but a national one.'[190] In response, the Home Secretary, Sir George Cave, stated that the Magistrates' decision was regrettable since they had not addressed the Chief Constable's request to obtain additional persons to act as special constables. However, due to a recommendation from the Advisory Committee of the Home Office, the Buckfast monks were exempt from internment, and their movements were restricted to the Abbey and the grounds.[191]

On the same day, Captain Vyvyan reported the decision of the Totnes Magistrates to the Devon Standing Joint Committee who had also received a letter from the Home Office following the communication they had received from Buckfastleigh's UDC. Committee member W. Vicary claimed that since there was so much talk about the monks amongst the local populations surrounding the Abbey, there was a lot of veiled suspicion that something wrong had been done despite the lack of proof.[192] The Committee's Chairman, G. C. Davie informed Vyvyan that they were unable to provide constables to monitor the Abbey because the Devonshire force was 92 police short.[193] Alongside the fact that they had no men to watch the monks voluntarily, Davie revealed that the county had no money to pay for the Abbey to be monitored. In his memoirs for the war years, Earl Fortescue recalled receiving a letter from a 'busy person at Buckfastleigh [who] wrote to me in a fuss about possible spying by the priests at Buckfast Abbey.'[194] Based on the difficulties of getting special constables to watch the Abbey, this letter was presumably from one UDC member who wrote to Devon's Lord Lieutenant to ask for his advice. In his reply, Fortescue proposed that keeping Buckfast's monks under observation would be an ideal job for the local VTC.[195]

On 26 February 1917, a group of nine members (an English priest, French priests and monks) of the Benedictine community wrote to DCC about how they felt distressed about the continued agitation against them despite the decision made by the Home Office.[196] Reverend Dom Savinien Louismet expressed similar sentiments in his letter to Captain Vyvyan. Louismet stressed that nothing disloyal occurred amongst the German monks and that the agitation against them was 'senseless and unjustifiable.'[197] However, the two letters contained a proposal to solve the problem of securing men to watch the Abbey. Although they hoped that special constables would soon be appointed, they also offered to act as special constables and effectively police themselves since they lived with the German portion of the community. As a priest and gentleman on the inside, Louismet also offered his services as a special constable under the direction of Captain Vyvyan to 'control and duly report about the doings of all or any of the German monks of Buckfast.'[198] Louismet avowed that the German monks spent their time dedicated to 'a life of study and prayer and the peaceful avocations of tilling the land and rebuilding the Abbey' just as they had done before the outbreak of war.[199]

Nevertheless, the UDC members tried to find new ways to justify removing the monks from the Abbey and sending them to an internment camp. During their meeting on 5 March 1917, the Council's Clerk, Edward Windeatt, revealed that one of the fundamental obstacles against interning the monks was that ecclesiastics should not be interned under international law. However, Windeatt stressed that, according to the Register, the monks were described as builders, masons, carpenters and students since they had received training in construction-based trades to help in their endeavours to rebuild the Abbey. Since the monks now possessed building skills under the Register, they could no longer be classed as ecclesiastics, removing this protection against their eviction from the Abbey.[200] However, the Home Office may not have engaged with these points because they considered the issue a matter between Captain Vyvyan and the Home Secretary.

After approaching Devon MPs to ask questions about the Buckfast monks in the House of Commons, the Council decided to liaise with the Conservative MP for Brentford, William Joynson-Hicks, for his assistance. In his letter to the Council, Joynson-Hicks advised the Council to pass a resolution that called for the interment of the German monks because they objected to the 'locality having to undertake the watching at Buckfast Abbey either by paid or by special constables.'[201] If the Council approved such a resolution, he promised to reference it in a question in the House of Commons.[202] After the Council passed this resolution on 2 April 1917, Joynson-Hicks raised the points of their motion in a Commons debate on

18 April 1917. In response, the Parliamentary Under-Secretary of State, William Brace, stated that if the Home Office tried to remove the German monks from the Abbey, they could easily claim repatriation to Germany since they were priests. Moreover, Brace argued that Buckfast's monks were doing 'very serviceable work for this nation.'[203] Yet Joynson-Hicks remained unsatisfied with this answer and later asked Brace in the Commons on 3 May 1917 to elaborate on this very serviceable work. Brace replied that alongside their religious activities, the monks produced a great deal of honey from their bee-keeping and utilised 45 acres for food production: 25 acres as grazing land for livestock whilst 20 acres was dedicated to crops, vegetables and fruit. Brace stressed that he had also heard from the Abbot that the monks had offered 'to help in all the farming in the district if they could be allowed to go outside the Abbey grounds for the purpose.'[204] Alongside the coverage of this Parliamentary debate in the national press and their Devon counterparts, Catholic newspapers in America and Australia reported on it. Newspapers such as the *Catholic Bulletin*, the *Catholic Advance* and the *Catholic Weekly* suggested that Hick's question was a disastrous attempt by the local council "bigots" to stir up a scare against the German Benedictines of Buckfast.[205]

Although the Council were described as the 'prime movers' in the agitation against the German monks, an anonymous official from the Home Office concluded that the Council had made 'no effort to find proper guardians over these *dangerous* monks.'[206] The evidence suggests that, while the Council received some offers from people willing to act as volunteers to watch the Abbey, some Buckfastleigh UDC members wanted to avoid having the responsibility of monitoring the German monks or the Abbey.[207] Faced with mounting local suspicions against these 'enemy aliens', the Council viewed them as irritants and tried to tactically use any pretext to get the Home Office to remove them from the locality. Sir Louis Dane, the head of the Home Office Special Commission, also came to this conclusion. In 1927, Dane visited Buckfast Abbey to see Abbot Vonier. He informed Vonier that he believed the Council members only wanted to "hoof" out the German monks from the Abbey and that 'patriotism had nothing to do with it.'[208]

An interesting point for comparison with the campaign of Buckfastleigh's UDC to have the monks removed from the locality were the efforts of Dunkeswell's Parish Council to request an increased police presence due to the large number of Portuguese labourers living in the east Devon parish. When the Council submitted their request to the Superintendent of police at Honiton in September 1918, the Council stressed that they needed these additional policemen because the 'Licensee [of the local public house] is a woman.'[209] Mrs Hornsey had taken over as the Licensee of the Royal Oak public house because her husband, the original Licensee, George Hornsey, had to join up after 17 May 1918.[210] However, the male members of the local Parish Council questioned whether Mrs Hornsey could manage the public house. Presumably, they believed that having these police officers would ease their concerns about the behaviour of these people in an environment involving alcohol. Therefore, they would effectively monitor the behaviour of the Portuguese labourers and provide assistance or possibly intervene if Mrs Hornsey failed to regulate the behaviour of the Portuguese labourers and the local patrons who regularly frequented the public house.

The Armistice

Facing the prospect of military collapse and the possibility of internal unrest in the autumn of 1918, Germany capitulated and signed the terms of the Armistice on 11 November. Like the desire for news of the July crisis, contemporaries across the British Isles sought to gain the most up-to-date information from national and local newspaper offices. Outside the *Western Morning News* newspaper office in Plymouth, a great crowd of the city's residents had assembled, waiting for the news. After seeing the confirmation of the Armistice posted in the office's window, many Plymothians waved British flags whilst several smiling citizens gave the announcement their thumbs up.[211] A similar congregation of people had assembled outside the offices of the *Express and Echo* in Exeter. Dorothy Holman noticed that once the notice of the Armistice went up in the window, the people reacted joyfully.[212] Meanwhile, in Ottery St Mary, Sir Ernest Satow noticed the residents draped Union Jacks outside their windows, and a great crowd assembled in the town square to celebrate the news with fireworks.[213] In their coverage of how people in Devon and Cornwall had responded to the Armistice, the *Western Morning News* argued that from a 'patriotic point of view' it was a credit to the people of the West Country that these Armistice celebrations had not got out of hand.[214]

Alongside those who viewed the Armistice as a cause for celebration, many Devonians were relieved and thankful upon hearing the news. A *Devon and Exeter Gazette* columnist observed that the prevailing mood amongst the majority of the citizens of Exeter was one of 'heartfelt thanksgiving.'[215] Speaking before a great audience assembled at the statue of Sir Redvers Buller, Sir James George Owen proclaimed that their hearts were filled with thankfulness for this momentous event. He also emphasised the Armistice held a religious dimension since Owen believed that all those present needed to offer thanks to God. Although the citizens of Exeter had done their best to help the war effort, he thought that it was only by God's divine authority that Britain had achieved victory against the '"invincible" German Army.'[216] Indeed, many Devonians went to their local churches to thank God for granting Britain victory after the ordeal of the past four years. The news of the Armistice meant that the religious intercession services at churches in Exeter, Plymouth and across the county for that day became thanksgiving services.[217] One three-year-old Devonian girl remembered her mother came to her nursery on 11 November to collect her so that she could be ready in her Sunday best to go to church that day to thank God for the Armistice.[218]

Yet the arrival of the Armistice was not a cause for thanksgiving or celebration for other Devonians. On the contrary, it was a sad occasion that brought forth a poignant recognition that the loved ones that they had lost would never return home. For Stephen Reynolds, the news of the Armistice overwhelmed him on 11 November with an emotional reflection about the human cost of the conflict. Although he was intensely relieved to hear that the war was over, the sight of crowds rejoicing the news in Sidmouth did not sit well with him. He wrote in a letter to H. G. Maurice that the joyful spectacle of people celebrating the Armistice that day in the streets of the seaside town gave him the morbid sensation of 'witnessing an orgie (sic) in a graveyard.'[219]

Conclusion

During 1917 and 1918, the initiatives taken in Devon were part of the larger mission to reinvigorate the support of the British population behind the war. However, the success of projects that constituted this second mobilisation or remobilisation of the British war effort depended on the involvement of local populations across Devon. Although tractors and set prices for arable crops sought to act as inducements to encourage the county's farmers to produce more cereals, many agriculturalists pushed back against these interventions. They did not want to comply with orders to till more pasture land for arable crops, resenting these measures and interpreting them as an unnecessary interference into their working practices. Under the auspices of remobilisation, some Devonians felt a renewed sense of imperative or mission to superintend the wartime behaviour of the county's citizens. In light of the food supply crisis and calls to increase domestic food production, individuals sought to superintend land use. These critics argued that the county's residents should use any patch of land for the patriotic purpose of growing food and deemed frivolous uses unpatriotic. However, some Devonian farmers felt aggrieved by these individuals who thought they knew better than them about how to farm their land and who sought to boss them around. Some Devonians objected to the intrusion of food inspectors or other officials who tried to police their activities and choices in the name of clamping down on unpatriotic food profiteering. The county's notables struggled to convince Devonians of the necessity of all of these heightened demands to secure the prospect of victory. For some Devonians, the directives that constituted remobilisation stood in opposition to the survival of their livelihoods. The crisis of food supplies amplified accusations of profiteering against farmers and food suppliers in the county and directly contributed to instances of disillusionment towards the war. Across Devon, the meetings of the NWAC gave Devon's local elite another avenue to disseminate their views on what constituted patriotism and prescribe acceptable behaviours to the county's citizens.

The success of the War Loan, War Bonds and War Savings campaigns in Devon reveals that remobilisation was very successful in economic terms in the county. The county's local elite persuaded their respective communities of the importance of these financial directives. In the applications for exemption, individual priorities continued to overrule many appeals for Devonians to consider the national interest. Meanwhile, the criticism from the county's population against Devon's tribunalists and the escalating demands of the military grew in the county during 1917 and 1918. For Devonians who submitted their critiques and information anonymously, Devon's Tribunalists argued that these authors needed to substantiate their allegations with names. They destroyed these letters rather than allow their contents to affect their deliberations. The process to 'comb out' additional men from Devon's agricultural sector for the 'clean cut' proved an arduous task for figures of Devon's elite who sat on the county's War Agricultural Executive Committee. Unsatisfied that the German and Austrian monks remained in Buckfast Abbey, members of Buckfastleigh's UDC employed new manoeuvres to have them removed from the Abbey and sent to an internment camp. However, like their earlier attempts, the Council's renewed campaign failed. Although many Devonians welcomed and celebrated the arrival of the Armistice, others reflected on the human cost of the war.

Conclusion

On 20 July 1915, the *Devon and Exeter Gazette* ran an article presenting a portrait of a 'stalwart young patriot.'[1] The article described a military-age man who believed he was a 'true patriot' because he was dedicated to following the war since it began ten months prior. He eagerly read the daily edition of *The Times* for the latest updates on the progress of the Allied armies and even proudly 'wore a patriotic button in his coat' to further demonstrate his patriotism.[2] Motivated by his deep interest in the war, he 'studied the recruitment returns diligently, and regretted that Devon, his native county, should be so backward, that its men should fail so obviously to realise how urgently England required them in the fighting line.'[3] However, when faced with the call to serve King and Country himself, the article's author suggested that the 'stalwart young patriot' would decline and list the many justifications as to why he could not possibly enlist, including his defective eyesight and delicate lungs holding him back from military service. The article's author clarified that since the 'stalwart young patriot' was reluctant to undertake military service himself, he was not a patriot but a shirker.[4]

This book has shown that, like the article's author, members of Devon's local elite sought to arbitrate upon the patriotism of men eligible for military service in the county. These patriotically minded men above military age believed it was up to them to do something about voluntary recruitment. They felt compelled to intervene in voluntary recruitment efforts and had taken it upon themselves to motivate the county's military-age men to enlist. Acting as the self-appointed arbiters of patriotism, they used their own sense of patriotism to arbitrate what it was for eligible men in wartime. Reynolds defined these figures as the 'provincial patriots' whose patriotism consisted solely of superintending eligible men's patriotism.[5] They behaved as John Loosemore had done towards military-age men still at home around South Molton, deciding who was patriotic and who was lacking in patriotism.[6] Many of Devon's elite presented prescriptions to eligible men, and their families, about their responsibilities and what they should do in wartime: ultimately, they should undertake military service. Patriotically minded women of Devon's civil society also acted as the 'superintendents of patriotism' since they attempted to enforce military service on younger men like older men had tried to do. Like the female volunteers of the White Feather Brigade who made value judgements about men still in civilian clothes by giving them white feathers, these women targeted eligible men and superintended their patriotism. As seen in Chapters 4 and 5, the introduction of conscription in the county provided another way in which Devon's 'provincial patriots' could superintend the patriotism of eligible men. The sessions of the local tribunals and the county's appeal tribunal allowed Devon's notable figures to arbitrate and commentate upon the patriotism of those seeking exemption from military service. However, Devon's 'provincial patriots' did not solely superintend the patriotism of those eligible for military service. These policemen and women of patriotism monitored and policed the patriotism of Devon's population, deciding what was patriotic or unpatriotic behaviour in wartime.

Although Reynolds described the behaviour of these figures as superintending patriotism, Devon's local elite would claim they were instead trying to fulfil their patriotic duty by providing wartime leadership. As the Mayor of Exeter through most of the war, James Owen provided wartime leadership in the city, letting 'no opportunity slip to stimulate the patriotism of the citizens' of Exeter.[7] Owen sought to encourage their patriotism across many wartime projects, including recruitment, food economy, war savings and other projects related to the war effort.[8] Earl Fortescue was another key civic figure who worked tirelessly to stimulate the patriotism of Devon's population. In his speeches and addresses at recruitment events, Fortescue emphasised that it was the patriotic duty of the county's eligible men to enlist because it was within his remit as Devon's Lord Lieutenant to gain recruits for the Army and the Territorials. Like Fortescue, other notable figures and Army recruiters employed recruitment strategies to define and stress what patriotism was for military-age men on the route marches and other recruiting events. Devon's 'provincial patriots' did not employ the same methods of coercive volunteerism as the APL had done in America. Instead, they sought to superintend the patriotism of military-age men through formal and informal means, like public addresses and encounters with the county's populace. Accordingly, Devon's 'provincial patriots' went to great lengths to influence and control the wartime discourses of patriotism. With conscription, the notable figures on Devon's tribunals made value judgements and arbitrated the patriotism of the county's menfolk in 1917 and 1918. Like the meetings of various wartime organisations in the county, the sessions of Devon's Appeal Tribunal provided the county's notables with a platform to broadcast their prescriptions and views of patriotism. The commentaries that accompanied the tribunal's verdicts also reveal how the county's notables used these rulings to encourage and prescribe the necessity of wartime measures for the sake of the national interest. Accordingly, Devon's 'provincial patriots' used the tribunals to offer prescriptions about the wartime behaviour of the county's population. For example, Devon's tribunalists prescribed the county's agriculturalists to take on women's labour as an essential wartime measure rather than keeping men on the land. The county's newspapers propagated the views, prescriptions, and assessments of 'patriotism' by Devon's 'provincial patriots' to a broader audience in their reporting of Devon's voluntary recruitment campaign. However, Devon's newspapers also played their own distinct part in arbitrating upon the patriotism of eligible men by contributing to the discourses of patriotism in the county. These tabloids achieved this by presenting criticism against Devonian men who unconsciously objected to volunteering at recruitment events in the county and used the recruiting figures of particular localities as the basis to determine their patriotism.

The evidence from Devon during the war years reinforces the argument that a patriot was an individual who made the right moral choice. The *Western Times* proposed that this was the case when the tabloid suggested on 19 October 1915 in that 'True patriotism consists in actions, good and wisely considered.'[9] Devon's 'provincial patriots' took it upon themselves to judge and police people's choices in the county. The validity of these choices was rooted in the socially and morally acceptable codes of conduct in wartime. Figures from Devon's local elite commended eligible men for enlisting because they had made the right moral choice. They praised men like Reverend S. J. K. Mills for volunteering since they had acted upon a sense of duty to defend the nation and had proven their patriotism. Men like Mills had, in turn, also chosen to sacrifice their own self-interest for the national interest. Alongside the county's newspapers, figures from Devon's local elite congratulated these men as true patriots since they had chosen to present their patriotism correctly by enlisting in the Army. The same was true for the men who volunteered for the Royal Navy since they had practically demonstrated their patriotism and fulfilled their obligation to defend the nation. At the same time, Devon's notables reprimanded military-age men who made the wrong and immoral choice by deciding to remain bystanders in the crowd. For non-combatants, cheering on soldiers, waving flags, wearing patriotic buttons and singing patriotic songs were important demonstrations of their patriotism. However, it was unacceptable for eligible men who remained at home to engage in such actions. If these men did, Devon's local elite interpreted these actions as self-absorbed performative gestures that were a poor substitute for undertaking their correct patriotic duty to fight for King and Country. These figures also superintended the patriotism of the county's farmers through their choices. For instance, if they decided against ploughing up their pasture land to grow cereals, their choice not to cooperate to grow more food for the national interest was deemed unpatriotic. Accordingly, the policing of patriotism in Devon neatly weaved into the dissemination of the language and representations of the social morality of wartime on a local level.

Devon's 'provincial patriots' saw their wartime activities as part of a campaign to educate the county's citizens and encourage them to make the patriotic choice to participate in mobilisation efforts. They sought to educate the county's population about patriotism, presenting a narrative of Devonian exceptionalism alongside examples of local patriotism for Devonians to emulate. In their wartime appeals to mobilise the county's population, figures from Devon's civil society integrated local identities and community affiliation in their appeals to give them a distinctly Devonian character. They used local cultural codes, such as the legend of Drake's Drum, alongside references to Devonshire's past, like the Spanish Armada and the county's illustrious men of action, such as Drake, hoping these would resonate with Devonian audiences. However, these locally rooted and historically framed appeals did not convince some Devonian men to enlist. The educative role of the county's local elite was evident in how they praised 'patriotic' responses from military-age men worthy of commendation in the discourses of patriotism. Men in Devon who enlisted functioned as 'patriotic' examples to educate and inform the county's population about patriotism and encourage other men to present their patriotism correctly. The contrast between demonstrating true patriotism and its opposite was also evident in the value judgements associated with the object of the white feather. Families with sons in the forces or volunteered were heralded as patriotic examples. Devon's elite attempted to promote and control their definition of patriotism by using specific patriotic examples. However, these attempts to educate people about patriotism were not always successful. As Reynolds identified in his definition of inspection, there was a negative perception of individuals acting as teachers trying to teach people how to live but having had no personal experience of the circumstances of the people they taught.[10] This sense of separation and unrelatability would explain why Devon's population pushed back against the efforts of Devon's local elite to educate them about their choices in wartime. Notable women from Devon's civil society tried to educate Devon's farmers about the validity of women's labour by using positive patriotic examples of women working on the land. Nevertheless, despite trumpeting the achievements of these women, many farmers remained unconvinced about the contribution that inexperienced women could make to agriculture. At the same time, Devon's notables promoted examples of unpatriotic behaviour to shame the misdemeanours of certain Devonians and act as a warning to others. The examples of 'patriotic' and 'unpatriotic' behaviour emphasised by these notable figures also reached a broader audience when published in Devon's local newspapers. The publication in the local press of the value judgements and views from Devon's Tribunalists about the lack of patriotism from some Devonians during tribunal hearings functioned as examples to inform and educate. The explicit exhortative role of Devon's local elite was also noticeable in their verdicts towards the appeals for exemption.

During the war years, Devonians developed their own rationalisations for abstaining from the behaviours that Devon's 'provincial patriots' prescribed for them. In the context of recruitment, many military-age men in Devon developed rationalisations against enlistment to justify their decision. When Army recruiters and Devon's 'provincial patriots' found men of military age not yet in uniform, they asked them to explain these rationalisations about why they had decided not to volunteer. Questions such as 'Why are you not in uniform?' could come across as a probing enquiry, whilst others like 'Don't you think you should be in the Army?' could be more challenging and judgemental. When faced with probing questions about their rationalisations against enlisting, some eligible men in Devon may have interpreted that these formed the basis for an interrogation, one person demanding an explanation like a police superintendent interrogating a potential suspect. Indeed, the experience probably left many eligible men feeling that these figures interrogated and treated them like suspects. Eligible men in Devon probably felt it was as if their patriotism was on trial by these 'superintendents of patriotism', and they needed to prove it to others. These figures arbitrated upon the validity of these rationalisations against military service, whether they were justifiable reasons for staying at home or flimsy excuses for not doing their obvious duty. After listening to some rationalisations, it appeared to Army recruiters and members of Devon's local elite that some men seemed to look for any pretext to justify not volunteering. These figures could also dismiss or mock these rationalisations to shame the lack of patriotism amongst these men. Fed up with these excuses, Apsley Petre Peter believed that a group of justices should arbitrate upon the reasonings that military-age men expressed to justify their decision not to enlist.[11] Under the MSA, local bodies of men and women from Devon's civil society did judge upon the explanations eligible men used to justify why they should gain exemption against military service. Many of Devon's tribunal panels contained figures from the county's civil society who were previously involved in the county's voluntary recruitment campaign, where they judged upon the rationalisations used by eligible Devon men to justify their decision not to volunteer. Now sitting on the tribunal panels, these figures assessed the justifications expressed by military-age men or those representing them as to why they should gain exemption from conscription.

As seen in Chapter 3, the fear of being cornered or pounced upon by Devon's local elite and Army recruiters helps explain why many eligible men decided to avoid recruitment events by hiding away. Some eligible men resented having to justify their reasons against military service to other people. They wanted to evade individuals who would likely tackle and question them about their rationalisations against military service. During the route marches and the Derby Scheme, many eligible men wanted to avoid Army enlistment. They tactically sought shelters from Army enlistment, by deciding to join the Royal Navy, seeking employment in munitions factories or Devonport dockyard. Whilst contemporaries suspected that the sons of the county's farmers hid on their farms, Fortescue acknowledged that there were men in every other class who had 'taken cover'.[12] Devon's notable figures tried to clamp down on men they deemed as shirkers since they had dodged military service.[13] According to Fortescue, the Northern Division of the Devon War Agricultural Executive Committee was 'unanimous in their desire to be down on any family that had shirked military service.'[14] However, Devon's local elite did not participate in the 'round-up' raids to hunt for shirkers that occurred in the county in September 1916, unlike the APL members who assisted American law enforcement officials on the slacker raids of 1918.

Despite the hopes of Devon's local elite that the county would set an exemplary patriotic standard for recruitment numbers, the reality was that voluntary recruitment for the Army was bad in Devon.[15] Embarrassed by the shame that Devon was letting the side down and infuriated that eligible men were indifferent about undertaking their obvious duty in wartime, many figures from the county's local elite felt helpless. They wrote letters published in the county's newspapers to vent their grievances and frustrations against Devon's eligible men who decided to stay at home rather than enlist. Whether submitted under their names, pen names or anonymously, these letters worked as denunciations and armchair critiques against these men. As presented in Chapter 2, these letters bemoaned that the county's young men had lost their patriotism since they had not fulfilled their duty. These critics also turned to Devonshire's past, using it as a yardstick to measure the patriotism, or lack thereof, of the present generation of Devon men. By comparing them to Devonshire's patriots of the past, men of pluck and action like Drake and Buller, these authors claimed that Devon's menfolk had failed to live up to the standards of patriotism and loyalty set by their forefathers. Some letters called for swift and decisive action to remedy the patriotic failings of these men, like sending them to Canada to learn what patriotism was. Anonymous letters through the war years also sought to chastise those who chose to use land in the county for unpatriotic uses and bring to the attention of the county's tribunalists about Devonian men who had gained exemptions unfairly.

The evidence from Devon reveals that self-mobilisation had distinct limitations in the county. As a form of self-mobilisation, Devon's voluntary recruitment campaign did not achieve universal success since many eligible men did not want to join the Colours. As shown in Chapters 2 and 3, despite their best efforts, Devon's notables faced an uphill struggle to mobilise the county's male population to enlist. The evidence from Devon indicates that the heightened demands of remobilisation during 1917 and 1918 were not unanimously well received by Devon's population. The tremendous social, economic, religious and political diversity within Devon and the county's outlying location in the South West of England helps explain why some corners of the county were partially resistant to the logic of modern industrial war. By scrutinising the effectiveness of mobilisation in Devon, the evidence from the war years reveals the striking contrast between the aspirations of mobilisation expressed in the appeals of Devon's elite and the reality of how Devonians responded to these appeals. The responses from Devonians to the different schemas of mobilisation reveal that the war effort was not an all-encompassing principle in the county. In many instances, Devon's population pushed back against state-driven totalisation. As seen in Chapter 4, conscription represented the state taking more significant intervention in the daily lives of civilians, and they did not take kindly to how it intruded upon their lives. The evidence presented in Chapters 4 and 5 reveals how some Devonian family businesses unconsciously objected to conscription interfering with their lives and complained about the war's interference in their business affairs. Many Devonians also viewed wartime measures as a form of obstructing interference, representing the war's intrusion upon their lives. These responses generate enquiries about the efficacy of Devon's elite as arbiters of the war effort across the county. Their campaigns to mobilise Devonians did not consistently achieve success and did not broadly unify the county's populace under shared wartime responsibilities. Indeed, some of the county's residents remained unconvinced about the importance of wartime directives.

Devon's elite achieved far greater success in encouraging the county's population to participate in charitable efforts and economic mobilisation. For Devonians, these were significant ways to support the war effort. Despite the problems with voluntary recruitment and conscription, the people of Devon were not generally disaffected towards the war effort since some forms of war mobilisation were undeniably successful in the county. Amongst Devonians outside the requirements for military service, the voluntary ethos continued to resonate throughout the war years. The success of wartime philanthropy in the county reinforces the deep commitment of Devon's civil society to this type of mobilisation and the humanitarian nature of Devon's patriotism. The philanthropic achievements of Devon's population were one of the significant features of Devon's war record.[16] In many instances, their involvement in the war effort was informed by what they considered an appropriate contribution. Many of the county's residents in rural areas presented their patriotism in practical ways. These included supporting war-related charities, donating food to local troops, donating eggs to the war effort and providing money to the war effort by investing in War Loans and other forms of War savings.

These practical demonstrations of support underscore the willingness of Devonians to support the war effort through charitable efforts and economic mobilisation rather than give their lives. Charitable efforts allowed these Devonians to claim citizenship in the wartime community and reflect the humanitarian sensibilities of the county's population. Accordingly, Devon's patriotism had a solid humanitarian dimension.

Reynolds' definition of Devon's elite as the 'provincial patriots' would suggest that they were a homogenous group similar to a local police force. Although they shared some similar attributes to the APL, this book has shown that Devon's local elite were a diverse assembly of individuals with different opinions, agendas, concerns and varied senses of authority. To envisage that they were a united group is to impose an artificial cohesion upon them. The lack of early effective coordination amongst Devon's elite helps to explain the limited success of voluntary recruitment efforts in some parishes and districts inside the county's administrative boundaries. As evident in Chapter 2, local councillors in Okehampton and Beer opposed setting up recruitment committees in their respective localities whilst other councillors were keen to establish them. As shown in Chapters 4 and 5, inconsistencies were also evident from the figures of the county's civil society who sat on the county's tribunals. The discretion of these figures to determine who received exemptions created an inconsistent system of conscription in the county. Fortescue complained that those administering exemptions on the county's rural tribunals who, due to their familiarity with farming, often prioritised agricultural concerns over those of the military.[17] As a result, Devon's notables on the Appeal Tribunal encountered great difficulties in administering a system of conscription.

As a unique observer, Reynolds noticed that people in Devon may have viewed the activities of the county's local elite differently than they intended. When faced with prescriptions to enlist from dignitaries exempted from military service, some working-class eligible men in Devon probably felt aggrieved that these figures thought they knew best about their patriotism and sought to superintend it. The frustrations of Devon's 'provincial patriots' who levelled accusations against eligible men in the county who they deemed lacked patriotism reveal the tension between the different generations and classes: those who, on account of their age or gender, could stay safe at home and the eligible men who lacked this advantage and begrudged being the subject of prescriptions that they needed to enlist. Many eligible men in

Devon resented these figures, directing them to enlist rather than fight the war themselves. Since many notables seemed to 'impose' their prescriptions onto them about volunteering, military-age men likely thought there was a divide: an 'us' versus 'them' mentality. As a result, some eligible men viewed these figures as armchair patriots. Earl Fortescue understood that, on account of his age, eligible men in the county could dismiss his appeals for recruits and view him as an armchair patriot. He sought to address this criticism by declaring that he would enlist were he a younger man and wanted to point out that he had two sons fighting overseas. As elders within their local communities, other older men may have also told military-age men who had not yet enlisted, 'If I were a younger man, I would join up'. Statements like this, alongside those from women who could declare that 'If I were a man, I would volunteer', sought to apply more significant pressure on eligible men and make them feel guilty about their decision to remain at home. However, hearing such declarations from individuals who would never face the prospect of military service was cold comfort for many eligible men in Devon. It was easy for older men to say they would enlist if they were younger or women to assert that they would volunteer if they were men since these figures were exempt from military service and did not need to prove their patriotism through military service. Thus, eligible men did not want to be 'lectured' or 'dictated' to by older men and women who would never face combat.

Another key argument of the critics against the county's notable figures was that Devon's 'provincial patriots' only paid lip service to the war effort. Like a superintendent taking charge and administrating over a concern, these figures ordered other people about without doing much themselves. Since these figures who worked on war-related bodies and committees ordered people about whilst sitting in their chairs, people in Devon viewed them as armchair patriots. These notable figures had taken the opportunity that the war afforded to take charge and instruct other people how to run their lives. Some eligible Devonian men resented the prescriptions of notables who had the 'advantage' of being exempt from military service and safe on the home front. The figures who served on the county's tribunals also experienced resentment when arbitrating who should receive exemptions for the same reasons. The men seeking exemption felt disempowered to control their fate as the county's tribunalists interrogated them about their motives and decided upon the sincerity of their application.

As the wartime authority of Devon's local elite increased, many Devonians confronted these figures since they viewed them as representatives of the state due to their elevated status as intermediaries of the war effort. Some Devonians felt aggrieved that these self-appointed figures were regulating their behaviour. New measures introduced in the name of the war effort were, in their view, yet another means to assert their authority in wartime by telling other people what to do. These figures did not miss an opportunity to prescribe what they should be doing. Some eligible men interpreted the involvement of the county's notable figures initially in recruitment efforts and later arbitrating over conscription in a conspiratorial light. They may have suspected that these self-important, nosy busybodies were seemingly united in opposition against eligible men to get them to enlist or take them away into the Army. Devonians suspected that hidden dealings occurred behind closed doors and complained that tribunalists were in league with the military representatives to get men for the Army.

Patriotism played a significant role in wartime mobilisation on the British home front, whether with efforts that constituted self-mobilisation or remobilisation. However, this book has shown that people in Devon held differing views about patriotism, and many parties contested it. The fact that patriotism was a disputed value on a local level made mobilisation efforts in Devon more challenging. For the gentry and figures ineligible for military service, the patriotism of eligible men was to serve, whilst those involved with agriculture and fishing were adamant that these industries needed to retain experienced people. Most of Devon's farmers disagreed with the idea that it was their patriotic duty to join the Army and believed that producing food was the best way to present their patriotism. However, other Devonians disagreed with these claims. Although it was a valid form of patriotism, Devon's notable figures thought the county's agriculturalists could better serve the nation by 'giving it men than by giving it meat.'[18] Since the definition of what constituted patriotism was a contested notion in Devon, there were multiple discourses of patriotism in the county, which were not solely driven by militaristic sentiment. Ultimately, this helps to explain why patriotism was a more challenging concept for Devon's local elite to try to police across the county since multiple parties in the county disputed over what was patriotic.

At the same time, some eligible Devonian men challenged the prescriptions of Devon's local elite and Army recruiters at recruitment events, arguing that they should go off to fight instead of canvassing for recruits. The fact that

Devonians expressed vocabularies of counter mobilisation such as 'It is not a working man's war' and 'Let those who started the war go and fight it' reveals that many in the county believed that the conflict was not everybody's war. Despite the well-meaning intentions of the county's notable figures, some Devonians regarded them as interfering, nosy busybodies since they resented their efforts to recruit their menfolk. Although Charles Alfred Thomas Fursdon recognised that the residents of Cheriton Bishop protested against being "dictated" to by war-related Committees, Loosemore discovered this violent feeling first-hand after denouncing Passmore's sons. However, many Devonians took umbrage with these prescriptions from the self-appointed authority of the county's local elite, who took to bossing or ordering them about since it was none of their business. Like Thomas Hardy superintending the activities of Dorchester's shopkeepers, Devon's population resented figures interfering in their affairs. They felt aggrieved by figures, like food inspectors, taking charge and ordering them about.

Devon's population also objected towards the prescriptions from Army recruiters and members of the county's local elite that their menfolk should enlist. Some Devonians directly confronted Devon's notable figures and Army recruiters as they represented an unwelcome intrusion into their affairs. Indeed, they regarded these figures' prescriptions as a form of outside interference. Fathers like Richard Miles tried to stop Army recruiter Sergeant Williman from pouncing upon his sons, pressuring them into enlisting and taking them away. Many mothers in Devon, like Mrs Triggs, shared Miles's views and would not consent to their military-age sons volunteering, objecting to Army recruiters interfering in matters which did not concern them. Based on this logic, they directly challenged the authority and appeals of figures that they viewed as interfering busybodies who only sought recruits for the Army. The nature of the relationship in Devon from both above and below was strained in numerous instances as Devon's 'provincial patriots' did not address the tension between local and national priorities. Throughout the war years, there was still a great divide in the county between those who prioritised their own self-interest over that of the nation. Devon's farmers were one such group who faced accusations that they were primarily concerned about the survival of their farms as family businesses. Many Devon farmers, like William Tremlett, 'did not like being shunted' when faced with wartime measures.[19]

The attempts to monitor and police the patriotic behaviour of the county's population by Devon's 'provincial patriots' also fed into notions of public duty.

Like Hardy's experience as a JP informed how he approached his activities clamping down on profiteering in Dorchester from a judicial perspective, the same was true for Devon's notable figures in how they approached their duties in wartime since they held legal appointments, serving as magistrates or JPs. Members of Buckfastleigh's UDC claimed that they were motivated by the preservation of local stability when they campaigned to have the 'dangerous' German and Austrian monks at Buckfast Abbey removed from the Abbey and sent to an internment camp. The evidence in Chapters 4 and 5 indicates that the Councillors wanted to remove the monks from the locality since they viewed them as a tiresome problem. Local and national tabloids supported the actions of Buckfastleigh's UDC against the Buckfast monks and advocated for their internment on the grounds of national security. However, after reviewing the Council's petitions, the Home Office concluded that the monks did not pose a threat. They recommended a special agreement that confined the monks to the Abbey's grounds and kept them under surveillance by special constables. This compromise was intolerable for the Councillors who persisted in pressing for the removal of the German and Austrian monks from the Abbey. However, this new campaign was also unsuccessful.

Examining Devon's notables as the policemen and women of patriotism provides a valuable perspective on their activities to police against what these individuals defined as unpatriotic behaviour. The responses to the demands of the war effort reaffirmed the constant tension between individual priorities and those of the nation. The constant negotiation between Devon's 'provincial patriots' and appellants exhibited at tribunal hearings further emphasises the difficulties that the county's notables faced in organising Devon's population to the needs of the war effort. For many of the county's residents, individual and local concerns were more powerful impulses than the national interest through the war years. The clannish nature of Devon's population was a crucial factor in why Devonians placed individual priorities above those of the nation. Devonians were concerned about navigating and surviving through the Great War, a period of uncertainty where continuity outweighed change. To some Devonians, their reactions towards these appeals were rooted and informed by the impact of these demands upon the social and economic fabric of the county. The responses from Devon's populace indicate that some individuals considered the conflict a distant phenomenon. The First World War was not a priority for many Devonians who did not view the conflict as everybody's war.

Notes

Introduction: Superintending Patriotism on the Home Front

1. John Dalton Osborne, 'Stephen Reynolds, a biographical and critical study', University of London, PhD Thesis, 1978, p. 231.
2. Nigel Hyman, 'Inshore Fisheries in Wartime Devon' in *Food, Farming and Fishing in Devon during the First World War* (Exeter, 2017) pp. 77–79.
3. Christopher Scoble, *Fisherman's Friend: A Life of Stephen Reynolds* (Tiverton, 2000) p. 639.
4. Scoble, *Fisherman's Friend*, p. 639.
5. *Letters of Stephen Reynolds*, ed. by Harold Wright (Richmond, 1923) p. 291.
6. *Letters of Stephen Reynolds*, p. 291.
7. Angela Woollacott, '"Khaki Fever" and Its Control: Gender, Class, Age and Sexual Morality on the British Homefront in the First World War', *Journal of Contemporary History*, Vol. 29, No. 2 (April 1994) pp. 325, 329–333.
8. Devon Heritage Centre (DHC): 1262M/0/O/LD/129/227, Letter from Lord Fortescue to Sir W. Acland, 28 October 1914, p. 3.
9. DHC: 1262M/0/O/LD/129/227, Letter from Lord Fortescue to Sir W. Acland, p. 1.
10. DHC: 1262M/0/O/LD/129/227, Letter from Lord Fortescue to Sir W. Acland, p. 2.
11. Maureen Healy, *Vienna and the Fall of the Habsburg Empire: Total War and Everyday Life in World War I* (Cambridge, 2004) p. 5.
12. John Horne, 'Soldiers, Civilians and the Warfare of Attrition: Representations of Combat in France, 1914–1918' in F. Coetzee and M. Shevin-Coetzee (eds), *Authority, Identity and the Social History of the Great War* (Providence, 1995) p. 224.
13. *Letters of Stephen Reynolds*, p. 291.
14. John Morton Osborne, *The Voluntary Recruiting Movement in Britain, 1914–1916* (New York, 1982) p. 25.
15. Trevor Wilson, *The Myriad Faces of War: Britain and the Great War, 1914–1918* (Cambridge, 1986) p. 400.
16. *Crediton Chronicle and North Devon Gazette (CCNDG)*, 29 April 1916, p. 6.
17. *CCNDG*, 29 April 1916, p. 6.
18. *CCNDG*, 29 April 1916, p. 6.
19. *CCNDG*, 29 April 1916, p. 6.
20. *CCNDG*, 29 April 1916, p. 6.
21. *CCNDG*, 29 April 1916, p. 6.
22. *CCNDG*, 29 April 1916, p. 6.
23. *CCNDG*, 29 April 1916, p. 6.
24. Gerard DeGroot, *Back in Blighty: The British at Home in World War I* (London, 2014) p. 262
25. *Devon and Exeter Gazette (DEG)*, 12 August 1915, p. 3.
26. *Letters of Stephen Reynolds*, p. 291.

27. Stephen Reynolds, Bob Woolley and Tom Woolley, *Seems So! A Working Class View of Politics*, Shilling edn (London, 1913) p. 27
28. *Western Evening Herald* (*WEH*), 27 May 1915, p. 1.
29. John Williams, *The Home Fronts: Britain, France and Germany, 1914–1918* (London, 1972); Arthur Marwick, *The Deluge: British Society and the First World War*, 2nd edn. (Basingstoke, 2006).
30. Jay Winter, 'Paris, London, Berlin, 1914–1919: capital cities at war', in J. Winter and J-L. Robert (eds), *Capital Cities at War: Paris, London, Berlin, 1914–1919* (Cambridge, 1999) p. 3.
31. Pierre Purseigle, 'Beyond and Below the Nations: Towards a Comparative History of Local Communities at War' in J. Macleod and P. Purseigle (eds), *Uncovered Fields: Perspectives in First World War Studies* (Leiden, 2004) p. 109.
32. Stuart Dalley, 'The response in Cornwall to the outbreak of the First World War', *Cornish Studies*, Vol. 11, (2003) pp. 85–109; Keith Grieves ed., *Sussex in the First World War* (Lewes, 2004); Linda K. Riddell, *Shetland and the Great War* (Lerwick, 2015).
33. Keith Grieves, 'The quiet of the country and the restless excitement of the towns: rural perspectives on the home front, 1914–1918' in M. Tebbutt (ed), *Rural and Urban Encounters in the Nineteenth and Twentieth Centuries: Regional Perspectives* (Manchester, 2004) p. 80.
34. Grieves, 'The quiet of the country and the restless excitement of the towns', pp. 81–82; *Sussex in the First World War*, p. ix; Helen B. McCartney, *Citizen Soldiers: The Liverpool Territorials in the First World War* (Cambridge, 2005) pp. 3, 57–88, 117; Purseigle, 'Beyond and Below the Nations', pp. 99–103.
35. Tammy M. Proctor, *Civilians in a World at War, 1914–1918* (New York, 2010).
36. Purseigle, 'Beyond and Below the Nations', p. 96.
37. Peter Martin, '*Dulce et Decorum*: Irish Nobles and the Great War, 1914–19' in A. Gregory and S. Pašeta (eds), *Ireland and the Great War: 'A war to unite us all'?* (Manchester, 2002) pp. 31–39.
38. Martin, '*Dulce et Decorum*, p. 34.
39. Peter Gatrell, *Russia's First World War: A Social and Economic History* (Harlow, 2005) pp. 50, 56.
40. John Horne, 'Introduction: mobilizing for "total war", 1914–1918' in J. Horne (ed), *State, Society and Mobilization in Europe during the First World War* (Cambridge, 1997) p. 1.
41. Horne, 'Introduction', p. 5.
42. Horne, 'Introduction', p. 5.
43. Pierre Purseigle, 'Between Participation and Victimization: World War I Urban Mobilization in Comparative Perspective' in F. Lenger ed., *Kollektive Gewalt in der Stadt: Europa 1890–1939* (Munich, 2013) p. 51.
44. Matteo Ermacora, 'Civilian Morale', *International Encyclopaedia of the First World War*, August 2015, <https://encyclopedia.1914-1918-online.net/article/civilian_morale> [Accessed 19 February 2020].
45. John Horne, 'Remobilizing for "total war": France and Britain, 1917–1918' in J. Horne (ed), *State, Society and Mobilization in Europe during the First World War* (Cambridge, 1997) p. 198.
46. Purseigle, 'Beyond and Below the Nations', p. 120.
47. Purseigle, 'Beyond and Below the Nations', p. 98.
48. Purseigle, 'Beyond and Below the Nations', p. 96–99.

49. Purseigle, 'Between Participation and Victimization', p. 55.
50. Purseigle, 'Between Participation and Victimization', p. 55.
51. Purseigle, 'Beyond and Below the Nations', p. 96.
52. Pierre Purseigle, 'Introduction: Warfare and Belligerence: Approaches to the First World War' in P. Purseigle ed., *Warfare and Belligerence: Perspectives in First World War Studies* (Leiden, 2005) p. 25.
53. Catriona Pennell, *A Kingdom United: Popular Responses to the Outbreak of the First World War in Britain and Ireland* (Oxford, 2012) p. 159.
54. Christopher Capozzola, *Uncle Sam Wants You: World War I and the Making of the Modern American Citizen* (New York, 2008) p. 42.
55. Emerson Hough, *The Web: A Revelation of Patriotism* (Chicago, 1919) pp. 142–143.
56. Capozzola, *Uncle Sam Wants You*, p. 42.
57. Capozzola, *Uncle Sam Wants You*, p. 43.
58. Horne, 'Introduction', p. 11.
59. John Horne, 'Social Identity in War: France, 1914–1918' in T. G. Fraser and K. Jeffrey (eds), *Men, Women and War* (Dublin, 1993) p. 119
60. Horne, 'Social Identity in War', p. 130.
61. Winter, 'Paris, London, Berlin 1914–1919', p. 17; David Silbey, *The British Working Class and Enthusiasm for War, 1914–1916* (London, 2005) pp. 7–13; John Horne, 'Patriotism and the Enemy: Political Identity as a Weapon' in N. Wouters and L. van Ypersele eds., *Nations, Identities and the First World War: Shifting Loyalties to the Fatherland* (London, 2018) p. 23.
62. *CCNDG*, 17 December 1914, p. 5.
63. Derek Rutherford Young, 'Voluntary Recruitment in Scotland, 1914–1916', University of Glasgow, PhD Thesis, 2001, p. 390.
64. *Western Times (WT)*, 4 January 1915, p. 2.
65. *CCNDG*, 29 April 1916, p. 6.
66. *Hartland and Westcountry Chronicle*, 29 May 1915, p. 4.
67. Dalley, 'The response in Cornwall to the outbreak of the First World War', p. 106
68. *The Queen*, 11 December 1915, p. 29.
69. J. M. Winter, 'Propaganda and the Mobilization of Consent' in H. Strachan (ed), *The Oxford Illustrated History of the First World War* 2nd ed (Oxford, 2014) p. 217.
70. Horne, 'Introduction', p. 12.
71. *North Devon Herald (NDH)*, 6 January 1916, p. 4.
72. Adrian Gregory, *The Last Great War: British Society and the First World War* (Cambridge, 2008) p. 229
73. Paul Rusiecki, *The Impact of Catastrophe: The people of Essex and the First World War (1914–1918)*, (Chelmsford, 2008) p. 390.
74. Roger Chickering, *The Great War and Urban Life in Germany: Freiburg, 1914–1918* (Cambridge, 2007) pp. 181–182; Benjamin Ziemann, *War Experiences in Rural Germany, 1914–1923*, trans. by Alex Skinner (Oxford, 2007) pp.184, 194–196.
75. Chickering, *The Great War and Urban Life in Germany*, p. 181.
76. Plymouth Archives, The Box (PA, TB): 1306/24, Miss Edrica de la Pole, of Tremar, Kingston, Diary, 1916, 12 January 1916; *Western Morning News (WMN)*, 20 April 1917, p. 3.
77. *The Daily Mail*, 8 September 1916, p. 6.
78. Olive Hockin, *Two Girls on the Land: Wartime on a Dartmoor Farm* (London, 1918) p. 77.

79. Hockin, *Two Girls on the Land*, p. 8.
80. *WT*, 1 September 1914, p. 3; *The Bystander*, 20 June 1917, p. 630.
81. Grieves, 'The quiet of the country and the restless excitement of the towns', pp. 79–97; Chickering, *The Great War and Urban Life in Germany*, pp. 181–182.
82. Matteo Ermacora, 'Rural Society' *International Encyclopaedia of the First World War*, January 2015, <https://encyclopedia.1914-1918-online.net/article/rural_society> [Accessed 19 February 2020]; Jay Winter and Antoine Prost, *The Great War in History: Debates and Controversies, 1914 to the Present*, 2nd edn (Cambridge, 2020) p. 165.
83. Pamela Horn, *Rural Life in England in the First World War* (Dublin, 1984); Ziemann, *War Experiences in Rural Germany*.
84. Grieves, *Sussex in the First World War*, pp. ix-xxv; Rusiecki, *The Impact of Catastrophe*.
85. Bonnie White, 'War and the Home Front: Devon in the First World War', McMaster University, PhD Thesis, 2008; David Parker, *The People of Devon in the First World War* (Stroud, 2013)
86. Henry French, 'Introduction' in *Food, Farming and Fishing in Devon during the First World War* (Exeter, 2017) pp. vii-ix; Henry French, 'Introduction', *The Devon Historian*, Vol. 86, (2017) pp. 1–3
87. Examples include Emil Sokolov, 'The Many Faces of the Great War: Local Patriotism and Recruitment in Ilfracombe, 1914–1918', *Devon during the First World War* (Exeter, 2018) pp. 119–121; Julia Neville, 'Devon County Council and First World War Food Production Policy: A Challenge to Landlordism and Squirearchy?', *The Devon Historian* Vol. 86, (2017) pp. 63–75.
88. Grieves, 'The quiet of the country and the restless excitement of the towns', p. 81.
89. *A Lord Lieutenant in Wartime: The Experiences of the Fourth Earl Fortescue during the First World War* ed. by Richard Batten (Woodbridge, 2018) pp. 21–32.
90. *Letters of Stephen Reynolds*, p. v.
91. Christopher Scoble, 'Reynolds, Stephen Sydney (1881–1919)', *Oxford Dictionary of National Biography*, Oxford University Press, 2004; online edition, Jan 2008, <https://doi-org.uoelibrary.idm.oclc.org/10.1093/ref:odnb/47513>, [Accessed 9 November 2020].
92. Scoble, 'Reynolds, Stephen Sydney (1881–1919)'.
93. Scoble, *Fisherman's Friend*, p. 672.
94. Stephen Vella, 'Newspapers' in M. Dobson and B. Ziemann eds., *Reading Primary Sources: The Interpretation of Texts from Nineteenth- and Twentieth-Century History*, 2nd edn (Abingdon, 2020) p. 218.
95. Vella, 'Newspapers', p. 218.
96. *DEG*, 2 January 1915, p. 3.

Chapter 1: Devon by 1914

1. *Kelly's Directory of Devon, 1902* (London, 1902) pp. 1–3.
2. Robin Stanes, *A History of Devon* (Chichester, 1986) pp. 14–16.
3. *DEG*, 28 October 1910, p. 14; 'A Devonshire Garland' in R. Pearse Chope (ed), *The London Devonian Year Book for the Year 1910* (London, 1910) pp. 91–108.
4. Great Western Railway Company, *Devon: The Shire of the Sea Kings* (London, 1906) pp. 7–9, 25, 48, 50, 67, 72, 90, 102.
5. 'Sociamur amore Devoniæ.' in R. Pearse Chope (ed), *The London Devonian Year Book for the Year 1910* (London, 1910) p. 20; 'Devon to Me!' in R. Pearse Chope (ed), *The Devonian Year Book for the Year 1911* (London, 1911) p. 41.
6. 'A Devonshire Garland', pp. 91–108.

7. Pierre Purseigle, '"Wither the Local?" Nationalization, Modernization, and the Mobilization of Urban Communities in England and France, c. 1900–18' in W. Whyte and O. Zimmer (eds), *Nationalism and the reshaping of Urban Communities in Europe, 1848–1914* (Basingstoke, 2011) pp. 187–188.
8. K. D. M. Snell, *Parish and Belonging: Community, Identity and Welfare in England and Wales, 1700–1950* (Cambridge, 2009) pp. 6–15, 25.
9. Thomas Westcote, *A View of Devonshire in MDCXXX, with a Pedigree of Most of its Gentry* (Exeter, 1845) p. 19.
10. Francis A. Knight and Louie M. (Knight) Dutton, *Devonshire* (Cambridge, 1910) p. 6.
11. A. R. Hope Moncrieff, *Black's Guide to Devonshire*, 17th edn (London, 1902) pp. xi-xix; Lord Bishop of Exeter, 'Address of the President', *Reports and Transactions of the Devonshire Association for the Advancement of Science, Literature and Art*, Vol. 39 (July 1907) pp. 46–48.
12. J. Henry Harris, *My Devonshire Book: "In the Land of Junket and Cream"'* (Plymouth, 1907) pp. 34–36.
13. Cecil R. M. Clapp, 'The Rivers of the Moor' in R. Pearse Chope (ed), *The Devonian Year Book for the Year 1911* (London, 1911) p. 75.
14. 'A Song of Devon', *Devonia: The Official Organ of the United Devon Association*, Vol. 6, 4 (June 1907) p. 88; 'O Devon! Fair Devon', *Devonia: The Official Organ of the United Devon Association*, Vol. 6, 4 (June 1907) p.90.
15. *Pall Mall Gazette*, 7 September 1907, p.10.
16. W. G. Hoskins, *Devon* (Chichester, 2003) p. 516.
17. Todd Gray, *Uncle Tom Cobley and All: The history of 'Widdicombe Fair'* (Exeter, 2019) p. 62.
18. Nicholas Mansfield, *English Farmworkers and Local Patriotism, 1900–1930* (Aldershot, 2001) p. 13.
19. Hilderic Friend, *Bygone Devonshire* (London, 1898) p. 216; United Devon Association, *The Book of Fair Devon* (Exeter, 1899–1900) pp. 5–6.
20. 'A Devonshire Garland' p. 21.
21. 'Sociamur amore Devoniæ', p. 21.
22. Todd Gray, *Elizabethan Devon* (Exeter, 2001) p. 73.
23. Robert Hutchinson, *The Spanish Armada* (London, 2014)
24. Colin Martin and Geoffrey Parker, *Armada: The Spanish Enterprise and England's Deliverance in 1588* (New Haven, 2022) pp. 440–441.
25. Martin and Parker, *Armada*, pp. 500–502.
26. 'Armada Day' in R. Pearse Chope (ed), *The Devonian Year Book for the Year 1913* (London, 1913) pp. 28–29.
27. 'Armada Day' pp. 24–30.
28. Paul Readman, 'Commemorating the past in Edwardian Hampshire: King Alfred, Pageantry and Empire' in M. Taylor (eds) *Southampton: Gateway to the British Empire* (London, 2007) pp. 96–97, 104–107.
29. Bruce Wathen, *Sir Francis Drake: The Construction of a Hero* (Woodbridge: 2009) pp. 136–141.
30. *Reading Standard*, 22 July 1911, p. 8.
31. Lewis Butler, *Sir Redvers Buller* (London, 1909) p. 84; Stephen M. Miller, 'Redvers Buller' in S. J. Corvi & I. F. W. Beckett (eds), *Victoria's Generals* (Barnsley, 2009) pp. 51–73.
32. Geoffrey Powell, *Buller: A Scapegoat? A Life of General Sir Redvers Buller VC* (London, 1994) pp. 195, 207.
33. John W. Fortescue, *My Native Devon* (London, 1925) pp. 252–258.

34. M. Jacson, *The Record of A Regiment of the Line: Being a Regimental History of the 1st Battalion Devonshire Regiment during the Boer War, 1899–1902* (London, 1908) pp. xiii-xv, 75–77; 'Annual Dinner', p. 17.
35. Robert Newton, *Victorian Exeter, 1837–1914* (Leicester, 1968) p. 289.
36. Paul Readman, 'The Place of the Past in English Culture, c. 1890–1914' *Past and Present*, No. 186 (February 2005) p. 155.
37. W. J. H. Phipps, *Devon Worthies: Biographies arranged as a Reader for Secondary Schools and the Upper Standards of Elementary Schools* (Exeter, 1903); Alun Howkins, 'The discovery of rural England' in R. Colls & P. Dodd (eds), *Englishness, Politics and Culture, 1880–1920* 2nd ed (London, 2014) pp. 93–94.
38. Readman, 'The Place of the Past in English Culture', p. 175.
39. *North Devon Journal (NDJ)*, 6 January 1910, p. 6.
40. 'Annual Dinner' in R. Pearse Chope (ed), *The Devonian Year Book for the Year 1913* (London, 1913) p. 21.
41. *DEG*, 3 March 1911, p. 9.
42. 'The Years Work' in R. Pearse Chope (ed), *The Devonian Year Book for the Year 1912* (London, 1912) p. 11.
43. Celia Applegate, *A Nation of Provincials: The German Idea of Heimat* (Berkeley, CA, 1990) pp. 16–17, 41–44.
44. 'Annual Dinner', p. 20.
45. Dieter K. Buse, 'Urban and National Identity: Bremen, 1860–1920', *Journal of Social History*, Vol. 26, No. 3 (Spring 1997) pp. 521–537; Stephane Gerson, *The Pride of Place: Local Memories and Political Culture in Nineteenth-Century France* (Ithaca, 2003).
46. R. Pearse Chope, 'The Folklore of Devon' in R. Pearse Chope (ed), *The London Devonian Year Book for the Year 1910* (London, 1910) p. 133.
47. Cynthia Gaskell Brown, *The Battle's Sound: Drake's Drum and the Drake Flags* (Tiverton, 1996) pp. 32–35.
48. Lord Bishop of Exeter, 'Address of the President', pp. 44–50.
49. Wathen, *Sir Francis Drake*, pp. 123–141; Powell, *Buller*, p. 207.
50. *Census of England and Wales, 1911: Vol. I* (London, 1911) p. 107.
51. DHC: 1262M/0/FH/42, Typescript of work of Lord Fortescue during 1st World War, p. 2.
52. Francis A. Knight and Louie M. (Knight) Dutton, *Devonshire* (Cambridge, 1910) pp. 103, 243.
53. Hoskins, *Devon*, p. 12.
54. *Census of England and Wales, 1911: Vol. I*, p. 107.
55. F. B. May, 'Victorian and Edwardian Ilfracombe' in J. K. Walton and J. Walvin eds., *Leisure in Britain, 1780–1939*, (Manchester, 1983) pp. 191, 197; John K. Walton, *The British Seaside: Holidays and resorts in the twentieth century* (Manchester, 2000) p. 154.
56. Bruce Coleman, 'The Nineteenth Century: Nonconformity' in N. Orme (ed), *Unity and Variety: A History of the Church in Devon and Cornwall* (Exeter, 1991) p. 149.
57. H. Rider Haggard, *Rural England: Being an Account of Agricultural and Social Researches carried out in the years 1901 & 1902*, Vol. 1 (London, 1906) p. 200.
58. W. G. Hoskins, *Devon and its people* (Exeter, 1959) p. 159.
59. *Census of England and Wales, 1911: Vol. X* (London, 1911) p. 161.
60. Rider Haggard, *Rural England*, p. 176.
61. *Census of England and Wales, 1911: Vol. X*, p. 161.

62. DHC: 1262M/0/FH/42, Typescript of work of Lord Fortescue during 1st World War, p. 2; Stanes, *A History of Devon*, pp. 14–15.
63. William Pope, *Glimpses of the Past* (Tiverton, 1927) p. 85
64. Sarah Wilmot, 'The South-West: Wiltshire, Dorset, Somerset, Devon, and Cornwall' in E. J. T. Collins (ed), *The Agrarian History of England and Wales, Volume VII, 1850–1914, Part I* (Cambridge, 2000) p. 425.
65. Stanes, *A History of Devon*, p. 11.
66. Anthony Michael Dawson, 'Politics in Devon and Cornwall, 1900–1931', London School of Economics, PhD thesis, 1991, pp. 191–196.
67. Hoskins, *Devon and its people*, p. 159.
68. Nigel J. Morgan and Annette Pritchard, *Power and Politics at the Seaside: The Development of Devon's Resorts in the Twentieth Century* (Exeter, 1999) p. 68.
69. John F. Travis, *The Rise of Devon Seaside Resorts, 1750–1900* (Exeter, 1993) pp. 7–59.
70. Stanes, *A History of Devon*, pp. 113–114.
71. Travis, *The Rise of Devon Seaside Resorts*, pp. 125–129.
72. May, 'Victorian and Edwardian Ilfracombe' p. 200.
73. DHC: 1262M/0/FH/42, Typescript of work of Lord Fortescue during 1st World War, p. 2.
74. Hoskins, *Devon and its people*, p. 160.
75. Ken Gibbs, *The Steam Workshops of the Great Western Railway* (Stroud, 2014) pp. 111–117.
76. Stanes, *A History of Devon*, p. 114
77. *Census of England and Wales, 1911: Vol. X*, p. 161; Mark Porter, 'Devon's Fishing Industry, 1880–1990' in M. Duffy, S. Fisher, B. Greenhill, D. J. Starkey and J. Youings (eds), *The New Maritime History of Devon, Volume II: From the Late Eighteenth Century to the Present Day* (London, 1994) p. 247.
78. Knight and Dutton, *Devonshire*, p. 126
79. Scoble, 'Reynolds, Stephen Sydney (1881–1919)'.
80. Scoble, *Fisherman's Friend*, pp. 499–512.
81. Osborne, 'Stephen Reynolds', p. 219; *Brixham Western Guardian (BWG)*, 14 November 1912, p. 5.
82. *Parliament and Politics in the Age of Asquith and Lloyd George: The Diaries of Cecil Harmsworth, MP, 1909–1922* eds Andrew Thorpe and Richard Toye (Cambridge, 2016) pp. 13–14, 130–133.
83. Scoble, *Fisherman's Friend*, p. 525.
84. Osborne, 'Stephen Reynolds', p. 230.
85. Scoble, 'Reynolds, Stephen Sydney (1881–1919)'.
86. H. J. Yallop, *The History of the Honiton Lace Industry* (Exeter, 1999) pp. 135–156.
87. Moncrieff, *Black's Guide to Devonshire*, p. 184; Knight and Dutton, *Devonshire*, pp. 111–114.
88. *Census of England and Wales, 1911: Vol. X*, p. 163.
89. Peter Hilditch, 'Devon and Naval Strategy since 1815', in M. Duffy, S. Fisher, D. Greenhill, D. J. Starkey and J. Youings (eds), *The New Maritime History of Devon, Volume II: From the Late Eighteenth Century to the Present Day*, (London, 1994) p. 158.
90. Reynolds, Woolley and Woolley, *Seems So!*, p. 222.
91. *NDJ*, 10 December 1914, p. 2.
92. Nicholas Orme, 'The Twentieth Century, Part 2: Devon and General' in N. Orme (ed), *Unity and Variety: A History of the Church in Devon and Cornwall* (Exeter, 1991) p. 181–182.

93. Coleman, 'The Nineteenth Century', p. 154.
94. Henry Pelling, *Social Geography of British Elections: 1885–1910* (London, 1967) p. 161.
95. Coleman, 'The Nineteenth Century', p. 153.
96. Orme, 'The Twentieth Century, Part 2', p. 191.
97. R. G. Richards, *Through the Mists of Memory* (Bideford, 1995) pp. 36–42.
98. R. J. E. Boggis, *I Remember* (Exeter, 1947) p. 179.
99. Pelling, *Social Geography of British Elections*, pp. 160–161.
100. Orme, 'The Twentieth Century, Part 2', p. 192.
101. Dom John Stéphan, *A History of Buckfast Abbey* (Bristol, 1970) pp. 261–331.
102. Dom Leo Smith, 'The Life and Work of Abbot Anscar Vonier', *English Benedictine Congregation History Commission – Symposium 1996*, <http://www.monlib.org.uk/papers/ebch/1996smith.pdf>, [Accessed 20 March 2019] pp. 5–9.
103. Hoskins, *Devon*, p. 355.
104. Bernard Susser, *The Jews of South-West England: The Rise and Decline of their Medieval and Modern Communities* (Exeter, 1993) p. xxi.
105. F. W. S. Craig ed., *British Parliamentary Election Results, 1885–1918* (London, 1974) pp. 104, 109, 169, 255–262.
106. Dawson, 'Politics in Devon and Cornwall', p. 18.
107. Michael Kinnear, *The British Voter: An Atlas and Survey since 1885*, 2nd edn (London, 1981) p. 123.
108. Paul Lambe, 'The Politics of Place: Three Devon Constituencies and the 1900 General Election', *Southern History: A Review of the History of Southern England*, Vol. 23 (2001) p. 149.
109. Sophia Lambert, 'A Devon By-Election: South Molton, 1891', *Reports and Transactions of the Devonshire Association for the Advancement of Science, Literature and Art*, Vol. 142 (June 2010) pp. 238–239.
110. Lambert, 'A Devon By-Election', pp. 238–239, 259.
111. Ian Packer, *Lloyd George, Liberalism and the Land: The Land Issue and Party Politics in England, 1906–1914* (Woodbridge, 2001) p. 34.
112. Lambe, 'The Politics of Place', p. 149.
113. Michael Dawson, 'Liberalism in Devon and Cornwall, 1910–1931: "The Old-Time Religion"', *The Historical Journal*, Vol. 38, No. 2 (June 1995) p. 426.
114. Lambe, 'The Politics of Place', p. 149.
115. Ian Cawood, *The Liberal Unionist Party: A History* (London, 2012) p. 171.
116. Pelling, *Social Geography of British Elections*, p. 173.
117. Craig ed., *British Parliamentary Election Results, 1885–1918*, pp. 104, 109, 169, 255–262.
118. Pelling, *Social Geography of British Elections*, p. 163.
119. Peter Clarke, *Hope and Glory: Britain, 1900–2000*, 2nd edn (London, 2004) p. 20.
120. Lambe, 'The Politics of Place', pp. 149, 162–163, 165.
121. Dawson, 'Politics in Devon and Cornwall', p. 309.
122. Margherita Rendel, 'The Campaign in Devon for Women's Suffrage, 1866–1908', *Report and Transactions of the Devonshire Association for the Advancement of Science, Literature and Art*, Vol. 140, (2008) pp. 111–151.
123. Craig ed., *British Parliamentary Election Results, 1885–1918*, pp. 104, 109, 169, 255–262.
124. Craig ed., *British Parliamentary Election Results, 1885–1918*, pp. 104, 109, 169, 255–262.
125. Frank Retter, *An Exeter Boyhood* (Exeter, 1984) p. 16.
126. Hoskins, *Devon*, p. 190.
127. Pelling, *Social Geography of British Elections*, p. 163.

128. *DEG*, 9 November 1891, p. 7; *WMN*, 20 May 1910, p. 7.
129. Daniel M. Jackson, *Popular Opposition to Irish Home Rule in Edwardian Britain* (Liverpool, 2009) p. 168
130. Pelling, *Social Geography of British Elections*, p. 162.
131. *Kelly's Directory of Devon, 1902*, p. 11.
132. Jeffrey Stanyer, *A History of Devon County Council, 1889–1989* (Exeter, 1989) pp. 10–14.
133. *Whitaker's Peerage, Baronetage, Knightage and Companionage for the year 1909* (London, 1909) p. 338.
134. Denzil Fortescue, 'Denzil Fortescue b. 1893 Recollections 1974', < http://fortescue.org/site/wp-content/uploads/2012/11/DGFRecollections2.pdf>, [Accessed 20 February 2020], pp. 2–3, 11–13.
135. 'The Family of Fortescue' in R. Pearse Chope (ed), *The London Devonian Year Book for the year 1910* (London, 1910) p. 36.
136. Fortescue, 'Denzil Fortescue b. 1893 Recollections 1974', p. 2.
137. *WMN*, 31 October 1932, p. 3.
138. 'Obituary Notices: Hugh Fourth Earl Fortescue, KCB, TD, JP, CA', *Report and Transactions of the Devonshire Association for the Advancement of Science, Literature and Art*, Vol. 65, (1933) pp. 38–39.
139. *WT*, 4 November 1932, p. 10.
140. David Parker, *Edwardian Devon: Before the Lights Went Out* (Stroud, 2016) p. 79.
141. *DEG*, 13 July 1929, p. 10.
142. *WT*, 9 January 1931, p. 2.
143. W. Gore Allen, *John Heathcoat and His Heritage* (London, 1958) p. 145.
144. *NDJ*, 1 January 1942, p. 3; *WMN*, 11 March 1932, p. 8.
145. *DEG*, 14 July 1939, p. 14; *DEG*, 30 July 1943, p. 8.
146. *Who's who in Devonshire* (Hereford, 1934) p. 196
147. *New York Times*, 9 July 1939, p. 30.
148. Michael Dawson, 'Party Politics and the Provincial Press in Early Twentieth Century England: The Case of the South West', *Twentieth Century British History*, Vol. 9, No. 2 (1998) pp. 204–206; *NDJ*, 1 January 1942, p. 3; *DEG*, 14 July 1939, p. 14.
149. *WMN*, 5 September 1949, p. 3.
150. Dawson, 'Politics in Devon and Cornwall', pp. 175–176.

Chapter 2: Mobilizing for War, 1914

1. Annika Mombauer, 'July Crisis 1914', *International Encyclopaedia of the First World War*, September 2018, < https://encyclopedia.1914-1918-online.net/article/july_crisis_1914>, [Accessed 14 March 2021].
2. Hew Strachan, 'Pre-war Military Planning (Great Britain)', *International Encyclopaedia of the First World War*, February 2018, <https://encyclopedia.1914-1918-online.net/article/pre-war_military_planning_great_britain>, [Accessed 14 March 2021].
3. Winston Churchill, *The World Crisis, 1911–1918*, Vol 1. (London, 1938) pp. 171–172.
4. *Letters of Stephen Reynolds*, pp. 191–192.
5. *Letters of Stephen Reynolds*, p. 191.
6. DHC: 1262M/0/FH/42, Typescript of work of Lord Fortescue during 1st World War, p. 3.
7. K. W. Mitchinson, *England's Last Hope: The Territorial Force, 1908–1914* (Basingstoke, 2008) p. 221.
8. *Letters of Stephen Reynolds*, p. 191.

9. T. G. Otte, *July Crisis: The World's Descent into War, Summer 1914* (Cambridge, 2014) p. 468–469.
10. DHC: 1262M/0/FD/46, Personal Diary of the 3rd Lord Ebrington, 1914–1916, 2 August 1914.
11. Bruno Cabanes, *August 1914: France, the Great War, and a Month that Changed the World Forever*, trans. by Stephanie O'Hara (New Haven, 2016) p. 197.
12. DHC: 1262M/0/FH/42, Typescript of work of Lord Fortescue during 1st World War, p. 3.
13. Pennell, *A Kingdom United*, p. 33.
14. *Letters of Stephen Reynolds*, p. 192.
15. Alfred T. Gregory, *Recollections of a Country Editor* (Tiverton, 1932) p. 60.
16. Keith Grieves, '"Lowther's Lambs": Rural Paternalism and Voluntary Recruitment in the First World War', *Rural History*, Vol. 4, No. 1 (1993) p. 68.
17. *The Diaries of Albert Best: A resident of Teignmouth: Part 3, 1st January 1914 to 9th September 1920*, ed. by Alan Best (Torquay, 2009) 2 August 1914, p. 9; Eric R. Delderfield, *Exmouth Milestones: A History* (Exmouth, 1946) p. 226.
18. *Letters of Stephen Reynolds*, p. 192.
19. PA, TB: 2173, J S Wellington of Plymouth, 1913–1957, 4 August 1914; Dalley, 'The response in Cornwall', p. 87.
20. University of Leeds: Liddle Collection, DF 148, Recollections relating to the Domestic Front: Transcript of Tape 916, Lincoln, F. A., 15 July 1993, p. 1.
21. *The Diaries of Sir Ernest Satow, 1912–1920: Volume 1 (1912–1916)* ed. by Ian Ruxton (Morrisville, NC, 2018) 4 August 1914, p. 242
22. *WT*, 5 August 1914, p. 3.
23. *WT*, 5 August 1914, p. 3.
24. DHC: Exeter City Council Minutes, Volume 2, 1914, p. 233.
25. *DEG*, 5 August 1914, p. 2.
26. *WT*, 5 August 1914, p. 3.
27. Francis Thoday and Tom Anstey, *The 4th Devons: A History of the 4th (Territorial) Battalion, The Devonshire Regiment, 1852–1952* (Exeter, 1952) p. 87; Daw, *Exeter Citizen*, p. 4.
28. *DEG*, 5 August 1914, p. 5.
29. Purseigle, 'Beyond and Below the Nations', p. 99.
30. Purseigle, 'Beyond and Below the Nations', pp. 99–101.
31. *DEG*, 5 August 1914, p. 5.
32. Adrian Gregory, 'Railway stations: gateways and termini' in J. Winter and J-L. Robert (eds), *Capital Cities at War: Paris, London, Berlin, 1914–1919, Volume 2: A Cultural History* (Cambridge, 2007) p. 29.
33. Pennell, *A Kingdom United*, p. 227.
34. DHC: 1262M/0/FD/46, Personal Diary of the 3rd Lord Ebrington, 4 August 1914.
35. Gregory, *Recollections of a Country Editor*, p. 60.
36. Pennell, *A Kingdom United*, pp. 38–42.
37. *WT*, 5 August 1914, p. 3.
38. *DEG*, 5 August 1914, p. 5.
39. *WT*, 5 August 1914, p. 3.
40. *DEG*, 5 August 1914, p. 5.
41. Pennell, *A Kingdom United*, pp. 39, 42.
42. *DEG*, 5 August 1914, p. 5.

43. Pennell, *A Kingdom United*, pp. 143–144.
44. Osborne, *The Voluntary Recruiting Movement in Britain*, p. 11.
45. DHC: 3248A/13/75, Okehampton Borough Correspondence File, February 1914 – October 1914, Letter from Earl Fortescue, 18 August 1914.
46. Mansfield, *English Farmworkers and Local Patriotism*, p. 87.
47. Gregory, *Recollections of a Country Editor*, p. 62.
48. *DEG*, 21 August 1914, p. 10.
49. *NDJ*, 10 September 1914, p. 7.
50. Nicholas Mansfield, 'Farmworkers, the Marches and the impact of the Great War' in M. Tebbutt (ed), *Rural and Urban Encounters in the Nineteenth and Twentieth Centuries: Regional Perspectives* (Manchester, 2004) p. 102.
51. *BWG*, 26 November 1914, p. 6.
52. *DEG*, 26 August 1914, p. 2.
53. *WT*, 21 August 1914, p. 8.
54. *The Diaries of Sir Ernest Satow, 1912–1920: Volume 1 (1912–1916)*, 4 September 1914, pp. 250–251.
55. WMN, 7 September 1914, p. 6.
56. DHC: 1262M/0/O/LD/129/172, Letter to Lord Fortescue from AGW Grant, 30 September 1914, pp. 1–2.
57. *West Sussex Gazette*, 24 December 1914, p. 4
58. *DEG*, 19 January 1915, p. 6.
59. *Tiverton Gazette & East Devon Herald*, 8 December 1914, p. 3.
60. *DEG*, 3 February 1915, p. 3.
61. *WT*, 24 November 1914, p. 5.
62. G. M. Tucker, *Ottery St. Mary Congregational Church: A Short History* (Exeter, 1962) p. 20.
63. *WT*, 11 December 1914, p. 7.
64. Dorset History Centre: RON/2/2/Charmouth/4, '*A few Notes on the Eastern Portion of Charmouth Street including The Lower Sea Lane, The Higher Sea Lane and Some of the People who lived there* by R W J Pavey', 1 March 1969, pp. 14–15.
65. Nicoletta F. Gullace, 'White Feathers and Wounded Men: Female Patriotism and the Memory of the Great War', *Journal of British Studies*, Vol. 36, No. 2 (April 1997) pp. 178–183.
66. Bonnie J. White, 'Volunteerism and Early Recruitment Efforts in Devonshire, August 1914 – December 1915', *The Historical Journal*, Vol. 52, No. 3 (2009) pp. 662–665; *TPG*, 11 September 1914, p. 3.
67. *BWG*, 3 September 1914, p. 2.
68. Nicoletta F. Gullace, *"The Blood of Our Sons": Men, Women and the Renegotiation of British Citizenship during the Great War* (New York, 2002) pp. 74, 80–81.
69. *WMN*, 3 September 1914, p. 6.
70. White, 'Volunteerism and Early Recruitment Efforts in Devonshire', p. 663; *BWG*, 10 December 1914, p. 2.
71. DHC: 1262M/0/O/LD/153/5, Speech (incomplete), 1 December 1914, p. 1.
72. DHC: 1262M/0/O/LD/153/3, Table 1: Analysis of recruiting by War Office up to 10/10/1914, 10 October 1914, p. 2.
73. DHC: 1262M/0/O/LD/129/81, Letter to Lord Fortescue from WH Bolt, 5 September 1914; *NDJ*, 17 December 1914, p. 6.
74. *DEG*, 7 October 1914, p. 4.

75. PA, TB: 1305/10, Newspaper cuttings, 'Local Patriotism and Organisation in 1803 (By Dr. Trelawny-Ross)', 1914, p. 7.
76. *Tiverton Gazette & East Devon Herald*, 8 December 1914, p. 3.
77. 'Devonshire and the War' in R. Pearse Chope ed., *The Devonian Year Book for the Year 1915* (London, 1915) p. 42.
78. Parliamentary Debates, House of Commons, Vol. 109, 29 July 1918, Column 91.
79. *Echoes of the Great War: The Diary of the Reverend Andrew Clark, 1914–1919* ed. by James Munson (Oxford, 1985) p. 14.
80. *WT*, 8 December 1914, p. 8.
81. DHC: 1262M/0/O/LD/153/5, Speech (incomplete), p. 1.
82. Mansfield, *English Farmworkers and Local Patriotism*, p. 101.
83. *WT*, 25 September 1914, p. 5.
84. DHC: 1037M/LG4/5/6, Printed circular letter from Lord Fortescue about recruitment for the Navy and Army, 1914.
85. *WMN*, 28 September 1914, p. 2.
86. *BWG*, 3 September 1914, p. 6.
87. DHC: 1037M/LG4/5/6, Printed circular letter from Lord Fortescue about recruitment for the Navy and Army.
88. *DEG*, 16 December 1914, p. 5.
89. *DEG*, 16 December 1914, p. 5.
90. *WMN*, 10 December 1914, p. 4; *DEG*, 10 December 1914, p. 2.
91. *WMN*, 24 November 1914, p. 6.
92. Pennell, *A Kingdom United*, p. 81.
93. *NDH*, 28 January 1915, p. 5; *DEG*, 12 February 1915, p. 8; *NDJ*, 25 February 1915, p. 5.
94. *WMN*, 21 April 1915, p. 7.
95. Gregory, *The Last Great War*, p. 89.
96. PA, TB: 1306/22, Miss Edrica de la Pole, of Tremor, Kingston, Diary, 1914, 1 September 1914.
97. PA, TB: 1306/23, Miss Edrica de la Pole, of Tremar, Kingston, Diary, 1915, 3 January 1915.
98. *NDJ*, 31 December 1914, p. 8.
99. *NDJ*, 31 December 1914, p. 8.
100. *NDJ*, 31 December 1914, p. 8.
101. *NDJ*, 31 December 1914, p. 8.
102. White, 'Volunteerism and Early Recruitment Efforts in Devonshire', pp. 641–666.
103. *BWG*, 3 September 1914, p. 2.
104. *BWG*, 3 September 1914, p. 2.
105. *WT*, 2 October 1914, p. 7.
106. *Kentish Express*, 5 September 1914, p. 3
107. *WEH*, 1 September 1914, p. 3.
108. *NDJ*, 10 December 1914, p. 2.
109. *NDJ*, 10 December 1914, p. 2.
110. *NDJ*, 10 December 1914, p. 2; DHC: 1262M/0/O/LD/153/5, Speech (incomplete), p. 4.
111. *DEG*, 1 October 1914, p. 2.
112. *DEG*, 30 September 1914, p. 5.
113. *NDJ*, 31 December 1914, p. 2.

114. *Kentish Express*, 5 September 1914, p. 3.
115. *WEH*, 1 September 1914, p. 3.
116. *DEG*, 1 October 1914, p. 2.
117. *DEG*, 1 January 1915, p. 2.
118. DHC: 1262M/0/O/LD/153/2, Letter (fragment) about reluctance to enlist, 9 November 1914, p. 8.
119. *NDJ*, 10 December 1914, p. 7.
120. *WT*, 8 December 1914, p. 3.
121. *NDJ*, 10 December 1914, p. 7.
122. PA, TB: 1306/22, Miss Edrica de la Pole, 1 September 1914.
123. White, 'Volunteerism and Early Recruitment Efforts in Devonshire', p. 666.
124. PA, TB: 1306/22, Miss Edrica de la Pole, of Tremar, Kingston, Diary, 3 September 1914.
125. *WMN*, 14 September 1914, p. 2.
126. Catriona Pennell, 'Believing the Unbelievable: The Myth of the Russians with "Snow on their Boots" in the United Kingdom, 1914', *Cultural and Social History*, Vol. 11, 1 (2014) pp. 69–88.
127. *WMN*, 14 September 1914, p. 2.
128. *NDJ*, 26 November 1914, p. 2.
129. *WT*, 20 November 1914, p. 7.
130. *DEG*, 24 November 1914, p. 5.
131. *WT*, 3 December 1914, p. 3.
132. *WT*, 27 November 1914, p. 3.
133. *WT*, 11 December 1914, p. 8.
134. *WMN*, 25 November 1914, p. 8.
135. Jean-Jacques Becker, *The Great War and the French People*, trans. by Arnold Pomerans (Providence, 1985) pp. 13–17.
136. *DEG*, 11 December 1914, p. 13.
137. DHC: 1262M/0/O/LD/153/5, Speech (incomplete), p. 3; *BWG*, 26 November 1914, p. 6.
138. James Watson, 'Patriotism, Profits and Problems: New Zealand Farming during the Great War' in J. Crawford and I. McGibbon eds., *New Zealand's Great War: New Zealand, the Allies & the First World War* (Auckland, 2007) p. 548.
139. White, 'Volunteerism and Early Recruitment Efforts in Devonshire', p. 641.
140. 'Devonshire and the War', p. 42; *DEG*, 28 November 1914, p. 5.
141. DHC: 3248A/13/76, Okehampton Borough Correspondence File, November 1914 – December 1915, Letter from Colonel Alexander to Town Clerk, 25 November 1914.
142. DHC: 3248A/13/9, Letter book, Okehampton Borough Council, 18 August 1914 – 22 May 1917, Letter to Lieutenant Colonel Alexander, 28 December 1914, p. 39.
143. *DEG*, 10 November 1914, p. 7
144. *WT*, 2 March 1915, p. 3.
145. *WT*, 2 March 1915, p. 3.
146. Niamh Gallagher, *Ireland and the Great War: A Social and Political History* (London, 2020) p. 142.
147. DHC: 3248A/13/76, Okehampton Borough Correspondence File, November 1914 – December 1915, Letter from Colonel Alexander to Town Clerk, 25 November 1914.
148. Cited in Peter Simkins, *Kitchener's Army: The raising of the new armies, 1914–1916* (Barnsley, 2007) p. 127.
149. John Dennehy, *In a Time of War: Tipperary, 1914–1918* (Kildare, 2013) p. 129.

150. Cited in Simkins, *Kitchener's Army*, p. 127.
151. Keith Grieves, 'War Comes to the Fields: Sacrifice, Localism and Ploughing up the English Countryside in 1917' in I. F. W. Beckett (ed), *1917: Beyond the Western Front* (Leiden, 2009) p. 164.
152. Grieves, 'War Comes to the Fields', p. 164.
153. *Nuneaton Observer*, 2 October 1914, p. 4.
154. *Nuneaton Observer*, 2 October 1914, p. 4.
155. *Nuneaton Observer*, 2 October 1914, p. 4.
156. C. T. Atkinson, *The Devonshire Regiment, 1914–1918* (Exeter, 1926) p. 55.
157. Melanie James, 'Indifferent or Just Different? The Cornish Response to the Declaration of War in August 1914' in G. Tregidga and T. Fidler eds., *Cornwall and the Great War: Perspectives on Conflict and Peace* (Penryn, 2018) p. 19; Dalley, 'The Response in Cornwall', pp. 102–103.
158. *WT*, 19 November 1914, p. 2.
159. *WT*, 8 August 1916, p. 5.
160. *NDH*, 19 August 1915, p. 4.
161. DHC: 1262M/0/O/LD/153/13, Newspaper cutting, 1914.
162. *NDJ*, 10 December 1914, p. 2
163. DHC: 1262M/0/O/LD/153/128, Recruiting Statistics, 1915.
164. DHC: 1262M/0/O/LD/153/38, Letter from the Admiralty to Lord Fortescue, 26 March 1915.
165. DHC: 1262M/0/O/LD/153/128, Recruiting Statistics, 1915.
166. *WMN*, 2 September 1914, p. 6.
167. PA, TB: 1305/10, Newspaper cuttings, 'Local Patriotism and Organisation in 1803 (By Dr. Trelawny-Ross)', p. 6.
168. PA, TB: 1305/10, Newspaper cuttings, 'Local Patriotism and Organisation in 1803 (By Dr. Trelawny-Ross)', pp. 6–7.
169. *DEG*, 27 November 1914, p. 7.
170. *DEG*, 27 November 1914, p. 7.
171. *DEG*, 27 November 1914, p. 7.
172. *BWG*, 1 October 1914, p. 8.
173. *BWG*, 1 October 1914, p. 8.
174. *BWG*, 1 October 1914, p. 8.
175. Pieter M. Judson, *The Habsburg Empire: A New History* (Cambridge, MA, 2016) p. 405.
176. Tamara Scheer, 'Denunciation and the Decline of the Habsburg Home Front (1914–1918)', *European Review of History: Revue Europeene d'Histoire*, Vol. 24, 2 (2017) p. 219.
177. *BWG*, 15 October 1914, p. 4.
178. DHC: 1262M/0/O/LD/153/67, Anonymous letter to Lord Fortescue, c. 1915, p. 1.
179. *DEG*, 10 November 1914, p. 5.
180. *DEG*, 10 November 1914, p. 5.
181. *DEG*, 26 August 1914, p. 4.
182. *BWG*, 3 December 1914, p. 6.
183. *WT*, 27 November 1914, p. 5.
184. PA, TB: 1305/10, Newspaper cuttings, 'Local Patriotism and Organisation in 1803 (By Dr. Trelawny-Ross)', p. 7.
185. John McQuilton, *Rural Australia and the Great War: From Tarrawingee to Tangambalanga* (Victoria, 2001) p. 6
186. *DEG*, 4 September 1914, p. 8.

187. Matthew Taylor, 'The 1914–15 Season', *The Greater Game: A History of Football in World War I* (Oxford, 2014) p. 7.
188. *DEG*, 4 September 1914, p. 8.
189. *DEG*, 7 September 1914, p. 4.
190. *DEG*, 3 September 1914, p. 2.
191. *DEG*, 5 September 1914, p. 4.
192. Alexander Jackson, *Football's Great War: Association Football on the English Home Front, 1914–1918* (Barnsley, 2022) pp. 36–37.
193. *DEG*, 5 September 1914, p. 4.
194. *DEG*, 5 September 1914, p. 4.
195. *DEG*, 8 December 1914, p. 7.
196. *WT*, 8 December 1914, p. 8.
197. *DEG*, 12 December 1914, p. 2.
198. *WT*, 14 December 1914, p. 2.
199. *WT*, 14 December 1914, p. 2.
200. *WT*, 14 December 1914, p. 2.
201. *DEG*, 12 December 1914, p. 2.
202. *WT*, 14 December 1914, p. 2.
203. *WT*, 25 November 1914, p. 2.
204. *DEG*, 12 December 1914, p. 2.
205. *WT*, 25 November 1914, p. 2.
206. *WT*, 24 December 1914, p. 9.
207. *DEG*, 31 December 1914, p. 2.
208. Peter Grant, *Philanthropy and Voluntary Action in the First World War: Mobilizing Charity* (New York, 2014) pp. 22–35.
209. Ralph Richardson, *Through war to peace, 1914–1918: Being a short account of the part played by Tavistock and Neighbourhood in the Great War* (Tavistock, 1919) pp. 82–95.
210. 'Devonshire Patriotic Fund' in R. Pearse Chope ed., *The Devonian Year Book for the Year 1915* (London, 1915) p. 17.
211. DHC: 1262M/0/FH/42, Typescript of work of Lord Fortescue during 1st World War, p. 9.
212. Proctor, *Civilians in a World at War*, p. 181.
213. *WMN*, 29 September 1914, p. 2.
214. David Parker, *Hertfordshire Children in War and Peace, 1914–1939* (Hatfield, 2007) p. 69.
215. Rebecca Gill, 'Calculating Compassion in War: The "New Humanitarian" Ethos in Britain, 1870–1918', University of Manchester, PhD Thesis, 2005, p. 171.
216. Steve Marti, *For Home and Empire: Voluntary Mobilization in Australia, Canada, and New Zealand during the First World War* (Vancouver, 2019) pp. 17, 25, 32, 43.
217. Timothy C. Winegard, *Indigenous Peoples of the British Dominions and the First World War* (Cambridge, 2012) pp. 219–220.
218. Capozzola, *Uncle Sam Wants You*, p. 83.
219. Margaret H. Darrow, *French Women and the First World War: War Stories of the Home Front* (Oxford, 2000) p. 79.
220. Paul Ward, '"Women of Britain Say Go!": Women's patriotism in the First World War', *Twentieth Century British History*, Vol. 13, No. 1 (2001) p. 31.
221. *The Times*, 24 September 1914, p. 11.
222. *DEG*, 28 September 1914, p. 4; *NDJ*, 1 October 1914, p. 6.

223. DHC: 1262M/0/FH/42, Typescript of work of Lord Fortescue during 1st World War, p. 17.
224. *WT*, 26 November 1914, p. 2.
225. *WT*, 3 November 1914, p. 4.
226. *WT*, 3 November 1914, p. 4.

Chapter 3: The totalization of the conflict? 1915

1. Frank Meeres, *Norfolk in the First World War* (Chichester, 2004) pp. 91–92.
2. Susan R. Grayzel, *At Home and Under Fire: Air Raids and Culture in Britain from the Great War to the Blitz* (Cambridge, 2012) p. 26.
3. PA, TB: 3010/1, Journal of James Thomas Rogers of Plymouth, 19 January 1915, p. 214.
4. *WMN*, 7 January 1915, p. 4.
5. Norman D. Cliff, *To Hell and Back with the Guards* (Braunton, 1988) p. 13
6. DHC: 1262M/0/O/LD/153/44, Itinerary and table for route march, 1915.
7. DHC: 1262M/0/O/LD/120/21, Notes of Recruiting meetings and marches, n.d. (c March 1915); *Tiverton Gazette & East Devon Herald*, 13 July 1915, p. 1.
8. DHC: 1262M/0/O/LD/153/42, Memorandum re route march, 1915.
9. DHC: 1262M/0/O/LD/153/57, Letter from T.E. Hopewell and W.S. Wade to Devon Parliamentary Recruiting Committee, 1915, pp. 3–4.
10. *WT*, 9 January 1915, p. 3.
11. *WMN*, 21 April 1915, p. 4.
12. *WMN*, 23 April 1915, p. 5.
13. *DEG*, 12 January 1915, p. 5; *WMN*, 17 February 1915, p. 7.
14. *Teignmouth Post and Gazette (TPG)*, 23 April 1915, p. 4.
15. *WT*, 3 September 1915, p. 5.
16. Helen Townsley, 'The First World War and Voluntary Recruitment: A forum for regional identity? An analysis of the nature, expression and significance of regional identity in Hull, 1900 -1916', University of Sussex, PhD Thesis, 2008, p. 234.
17. *DEG*, 29 January 1915, p. 7
18. *NDJ*, 18 February 1915, p. 5.
19. *WMN*, 21 April 1915, p. 7.
20. *NDJ*, 3 June 1915, p. 2.
21. *TPG*, 3 September 1915, p. 4.
22. *DEG*, 16 February 1915, p. 4.
23. *WT*, 2 March 1915, p. 6.
24. *DEG*, 5 November 1915, p. 12.
25. Dudley Clark, 'For Dartymoor' in R. Pearse Chope (ed), *The Devonian Year Book for the Year 1916* (London, 1916) p. 22.
26. *NDJ*, 29 April 1915, p. 3.
27. *WEH*, 17 June 1915, p. 1.
28. DHC: 1262M/0/O/LD/120/30, The War: An Appeal to Devon Men and Women issued by the Devon Parliamentary Recruiting Committee, 1 February 1915, p. 1.
29. DHC: 1262M/0/O/LD/120/30, The War, pp. 4–8.
30. DHC: 1262M/0/O/LD/120/30, The War, p. 2.
31. *DEG*, 23 October 1915, p. 4.
32. *WEH*, 24 April 1915, p. 4.
33. DHC: 1262M/0/FD/46, Personal Diary of the 3rd Lord Ebrington, 15 January 1915.

34. *WT*, 27 February 1915, p. 2.
35. *WT*, 2 September 1915, p. 3.
36. *WT*, 2 March 1915, p. 3; *WEH*, 6 September 1915, p. 3.
37. DHC: 1262M/0/FH/42, Typescript of work of Lord Fortescue during 1st World War, p. 32.
38. *WT*, 19 June 1915, p. 4.
39. *DEG*, 16 June 1915, p. 5.
40. *The Diaries of Sir Ernest Satow, 1912–1920: Volume 1 (1912–1916)*, 14 June 1915, p. 313.
41. *WMN*, 21 June 1915, p. 3.
42. *WT*, 19 June 1915, p. 4.
43. *DEG*, 17 June 1915, p. 5.
44. *DEG*, 17 June 1915, p. 3.
45. *DEG*, 8 January 1915, p. 7.
46. Young, 'Voluntary Recruitment in Scotland, 1914–1916', p. 173
47. *DEG*, 22 June 1915, p. 9.
48. *DEG*, 10 September 1915, p. 9.
49. *DEG*, 10 September 1915, p. 9.
50. *WMN*, 18 February 1915, p. 3.
51. *WT*, 19 February 1915, p. 6.
52. *WT*, 17 July 1915, p. 2.
53. *TPG*, 23 April 1915, p. 4.
54. Hoskins, *Devon*, p. 516.
55. *TPG*, 23 April 1915, p. 4
56. *WT*, 27 February 1915, p. 2.
57. DHC: 1262M/0/O/LD/153/41, Letter from Lord Fortescue to Colonel Western, 31 March 1915, p. 4.
58. DHC: 1262M/0/O/LD/153/41, Letter from Lord Fortescue to Colonel Western, p. 3.
59. *WT*, 4 December 1914, p. 16; DHC: 1262M/0/O/LD/153/41, Letter from Lord Fortescue to Colonel Western, p. 3.
60. DHC: 1262M/0/O/LD/153/25, Recruitment of non conformists, Letter from Gulland to Steel Maitland, 13 May 1915, p. 1.
61. DHC: 1262M/0/O/LD/153/25, Recruitment of non conformists, Letter from Gulland to Steel Maitland, p. 1.
62. DHC: 1262M/0/O/LD/153/41, Letter from Lord Fortescue to Colonel Western, p. 3.
63. *Hartland and West Country Chronicle*, 12 March 1915, p. 12.
64. *WMN*, 19 February 1915, p. 8.
65. *WMN*, 19 February 1915, p. 8.
66. *WMN*, 19 February 1915, p. 8.
67. *DEG*, 20 February 1915, p. 3.
68. *DEG*, 20 February 1915, p. 3.
69. *DEG*, 20 February 1915, p. 3.
70. *WMN*, 19 February 1915, p. 8.
71. Dalley, 'The response in Cornwall', pp. 98–99.
72. *WMN*, 15 April 1915, p. 8.
73. *NDJ*, 18 February 1915, p. 5.
74. *NDJ*, 18 February 1915, p. 5.
75. *WMN*, 18 February 1915, p. 3.
76. White, 'Volunteerism and Early Recruitment Efforts in Devonshire', p. 665.

77. *DEG*, 4 August 1915, p. 3. *WT*, 6 August 1915, p. 6.
78. *DEG*, 4 August 1915, p. 3.
79. *WMN*, 20 February 1915, p. 6; *WT*, 3 September 1915, p. 5.
80. *WMN*, 2 March 1915, p. 6.
81. *DEG*, 20 February 1915, p. 3.
82. PA, TB: 1306/23, Miss Edrica de la Pole, 22 April 1915.
83. *NDJ*, 10 June 1915, p. 2.
84. *WT*, 3 September 1915, p. 5.
85. *WT*, 16 July 1915, p. 5; *WT*, 3 September 1915, p. 5.
86. DHC: 1262M/0/O/LD/114/5, Letter to Fortescue from Gretton, 15 July 1915, p. 2.
87. *DEG*, 5 June 1915, p. 5.
88. *WT*, 3 September 1915, p. 5.
89. *NDJ*, 18 February 1915, p. 6.
90. *WMN*, 19 February 1915, p. 8; *WT*, 16 July 1915, p. 5.
91. *WMN*, 17 February 1915, p. 7; *DEG*, 3 September 1915, p. 2.
92. DHC: 1262M/0/O/LD/153/21, Letter from C. Fursdon to Lord Fortescue, 18 January 1915, p. 2; *South Devon Weekly Express (SDWE)*, 16 July 1915, p. 4.
93. DHC: 1262M/0/O/LD/153/24, Letter from Lord Fortescue to Deputy Lieutenants, 1915, p. 1.
94. *WT*, 3 September 1915, p. 5.
95. *DEG*, 3 September 1915, p. 10; *DEG*, 24 September 1915, p. 14.
96. Joe Harris Lunn, 'Kande Kamara Speaks: An Oral History of the West African Experience in France, 1914–18' in M. E. Page ed., *Africa and the First World War* (Basingstoke, 1987) p. 32.
97. *DEG*, 19 March 1915, p. 13.
98. *NDJ*, 9 September 1915, p. 8.
99. *WT*, 31 August 1915, p. 5.
100. *WMN*, 15 January 1915, p. 6.
101. *WT*, 19 February 1915, p. 5.
102. *WMN*, 23 April 1915, p. 5.
103. *DEG*, 4 October 1915, p. 3.
104. *DEG*, 3 September 1915, p. 2.
105. *WT*, 4 November 1915, p. 3.
106. *WT*, 6 September 1915, p. 2.
107. *WT*, 3 September 1915, p. 5.
108. *WMN*, 8 January 1915, p. 1; *SDWE*, 8 January 1915, p. 4.
109. DHC: 1262M/0/O/LD/120/30, The War, p. 10.
110. Gregory, *The Last Great War*, p. 90.
111. *WMN*, 23 April 1915, p. 5.
112. *WMN*, 23 April 1915, p. 5.
113. *WMN*, 21 June 1915, p. 3.
114. DHC: 1262M/0/O/LD/153/53, Letter from Apsley Petre Peter, 1915.
115. DHC: 1262M/0/O/LD/153/53, Letter from Apsley Petre Peter, 1915.
116. DHC: 1262M/0/O/LD/153/53, Letter from Apsley Petre Peter, 1915.
117. *WMN*, 17 March 1915, p. 5.
118. *WT*, 10 November 1915, p. 2.
119. *WT*, 20 May 1915, p. 2.
120. DHC: 1262M/0/O/LD/153/21, Letter from C. Fursdon to Lord Fortescue, p. 1.

121. DHC: 1262M/0/O/LD/153/21, Letter from C. Fursdon to Lord Fortescue, p. 2.
122. DHC: 1262M/0/O/LD/153/21, Letter from C. Fursdon to Lord Fortescue, p. 2.
123. *The Diaries of Sir Ernest Satow, 1912–1920: Volume 1 (1912–1916)*, 8 April 1916, p. 386.
124. *NDJ*, 18 February 1915, p. 6.
125. *WT*, 16 July 1915, p. 5.
126. *NDJ*, 13 May 1915 p. 2.
127. *DEG*, 14 May 1915 p. 3.
128. *WMN*, 18 February 1915, p. 3.
129. *WMN*, 18 February 1915, p. 3.
130. *WMN*, 18 February 1915, p. 3.
131. *WMN*, 18 February 1915, p. 3.
132. *DEG*, 4 June 1915, p. 15.
133. *DEG*, 4 June 1915, p. 15.
134. DHC: 1262M/0/O/LD/153/41, Letter from Lord Fortescue to Colonel Western, p. 3.
135. DHC: 1262M/0/O/LD/153/41, Letter from Lord Fortescue to Colonel Western, p. 3.
136. *SDWE*, 16 July 1915, p. 4.
137. *DEG*, 16 July 1915, p. 2.
138. *WT*, 17 July 1915, p. 2.
139. *DEG*, 16 July 1915, p. 2.
140. *WMN*, 16 July 1915, p. 5.
141. *DEG*, 16 July 1915, p. 2.
142. *DEG*, 16 July 1915, p. 2.
143. *DEG*, 16 July 1915, p. 2.
144. *WT*, 17 July 1915, p. 2; *WMN*, 16 July 1915, p. 5.
145. *DEG*, 17 July 1915, p. 3.
146. *John Bull*, 31 July 1915, p. 6
147. DHC: 1262M/0/FH/42, Typescript of work of Lord Fortescue during 1st World War, p. 32.
148. Peter Simkins, 'Pals Battalions', *International Encyclopaedia of the First World War*, March 2018, <https://encyclopedia.1914-1918-online.net/article/pals_battalions>, [Accessed 20 February 2020]
149. Grieves, '"Lowther's Lambs"', pp. 62–64.
150. DHC: 1262M/0/O/LD/153/41, Letter from Lord Fortescue to Colonel Western, 31 March 1915, p. 2.
151. *A Lord Lieutenant in Wartime*, pp. 212–220.
152. DHC: 1262M/0/FH/42, Typescript of work of Lord Fortescue during 1st World War, p. 32.
153. Mansfield, 'Farmworkers, the Marches and the impact of the Great War', p. 102.
154. DHC: 1262M/0/O/LD/153/54, Letter from Apsley Petre Peter, 1915, p. 1.
155. Wilson, *The Myriad Faces of War*, p. 167.
156. *WT*, 17 July 1915, p. 2.
157. Wilson, *The Myriad Faces of War*, pp. 167–168.
158. Osborne, *The Voluntary Recruiting Movement in Britain*, p. 67.
159. Nicholas Mansfield, 'Volunteers and Recruiting' in G. Gliddon (ed), *Norfolk & Suffolk in the Great War* (Norwich, 1988) p. 26.
160. *WMN*, 21 October 1915, p. 3.
161. *WMN*, 12 November 1915, p. 8.
162. DHC: 1262M/0/FD/46, Personal Diary of the 3rd Lord Ebrington, 28 October 1915.

163. DHC: 1037M/LG4/5/13, Letter to Mr Ford from Mr Steele King of Branscombe Vicarage regarding 'Lord Derby's Scheme' and a meeting for the Honiton division to select canvassers', c1915, p. 1.
164. *WT*, 3 December 1915, p. 14.
165. William Collins, *Herefordshire and the Great War, with the City and County's Roll of Honour* (Hereford, 1919) p. 47.
166. DHC: 1262M/0/O/LD/153/74, Acknowledgement of role as Canvasser of Recruits, 2 November 1915.
167. *WT*, 23 October 1915, p. 3.
168. *DEG*, 5 November 1915, p. 10.
169. *SDWE*, 12 November 1915, p. 3; *DEG*, 19 November 1915, p. 11.
170. DHC: 1262M/0/O/LD/116/27, Letter to Fortescue from Rowell, 22 November 1915.
171. *DEG*, 16 November 1915, p. 5.
172. DHC: 1262M/0/O/LD/153/85, Letter from King's Nympton Rectory to Lord Fortescue, 1915, p. 3.
173. PA, TB: 1306/23, Miss Edrica de la Pole, 20 November 1915.
174. PA, TB: 1306/23, Miss Edrica de la Pole, 20 November 1915.
175. PA, TB: 1306/23, Miss Edrica de la Pole, 8 December 1915.
176. DHC: 1262M/0/O/LD/116/24, Letter to Fortescue from Hugh Breton, 20 November 1915, p. 2.
177. DHC: 1262M/0/O/LD/153/84, Letter from James Bucknell to Lord Fortescue, 1915, p. 3.
178. DHC: 1262M/0/O/LD/153/84, Letter from James Bucknell to Lord Fortescue, 1915, p. 3.
179. *WMN*, 2 December 1915, p. 3.
180. DHC: 1262M/0/O/LD/153/74, Acknowledgement of role as Canvasser of Recruits, p. 2.
181. DHC: 1262M/0/O/LD/116/25, Typed Letter from Fortescue to Derby containing some handwritten notes, p. 3.
182 DHC: 1262M/0/O/LD/153/74, Acknowledgement of role as Canvasser of Recruits, p. 2.
183. *TPG*, 22 October 1915, p. 3.
184. *WT*, 30 October 1915, p. 2.
185. Rusiecki, *The Impact of Catastrophe*, p. 87.
186. *WMN*, 13 November 1915, p. 3.
187. *Echoes of the Great War*, p. 92.
188. *WT*, 23 October 1915, p. 3.
189. *WMN*, 12 November 1915, p. 8.
190. DHC: 1262M/0/O/LD/116/25, Typed Letter from Fortescue to Derby containing some handwritten notes, 20 November 1915, p. 1.
191. DHC: 1262M/0/O/LD/116/25, Typed Letter from Fortescue to Derby containing some handwritten notes, p. 1.
192. DHC: 1262M/0/O/LD/116/25, Typed Letter from Fortescue to Derby containing some handwritten notes, p. 2.
193. DHC: 1262M/0/O/LD/116/25, Typed Letter from Fortescue to Derby containing some handwritten notes, p. 3.
194. DHC: 1262M/0/O/LD/116/25, Typed Letter from Fortescue to Derby containing some handwritten notes, p. 1.

195. DHC: 1262M/0/O/LD/116/25, Typed Letter from Fortescue to Derby containing some handwritten notes, p. 3.
196. DHC: 1262M/0/O/LD/116/31, Letter from Fortescue to Carnegie, 23 November 1915, p. 1.
197. *WMN*, 20 November 1915, p. 8.
198. *WT*, 26 November 1915, p. 9.
199. DHC: 1262M/0/O/LD/116/25, Typed Letter from Fortescue to Derby containing some handwritten notes, p. 2.
200. DHC: 1262M/0/O/LD/116/25, Typed Letter from Fortescue to Derby containing some handwritten notes, p. 2.
201. *WMN*, 11 December 1915, p. 8.
202. *Hull Daily Mail*, 15 December 1915, p. 2.
203. *WMN*, 11 December 1915, p. 8.
204. *First World War Military Service Tribunals: Warwick District Appeal Tribunal, 1916–1918*, Philip and Julie Sprinks (eds.) (Stratford Upon Avon, 2017) p. 7.
205. *WT*, 1 November 1915, p. 4.
206. *DEG*, 31 December 1915, p. 16.
207. *WMN*, 9 December 1915, p. 4.
208. *Hull Daily Mail*, 15 December 1915, p. 2.
209. *Farnworth Chronicle*, 22 January 1916, p. 6.
210. *WEH*, 21 January 1916, p. 5.
211. *Illustrated Police News*, 27 January 1916, p. 3.
212. *Globe*, 20 January 1916, p. 8.
213. *Globe*, 20 January 1916, p. 8.
214. *The Times History of the War*, Vol. VI (London, 1916) p. 302.
215. *NDJ*, 9 March 1916, p. 2.
216. *Echoes of the Great War*, p. 91.
217. *Echoes of the Great War*, p. 92.
218. *WMN*, 25 November 1915, p. 3; *DEG*, 10 May 1918, p. 6.
219. *WMN*, 29 March 1915, p. 6.
220. Peter Hilditch, 'The Dockyard in the Local Economy', in M. Duffy, S. Fisher, D. Greenhill, D. J. Starkey and J. Youings (eds), *The New Maritime History of Devon, Volume II: From the Late Eighteenth Century to the Present Day*, (London, 1994) p. 216.
221. *WMN*, 29 October 1915, p. 5.
222. *DEG*, 10 May 1918, p. 6.
223. *WMN*, 29 March 1915, p. 6.
224. Andy Gale, 'The Westcountry and the First World War: Recruits & Identities', Lancaster University, PhD Thesis, 2010, p. 369.
225. DHC: 1262M/0/O/LD/153/81, Letter from Lord Fortescue to Lord Derby, 1915, p. 1.
226. *WEH*, 20 November 1915, p. 4.
227. *Letters of Stephen Reynolds*, p. 210.
228. *WMN*, 24 November 1915, p. 5.
229. DHC: 1262M/0/O/LD/116/35, Letter to Fortescue from Powell-Williams, 10 December 1915.
230. *WT*, 17 December 1915, p. 7.
231. DHC: 1262M/0/O/LD/153/128, Recruiting Statistics, 1915.
232. DHC: 1262M/0/O/LD/153/128, Recruiting Statistics, 1915.

233. DHC: 1262M/0/O/LD/153/128, Recruiting Statistics, 1915.
234. DHC: 3601A/8/PZ/2, Notice of recruiting route march by detachment of 3rd Battalion of the Devonshire Regiment, 20 April 1915.
235. Young, 'Voluntary Recruitment in Scotland', p. 170
236. *SDWE*, 23 April 1915, p. 2.
237. *WMN*, 26 April 1915, p. 8.
238. *DEG*, 25 June 1915, p. 2
239. DHC: 1262M/0/FD/46, Personal Diary of the 3rd Lord Ebrington, 3 June 1915; *DEG*, 4 June 1915, p. 15.
240. *DEG*, 16 July 1915, p. 2.
241. *SDWE*, 23 April 1915, p. 2.
242. *DEG*, 3 September 1915, p. 10.
243. *WT*, 29 December 1914, p. 5.
244. *WT*, 20 December 1915, p. 3.
245. Darrow, *French Women and the First World War*, pp. 53–97.
246. Darrow, *French Women and the First World War*, p. 78.
247. *WT*, 23 April 1915, p. 2.
248. *WT*, 23 April 1915, p. 2.
249. *DEG*, 6 August 1915, p. 12.
250. *WT*, 6 August 1915, p. 11.
251. Ward, '"Women of Britain Say Go!"', p. 38; Darrow, *French Women and the First World War*, p. 78.
252. Peter Cooksley, *The Home Front: Civilian Life in World War One* (Stroud, 2006) p. 24.
253. *WT*, 24 August 1915, p. 5.
254. *WT*, 23 December 1915, p. 3.
255. Richardson, *Through war to peace*, pp. 85–95.
256. *SDWE*, 25 June 1915, p. 3.
257. Rachel Duffett, 'A War Unimagined: Food and the rank and file soldier of the First World War' in J. Meyer (ed), *British Popular Culture and the First World War* (Leiden, 2008) pp. 61–68.

Chapter 4: The Shift from Self-Mobilisation to Remobilisation, 1916

1. *DEG*, 5 January 1916, p. 1.
2. Laura Ugolini, *Civvies: Middle-class men on the English Home Front, 1914–18* (Manchester, 2013) pp. 141–145.
3. Collins, *Herefordshire and the Great War*, p. 47.
4. *NDJ*, 27 January 1916, p. 4.
5. PA, TB: 1306/24, Miss Edrica de la Pole, of Tremar, Kingston, Diary, 1916, 12 January 1916.
6. PA, TB: 1306/24, Miss Edrica de la Pole, 12 January 1916.
7. PA, TB: 1306/24, Miss Edrica de la Pole, 22 November 1916.
8. PA, TB: 1306/24, Miss Edrica de la Pole, 12 January 1916.
9. PA, TB: 1306/24, Miss Edrica de la Pole, 13 January 1916.
10. David Stevenson, *1914–1918: The History of the First World War* (London, 2005) p. 203.
11. Simkins, *Kitchener's Army*, p. 156.
12. Gregory, *Recollections of a Country Editor*, p. 63; *WT*, 15 September 1916, p. 5.
13. *First World War Military Service Tribunals: Warwick District Appeal Tribunal, 1916–1918*, p. 13; DHC: R4582A/2/BZ/2, Local Military Tribunal Minute book, 1915–1916, p. 9.

14. Adrian Gregory, 'Military Service Tribunals: Civic Society in Action, 1916–1918' in J. Harris (ed), *Civil Society in British History: Ideas, Identities, Institutions* (Oxford, 2005) pp. 181, 190.
15. Gregory, *The Last Great War*, p. 101.
16. Ivor Slocombe, 'Recruitment into the Armed Forces during the First World War. The work of the Military Tribunals in Wiltshire, 1915–1918', *The Local Historian* Vol. 30, 2 (May 2000) p. 107
17. *First World War Military Service Tribunals: Warwick District Appeal Tribunal, 1916–1918*, p. 11.
18. *DEG*, 4 March 1916, p. 6; *DEG*, 18 March 1916, p. 3.
19. Gullace, *"The Blood of Our Sons"*, p. 114
20. *DEG*, 10 June 1916, p. 5.
21. David Littlewood, *Military Service Tribunals and Boards in the Great War* (Abingdon, 2018) p. 72
22. *WT*, 10 June 1916, p. 2.
23. *NDJ*, 13 July 1916, p. 8.
24. *WT*, 14 July 1916, p. 3.
25. *WT*, 14 July 1916, p. 3.
26. *BWG*, 30 March 1916, p. 3.
27. Lois B. Bibbings, *Telling Tales about Men: Conceptions of Conscientious Objectors to Military Service during the First World War* (Manchester, 2009) pp. 29–30.
28. Robin Barlow, 'Military Tribunals in Carmarthenshire, 1916–1917' in N. Mansfield and C. Horner eds, *The Great War: Localities and Regional Identities* (Newcastle Upon Tyne, 2014) p. 23
29. *BWG*, 30 March 1916, p. 3.
30. *DEG*, 13 March 1916, p. 4.
31. *WMN*, 28 February 1916, p. 7; *Pioneer*, 4 March 1916, p. 2.
32. *WT*, 13 March 1916, p. 2.
33. *WT*, 1 April 1916, p. 2.
34. *WMN*, 1 April 1916, p. 8; *The Northwest Worker*, 18 May 1916, p. 1; *The Maoriland Worker*, Vol. 7, 280, 28 June 1916, p. 1.
35. *WT*, 15 March 1916, p. 3.
36. *WMN*, 15 April 1916, p. 7.
37. *DEG*, 19 June 1916, p. 3.
38. *WMN*, 16 December 1916, p. 8.
39. William Stone, *Hero of the Fleet: Two World Wars, One extraordinary life – The Memoirs of Centenarian* (Edinburgh, 2009) p. 49.
40. WT, 9 October 1916, p. 3.
41. *NDJ*, 12 October 1916, p. 2.
42. *WEH*, 27 September 1916, p. 1.
43. *WMN*, 28 September 1916, p. 8.
44. *WT*, 18 July 1916, p. 2.
45. *WMN*, 11 October 1916, p. 7.
46. *WMN*, 11 October 1916, p. 7.
47. Rusiecki, *The Impact of Catastrophe*, pp. 103–104.
48. Dorset History Centre: D1576/2/8/3/1, Letter to Charles Barnes from his fiancée Frances Ched of Prime Farm, Marshwood, 5 October 1916, p. 1.
49. Purseigle, 'Introduction', p. 31

50. James McDermott, *British Military Service Tribunals, 1916–1918: 'A very much abused body of men'* (Manchester, 2011) pp. 156–157.
51. McDermott, *British Military Service Tribunals*, p. 157.
52. *DEG*, 19 August 1916, p. 4.
53. *DEG*, 19 August 1916, p. 4.
54. *DEG*, 19 August 1916, p. 4.
55. *WMN*, 19 August 1916, p. 7.
56. *DEG*, 19 August 1916, p. 3.
57. DeGroot, *Back in Blighty*, p. 141.
58. *WT*, 1 August 1916, p. 3.
59. *WT*, 7 April 1916, p. 2.
60. *Daily Telegraph*, 14 March 1916, p. 7.
61. *DEG*, 17 August 1916, p. 5.
62. *NDJ*, 17 August 1916, p. 5.
63. *DEG*, 17 August 1916, p. 3.
64. *DEG*, 17 August 1916, p. 3.
65. *WT*, 10 June 1916, p. 2.
66. Jeanette Keith, *Rich Man's War, Poor Man's Fight: Race, Class, and Power in the Rural South during the First World War* (Chapel Hill, 2004) p. 116.
67. *WT*, 21 July 1916, p. 3.
68. DHC: 1262M/0/O/LD/155/45, Typed notes, entitled – as to the Clean Cut in Devonshire and additional hand written notes, June 1918, p. 1.
69. DHC: 1262M/0/O/LD/155/45, Typed notes, p. 1.
70. McDermott, *British Military Service Tribunals*, p. 157.
71. *Daily Mail*, 1 September 1916, p. 3
72. *The Diaries of Sir Ernest Satow, 1912–1920: Volume 2 (1917–1920)* ed. by Ian Ruxton (Morrisville, NC, 2018) 1 February 1917, p. 31.
73. *Daily Mail*, 1 September 1916, p. 3
74. *Daily Mail*, 2 September 1916, p. 3.
75. *The Times*, 27 October 1916, p. 9; Gregory, *The Last Great War*, p. 122.
76. *CCNDG*, 9 September 1916, p. 2.
77. *DEG*, 4 September 1916, p. 3.
78. *DEG*, 9 September 1916, p. 3.
79. DHC: R4582A/2/BZ/2, Local Military Tribunal Minute book, 1915–1916, 16 June 1916.
80. John Morton Osborne, 'Defining Their Own Patriotism: British Volunteer Training Corps in the First World War', *Journal of Contemporary History*, Vol. 23, No. 1 (January 1988) pp. 59–75.
81. DHC: R4582A/2/BZ/2, Local Military Tribunal Minute book, 28 July 1916.
82. McDermott, *British Military Service Tribunals*, p. 214.
83. DHC: R4582A/2/BZ/2, Local Military Tribunal Minute book, 3 November 1916.
84. DHC: R4582A/2/BZ/2, Local Military Tribunal Minute book, pp. 91, 93–94.
85 DHC: R4582A/2/BZ2, Local Military Tribunal Minute book, 8 December 1916.
86. *WEH*, 16 September 1916, p. 3.
87. *Middlesex Chronicle*, 2 September 1916, p. 7.
88. Theodore Kornweibel Jr, *'Investigate Everything': Federal Efforts to Compel Black Loyalty during World War I* (Bloomington, IN, 2002) pp. 98–99.
89. *Philadelphia Inquirer*, 16 August 1918, p. 5; *Hudson Observer, New Jersey*, 16 August 1918, p. 1.

90. Capozzola, *Uncle Sam Wants You*, p. 43.
91. *Evening Sun*, 29 August 1918, p. 24.
92. *Republican-Gazette*, 11 July 1918, p. 6.
93. David J. Bettez, *Kentucky and the Great War: World War I on the Home Front* (Lexington, KY, 2016) p. 35.
94. *WT*, 26 September 1916, p. 8.
95. *WT*, 25 September 1916, p. 2.
96. *WT*, 25 September 1916, p. 2; *BWG*, 28 September 1916, p. 3.
97. *WT*, 26 September 1916, p. 8
98. *WEH*, 16 September 1916, p. 3.
99. *WMN*, 16 September 1916, p. 5.
100. *WEH*, 16 September 1916, p. 3.
101. *WMN*, 23 September 1916, p. 5.
102. *WMN*, 23 September 1916, p. 5.
103. *WMN*, 28 September 1916, p. 6.
104. *WT*, 3 October 1916, p. 6.
105. *WT*, 3 October 1916, p. 6.
106. *WMN*, 11 September 1916, p. 8.
107. *WMN*, 11 September 1916, p. 8.
108. *WMN*, 11 September 1916, p. 8.
109. *WMN*, 11 September 1916, p. 8.
110. *WT*, 16 September 1916, p. 4.
111. *NDJ*, 21 September 1916, p. 5.
112. *WT*, 16 September 1916, p. 4.
113. *WT*, 18 October 1916, p. 3.
114. Wilson, *The Myriad Faces of War*, p. 400.
115. *Tiverton Gazette & East Devon Herald*, 31 October 1916, p. 7.
116. *WMN*, 13 September 1916, p. 4.
117. *Taunton Courier and Western Advertiser*, 20 September 1916, p. 5.
118. *North Wales Weekly News*, 14 September 1916, p. 5.
119. *WMN*, 29 September 1916, p. 3.
120. *Bolton Journal & Guardian*, 20 October 1916, p. 5.
121. *Bolton Journal & Guardian*, 20 October 1916, p. 5.
122. *Bolton Journal & Guardian*, 20 October 1916, p. 5.
123. Gullace, *'The Blood of Our Sons'*, p. 159.
124. *WT*, 25 January 1916, p. 3.
125. *WT*, 25 January 1916, p. 3.
126. Julia Neville, 'Mary Sylvia Calmady-Hamlyn (1881–1962)' in J. Neville, M. Auchterlonie, P. Auchterlonie & A. Roberts (eds), *Devon Women in Public and Professional Life, 1900–1950: Votes, Voices and Vocations* (Exeter, 2021) pp. 207–211.
127. *NDJ*, 10 February 1916, p. 7.
128. *WT*, 8 February 1916, p. 3.
129. *NDJ*, 10 February 1916, p. 7.
130. *WMN*, 23 December 1916, p. 6.
131. Parliamentary Debates, House of Commons, Fifth Series, Vol. 82, 22 May 1916, Column 1855.
132. *The Times*, 3 June 1916, p. 9.
133. *NDJ*, 3 February 1916, p. 6.

134. *NDJ*, 3 February 1916, p. 6.
135. *NDJ*, 3 February 1916, p. 6.
136. *NDJ*, 3 February 1916, p. 6.
137. *WT*, 6 July 1917, p. 9.
138. The National Archives (TNA): MAF 80/4998, Devon War Agricultural Committee, 4 August 1916, folio 11.
139. W. A. Armstrong, 'Kentish Rural Society during the First World War' in B. A. Holdness and M. Turner (eds), *Land, Labour and Agriculture, 1790–1920: Essays for Gordon Mingray* (London, 1991) p. 117.
140. TNA: MAF 80/4998, Devon War Agricultural Committee, 4 August 1916, folio 11.
141. *The Diaries of Sir Ernest Satow, 1912–1920: Volume 1 (1912–1916)*, 23 December 1915.
142. Tiverton Museum of Mid Devon Life: 88/1158/1, J. Heathcoat-Amory factory Logbook, 8 March 1916, p. 174.
143. *Letters of Stephen Reynolds*, p. 210.
144. *NDJ*, 18 May 1916, p. 2.
145. *WT*, 25 January 1916, p. 3.
146. Hockin, *Two Girls on the Land*, p. 8.
147. Bonnie White, 'Sowing the seeds of patriotism? The Women's Land Army in Devon, 1916–1918', *The Local Historian*, Vol. 41, No. 1 (February 2011) p. 17.
148. Imperial War Museum (IWM): 506, Lees, Mary (Oral History), Transcript, 1974, p. 36.
149. *NDJ*, 25 May 1916, p. 8
150. *DEG*, 18 August 1916, p. 10.
151. *CCNDG*, 29 January 1916, p. 3.
152. *CCNDG*, 29 January 1916, p. 3.
153. *CCNDG*, 29 January 1916, p. 3.
154. *NDJ*, 10 February 1916, p. 7.
155. *WT*, 21 October 1916, p. 2.
156. *WT*, 21 October 1916, p. 2.
157. *WT*, 21 October 1916, p. 2.
158. Parliamentary Debates, House of Commons, Fifth Series, Vol. 86, 17 October 1916, Column 457.
159. Parliamentary Debates, House of Commons, Fifth Series, Vol. 86, 17 October 1916, Column 456.
160. Julie Moore, 'Feeding the city' in J. Mein, A. Wares & S. Mann eds., *St Albans: Life on the Home Front, 1914–1918* (Hatfield, 2016) pp. 176–177; Val Argue, 'Heath Farm Dairy and the St Albans Military Tribunal', 24 April 2019, St Albans & Hertfordshire Architectural & Archaeological Society, <https://www.stalbanshistory.org/social-history/war-and-its-impact-on-st-albans/the-home-front-in-st-albans-during-the-first-world-war/heath-farm-dairy-and-the-st-albans-military-tribunal>, [Access 5 May 2022]
161. Richard Bessel, 'Mobilization and demobilization in Germany, 1916–1919' in J. Horne (ed), *State, Society and Mobilization in Europe during the First World War* (Cambridge, 1997) p. 219.
162. Elizabeth B. Jones, *Gender and Rural Modernity: Farm Women and the Politics of Labor in Germany, 1871–1933* (Farnham, 2009) pp. 98–110; Ziemann, *War Experiences in Rural Germany,* pp. 156–158.
163. Fionnuala Walsh, *Irish Women and the Great War* (Cambridge, 2020) pp. 142–143.
164. *NDJ*, 18 May 1916, p. 2.

165. Bonnie White, *The Women's Land Army in First World War Britain* (Basingstoke, 2014) p. 37.
166. *WT*, 17 March 1916, p. 8.
167. Nicola Verdon, *Working the Land: A History of the Farmworker in England from 1850 to the Present Day* (London, 2017) p. 138.
168. *The Times*, 28 April 1916, p. 7.
169. TNA: MAF 59/1, Women's County Committees - organisation of labour, September 1916, p. 4.
170. PA, TB: 1306/24, Miss Edrica de la Pole, 6 November 1916.
171. TNA: MAF 80/4998, Devon War Agricultural Committee, War Agricultural Committee Minutes of 6 May 1916, 6 May 1916, p. 2.
172. DHC: R7/9/0/C/7, Rural District Council Minutes, 22 May 1915 – 10 December 1921, 21 May 1916, p. 72.
173. Panikos Panayi, *The Enemy in our Midst: Germans in Britain during the First World War* (Oxford, 1991) pp. 40–41, 153–157.
174. Dom Ernest Graf, *Anscar Vonier, Abbot of Buckfast: with some account of the restoration of the Abbey and its Church* (London, 1957) p. 55.
175. *The Tablet*, 23 January 1915, p. 113.
176. Augustine Clark, 'Vonier, Martin [*name in religion* Anscar] (1875–1938)', Oxford University Press, 2004; online edition, September 2004, <https://doi.org/10.1093/ref:odnb/65088>, [Access 9 November 2020]; *The Tablet*, 23 January 1915, p. 113.
177. Graf, *Anscar Vonier*, p. 58.
178. Smith, 'The Life and Work of Abbot Anscar Vonier', p. 10.
179. Panikos Panayi, *Prisoners of Britain: German civilian and combatant internees during the First World War* (Manchester, 2012) p. 78–114.
180. TNA: HO 45/23540, part 49, ALIENS (See separate headings for NATIONALITY and NATURALISATION): monks of German origin at Buckfast Abbey: restriction measures, Aliens at Buckfast Abbey (Devon), 17 November 1919, p. 1.
181. TNA: HO 45/23540, part 49, ALIENS (See separate headings for NATIONALITY and NATURALISATION): monks of German origin at Buckfast Abbey: restriction measures, pp. 1–2.
182. Proctor, *Civilians in a World at War, 1914–1918*, p. 205.
183. *WMN*, 31 January 1916, p. 4.
184. *DEG*, 13 January 1916, p. 3.
185. *WMN*, 16 February 1916, p. 8.
186. *WMN*, 8 February 1916, p. 3.
187. *WMN*, 8 February 1916, p. 3.
188. *WMN*, 11 February 1916, p. 3.
189. Hough, *The Web*, p. 430.
190. *The Courier-Journal*, 2 March 1918, p. 4.
191. *The Courier-Journal*, 2 March 1918, p. 4.
192. *WMN*, 8 February 1916, p. 3.
193. *WMN*, 8 February 1916, p. 3.
194. TNA: HO 45/23540, part 49, ALIENS (See separate headings for NATIONALITY and NATURALISATION): monks of German origin at Buckfast Abbey: restriction measures, p. 1.
195. DHC: R2372A/C12, Minutes of Buckfastleigh Urban District Council, 1915–1916, 3 April 1916, p. 54.

196. Parliamentary Debates, House of Commons, Fifth Series, Vol. 85, 16 August 1916, column 1862.
197. Parliamentary Debates, House of Commons, Fifth Series, Vol. 85, 16 August 1916, column 1862.
198. Graf, *Anscar Vonier,* pp. 59–60; *WMN*, 8 February 1916, p. 3.
199. *John Bull*, 19 August 1916, p. 4.
200. *John Bull*, 12 August 1916, p. 12; *John Bull*, 26 August 1916, p. 28.
201. *John Bull*, 29 July 1916, p. 5.
202. *The Times*, 9 October 1916, p. 5.
203. *The Times*, 9 October 1916, p. 5.
204. *John Bull*, 26 August 1916, p. 28.
205. *WMN*, 4 July 1916, p. 8.
206. *DEG*, 14 July 1916, p. 10.
207. *WEH*, 13 July 1916, p. 3.
208. *WT*, 13 July 1916, p. 3.
209. *WMN*, 13 July 1916, p. 8
210. *John Bull*, 12 August 1916, p. 12.
211. Parliamentary Debates, House of Commons, Fifth Series, Vol. 85, 16 August 1916, column 1862.
212. DHC: R2372A/C12, Minutes of Buckfastleigh Urban District Council, 11 October 1916, p. 113; *Catholic Times and Catholic Opinion*, 6 October 1916, p. 7; *WEH*, 9 October 1916, p. 3.
213. *WT*, 10 October 1916, p. 3.
214. *WT*, 10 October 1916, p. 3.
215. TNA: HO 45/23540, part 49, ALIENS (See separate headings for NATIONALITY and NATURALISATION): monks of German origin at Buckfast Abbey: restriction measures, pp. 1–2.
216. *WT*, 5 December 1916, p. 5.
217. *WMN*, 5 December 1916, p. 5.
218. *WMN*, 5 December 1916, p. 5.
219. *WMN*, 27 December 1916, p. 4.
220. TNA: HO 45/23540, part 49, ALIENS (See separate headings for NATIONALITY and NATURALISATION): monks of German origin at Buckfast Abbey: restriction measures, Home Office file, 17 November 1919, p. 1.
221. *Letters of Stephen Reynolds*, p. 203.
222. Scoble, *Fisherman's Friend*, p. 624.
223. *Letters of Stephen Reynolds*, p. 203.
224. Scoble, *Fisherman's Friend*, pp. 585–586.
225. *Letters of Stephen Reynolds*, p. 204.
226. *Letters of Stephen Reynolds*, p. 204.
227. Caroline Dakers, *Forever England: The Countryside at War, 1914–1918*, (London, 2016) pp. 65–66.

Chapter 5: The Effects of Remobilisation, 1917 and 1918

1. John Turner, *British Politics and the Great War* (New Haven, 1992) p. 131.
2. Wilson, *The Myriad Faces of War*, p. 412.
3. Richard Toye, *Lloyd George & Churchill: Rivals for Greatness* (London, 2007) p. 168.

4. PA, TB: 261/4, Robert Alfred John Walling, Notes, 1913–1920, 1 December 1916, pp. 3–4.
5. PA, TB: 261/4, Robert Alfred John Walling, Notes, 1 December 1916, p. 3.
6. DHC: 1262M/0/FD/47, Personal Diary of the 3rd Lord Ebrington, 1916–1918, 6 December 1916.
7. Toye, *Lloyd George & Churchill*, pp. 168–171.
8. PA, TB: 1306/24, Miss Edrica de la Pole, 8 December 1916.
9. *WT*, 23 December 1916, p. 2.
10. David Stevenson, *1917: War, Peace & Revolution* (Oxford, 2017) pp. 14–35.
11. Alun Howkins, *The Death of Rural England: A Social History of the Countryside Since 1900* (London, 2003) pp. 27–28.
12. DHC: 1262M/0/FD/47, Personal Diary of the 3rd Lord Ebrington, 18 April 1917.
13. DHC: 1262M/0/FD/47, Personal Diary of the 3rd Lord Ebrington, 18 April 1917.
14. TNA: MAF 80/4998, Devon War Agricultural Committee, 8 January 1917, folio 17.
15. *DEG*, 15 May 1917, p. 5.
16. Parliamentary Debates, House of Commons, Fifth Series, Vol. 90, 8 February 1917, Column 154.
17. Parliamentary Debates, House of Commons, Fifth Series, Vol. 90, 8 February 1917, Column 153.
18. *SDWE*, 26 January 1917, p. 2.
19. *SDWE*, 26 January 1917, p. 2.
20. *SDWE*, 26 January 1917, p. 2.
21. *SDWE*, 26 January 1917, p. 2.
22. *SDWE*, 26 January 1917, p. 2.
23. *CCNDG*, 18 August 1917, p. 2.
24. Peter Dewey, *British Agriculture in the First World War* (London, 1989) pp. 93–95
25. Jonathan Brown, 'Agricultural Policy and the National Farmers' Union, 1908–1939' in J. R. Wordie (ed), *Agriculture and politics in England, 1815–1939* (Basingstoke, 2000) p. 183.
26. University of Reading Special Collections: National Farmers Union Archive, AD1.2, Minutes of the Executive Committee, 18 September 1917, p. 53.
27. University of Reading Special Collections: National Farmers Union Archive, AD1.2, Minutes of the Executive Committee, 18 September 1917, p. 53.
28. Parliamentary Debates, House of Commons, Fifth Series, Vol. 90, 8 February 1917, Column 153.
29. Parliamentary Debates, House of Commons, Fifth Series, Vol. 90, 8 February 1917, Column 153.
30. Parliamentary Debates, House of Commons, Fifth Series, Vol. 90, 8 February 1917, Column 154.
31. *DEG*, 29 December 1917, p. 4.
32. *DEG*, 29 December 1917, p. 4.
33. *DEG*, 29 December 1917, p. 4.
34. *WT*, 29 December 1917, p. 3.
35. *WT*, 7 December 1917, p. 2.
36. *WT*, 7 December 1917, p. 2.
37. DHC: 1262M/0/O/LD/155/45, Typed notes, p. 1.
38. DHC: 1262M/0/O/LD/155/20, Typed report, Feb 1918, p. 1.
39. *The Diaries of Sir Ernest Satow, 1912–1920: Volume 2 (1917–1920)*, 25 February 1918.

40. *The Diaries of Sir Ernest Satow, 1912–1920: Volume 2 (1917–1920)*, 9 July 1918.
41. *WT*, 10 July 1918, p. 3.
42. DHC: 1262M/0/O/LD/155/45, Typed notes, p. 4
43. DHC: 1262M/0/O/LD/155/45, Typed notes, p. 4
44. PA, TB: 1306/26, Miss Edrica de la Pole, of Tremar, Kingston, Diary, 1918, 7 November 1918.
45. *NDJ*, 25 October 1917, p. 8.
46. DHC: 1262M/0/FH/42, Typescript of work of Lord Fortescue during 1st World War, p. 45.
47. C. D. Whetham, 'The Tractor' in C. D. Whetham (ed), *An Exeter Book of Verse* (Exeter, 1919) pp. 37–39.
48. *WMN*, 1 December 1917, p. 3.
49. DHC: 1262M/0/FH/42, Typescript of work of Lord Fortescue during 1st World War, p. 45.
50. TNA: MAF 80/4998, Devon War Agricultural Committee, 8 January 1917, folio 21.
51. DHC: 1122A/PP1, Minutes of West Alvington Parish Council, 1901–1940, 30 May 1917, p. 111; F. Ralph Penwill, *Paignton in Six Reigns: Being the History of Local Government in Paignton* (Paignton, 1953) p. 82.
52. *WMN*, 20 April 1917, p. 3.
53. *WT*, 8 February 1918, p. 10.
54. *WT*, 8 March 1918, p. 10.
55. *The Diaries of Sir Ernest Satow, 1912–1920: Volume 2 (1917–1920)*, 18 March 1918.
56. *The Diaries of Sir Ernest Satow, 1912–1920: Volume 2 (1917–1920)*, 18 March 1918–19 March 1918.
57. *The Diaries of Sir Ernest Satow, 1912–1920: Volume 2 (1917–1920)*, 18 March 1918.
58. *The Diaries of Sir Ernest Satow, 1912–1920: Volume 2 (1917–1920)*, 3 April 1918.
59. *WT*, 9 January 1917, p. 2.
60. *NDH*, 11 January 1917, p. 2.
61. *NDH*, 11 January 1917, p. 2.
62. Hockin, *Two Girls on the Land*, p. 116.
63. Peter Dewey, 'Nutrition and living standards in wartime Britain', in J. Winter and R. Wall (eds), *The Upheaval of War: Family, Work and Welfare in Europe, 1914–1918* (Cambridge, 2005) p. 204.
64. *WT*, 16 February 1917, p. 11.
65. *WMN*, 2 March 1917, p. 6.
66. *WMN*, 2 March 1917, p. 6.
67. Thierry Bonzon and Belinda Davis, 'Feeding the cities' in J. Winter and J-L. Robert (eds), *Capital Cities at War: Paris, London, Berlin, 1914–1919* (Cambridge, 1999), pp. 320, 332.
68. DHC: 4478M/F1, Letter to Dollie Hammond from Mabel Hammond, 27 February 1917, p. 2.
69. UL: Liddle Collection, DF 148, Recollections relating to the Domestic Front: Transcript of Tape 916, p. 3.
70. Claire Morelon, 'A Threat to National Unity? The urban-rural antagonism in Prague during the First World War in a comparative perspective' in W. Dornik, J. Walleczek-Fritz and S. Wedrac (eds) *Frontwechsel: Österreich-Ungarns "Großer Krieg"* (Vienna, 2014) p. 330.
71. DHC: 3248A/13/76, Okehampton Town Council Meeting, 7 April 1917, item 4.

72. Jean-Louis Robert, 'The image of the profiteer' in J. Winter and J-L Robert (eds), *Capital Cities at War: Paris, London, Berlin, 1914–1919* (Cambridge, 1999) pp. 104–132.
73. DHC: 3248A/13/76, Okehampton Town Council Meeting, 7 April 1917, item 4.
74. *WT*, 19 October 1917, p. 8.
75. *WT*, 19 October 1917, p. 8.
76. *WT*, 26 October 1917, p. 2.
77. Richardson, *Through war to peace,* p. 73.
78. *NDJ*, 18 July 1918, p. 8.
79. Edward J. Sampson, 'Thomas Hardy - Justice of the Peace', *Colby Library Quarterly*, Vol. 13, 4 (December 1977) p. 271.
80. *The Sphere*, 28 January 1928, p. 11.
81. *Letters of Emma and Florence Hardy* ed. by Michael Millgate (Oxford, 1996) p. 151.
82. *Derbyshire Times*, 3 November 1917, p. 8.
83. Roy Bullock, *Salford, 1914–1920: The County Borough and the First World War* (Manchester, 2001) p. 35.
84. *Western Gazette*, 18 September 1918, p. 6.
85. *Western Gazette*, 20 September 1918, p. 7.
86. *East London Observer*, 16 March 1918, p. 3.
87. *East London Observer*, 16 March 1918, p. 3.
88. *Pall Mall Gazette*, 9 March 1918, p. 5.
89. *Pall Mall Gazette*, 9 March 1918, p. 5.
90. *Pall Mall Gazette*, 9 March 1918, p. 5.
91. Cecil Torr, *Small talk at Wreyland* (Cambridge, 1918) p. 63.
92. Hockin, *Two Girls on the Land*, p. 76.
93. Hockin, *Two Girls on the Land*, p. 77.
94. PA, TB: 1306/25, Miss Edrica de la Pole, 10 February 1917.
95. TB: 3010/1, Journal of James Thomas Rogers of Plymouth, 13 June 1917.
96. *The Diaries of Albert Best*, 4 August 1917, p. 78.
97. Jay Winter, 'War and Anxiety in 1917' in M. Abbenhuis, N. Atkinson, K. Baird and G. Romano (eds), *The Myriad Legacies of 1917: A Year of War and Revolution* (Basingstoke, 2018) pp. 13–29.
98. Horne, 'Remobilizing for "total war"', p. 198.
99. Horne, 'Remobilizing for "total war"', p. 199
100. David Monger, *Patriotism and Propaganda in First World War Britain: The National War Aims Committee and Civilian Morale* (Liverpool, 2012) p. 183.
101. *CCNDG*, 1 December 1917, p. 2.
102. *WEH*, 21 February 1918, p. 1.
103. *DEG*, 7 January 1918, p. 3.
104. *WT*, 15 December 1917, p. 2.
105. *WT*, 18 December 1917, p. 2.
106. *WMN*, 20 December 1917, p. 4.
107. *NDH*, 27 December 1917, p. 2.
108. *NDJ*, 1 November 1917, p. 8.
109. *DEG*, 29 October 1917, p. 4.
110. *DEG*, 29 October 1917, p. 4.
111. *WT*, 30 October 1917, p. 2.
112. David Stevenson, *With Our Backs to the Wall: Victory and Defeat in 1918* (London, 2012) p. 467.

113. *WT*, 7 January 1918, p. 3.
114. *NDJ*, 1 November 1917, p. 8.
115. *WT*, 1 February 1917, p. 4.
116. DHC: Exeter City Archive, Town Clerk's Files, Box 3557 (Miscellaneous Papers), Town Clerk's Notes, 1919, p. 4.
117. DHC: Exeter City Archive, Town Clerk's Files, Box 3557 (Miscellaneous Papers), Town Clerk's Notes, pp. 4–5.
118. *WT*, 16 February 1917, p. 12.
119. DHC: Exeter City Archive, Town Clerk's Files, Box 3557 (Miscellaneous Papers), Town Clerk's Notes, p. 5
120. *WT*, 9 February 1917, p. 4.
121. *WT*, 25 September 1917, p. 5.
122. *WT*, 6 February 1917, p. 3.
123. *WT*, 16 February 1917, p. 12.
124. *DEG*, 16 March 1917, p. 9.
125. *DEG*, 2 February 1917, p. 9.
126. *Tiverton Gazette & East Devon Herald*, 13 November 1917, p. 3.
127. *WMN*, 12 December 1918, p. 8.
128. DHC: Exeter City Archive, Town Clerk's Files, Box 3557 (Miscellaneous Papers), Town Clerk's Notes, p. 3.
129. DHC: Exeter City Archive, Town Clerk's Files, Box 3557 (Miscellaneous Papers), Town Clerk's Notes, p. 3.
130. A. H. Rousham, *Exwick during the Great War, 1914–1919* (Exeter, 1920) p. 10.
131. *WT*, 15 February 1918, p. 10.
132. Gregory, *The Last Great War*, pp. 224, 226, 228.
133. *WT*, 7 December 1917, p. 8.
134. DHC: Exeter City Archive, Town Clerk's Files, Box 3557 (Miscellaneous Papers), Town Clerk's Notes, p. 5.
135. DHC: Exeter City Archive, Town Clerk's Files, Box 3557 (Miscellaneous Papers), Town Clerk's Notes, p. 5.
136. *DEG*, 15 December 1917, p. 3.
137. Adam J. Hodges, *World War I and Urban Order: The Local Class Politics of National Mobilization* (Basingstoke, 2016) p. 52.
138. *WMN*, 5 July 1918, p. 4.
139. *WMN*, 5 July 1918, p. 4.
140. *WMN*, 10 April 1917 p. 6.
141. *WMN*, 10 April 1917 p. 6.
142. *NDH*, 12 July 1917, p. 6.
143. *NDJ*, 12 July 1917, p. 6.
144. *DEG*, 10 March 1917, p. 3.
145. *WMN*, 8 May 1917, p. 6.
146. *WMN*, 8 May 1917, p. 6.
147. *WMN*, 8 May 1917, p. 6.
148. *WT*, 21 August 1918, p. 3.
149. *WT*, 21 August 1918, p. 3.
150. *WT*, 21 August 1918, p. 3.
151. *WMN*, 20 October 1917, p. 6.
152. *WMN*, 20 October 1917, p. 6.

153. *NDJ*, 5 April 1917, p. 3.
154. *NDJ*, 5 April 1917, p. 3.
155. *WT*, 18 July 1916, p. 2.
156. *WT*, 11 November 1916, p. 2.
157. *The Courier-Journal*, 3 August 1918, p. 4.
158. Diane M. T. North, *California at War: The State and the People during World War I* (Kansas, 2018) p. 228
159. *NDH*, 2 August 1917, p. 5.
160. *DEG*, 3 August 1917, p. 7.
161. *DEG*, 3 August 1917, p. 7.
162. *DEG*, 3 August 1917, p. 7.
163. *WT*, 2 August 1917, p. 3.
164. *DEG*, 10 May 1917, p. 3.
165. *WMN*, 1 February 1918, p. 3.
166. Caroline E. Playne, *Society at War: 1914–1916* (Boston, MA, 1931) p. 273.
167. Healy, *Vienna and the Fall of the Habsburg Empire*, pp. 271–272.
168. *NDH*, 31 January 1918, p. 3.
169. DHC: 1262M/0/FH/42, Typescript of work of Lord Fortescue during 1st World War, p. 47.
170. Keith Grieves, 'Military Tribunal Papers: The Case of Leek Tribunal in the First World War', *Archives* Vol. 16, No. 70 (October 1983) p. 147.
171. DHC: 1262M/0/FH/42, Typescript of work of Lord Fortescue during 1st World War, p. 44.
172. DHC: 1262M/0/O/LD/151/33, Letter to Lord Fortescue from Mr Ian Amory, 16 June 1918.
173. DHC: 1262M/0/O/LD/151/38, Letter to Lord Fortescue from Mr R. F. Woodcock and schedule, 20 June 1918, p. 1.
174. DHC: 1262M/0/O/LD/155/45, Typed notes, p. 3.
175. DHC: 1262M/0/O/LD/155/45, Typed notes, p. 3.
176. DHC: 1262M/0/FH/42, Typescript of work of Lord Fortescue during 1st World War, p. 47.
177. DHC: 1262M/0/FH/42, Typescript of work of Lord Fortescue during 1st World War, p. 47.
178. *DEG*, 10 May 1918, p. 6.
179. DHC: 1262M/0/O/LD/143/37, Draft letter from Chairman of Devon Agricultural Executive Committee discussing threat by disgruntled farmers to put cattle in fields laid up for hay. Table of police numbers and stations on the back of sheet, 30 May 1918.
180. *WMN*, 2 January 1917, p. 8.
181. *WMN*, 2 January 1917, p. 8.
182. *WMN*, 2 January 1917, p. 8; *WT*, 6 February 1917, p. 5.
183. *WT*, 13 February 1917, p. 5.
184. *WT*, 13 February 1917, p. 5.
185. *DEG*, 23 February 1917, p. 3.
186. *WT*, 20 February 1917, p. 5.
187. *WMN*, 20 February 1917, p. 6.
188. *WT*, 20 February 1917, p. 5.
189. *John Bull*, 10 March 1917, p. 7.
190. Parliamentary Debates, House of Commons, Fifth Series, Vol. 85, 27 February 1917, column 1846.

191. Parliamentary Debates, House of Commons, Fifth Series, Vol. 85, 27 February 1917, column 1846.
192. *DEG*, 28 February 1917, p. 3.
193. *DEG*, 28 February 1917, p. 3.
194. DHC: 1262M/0/FH/42, Typescript of work of Lord Fortescue during 1st World War, p. 36.
195. DHC: 1262M/0/FH/42, Typescript of work of Lord Fortescue during 1st World War, p. 37.
196. TNA: HO 45/23540, part 49, ALIENS, Letter to Devon County Council, 26 February 1917, p. 4.
197. TNA: HO 45/23540, part 49, ALIENS, Letter to Chief Constable of Devon, 27 February 1917, p. 3.
198. TNA: HO 45/23540, part 49, ALIENS, Letter to Chief Constable of Devon, 27 February 1917, p. 3.
199. TNA: HO 45/23540, part 49, ALIENS, Letter to Chief Constable of Devon, 27 February 1917, p. 3.
200. *WT*, 6 March 1917, p. 5.
201. *DEG*, 3 April 1917, p. 2.
202. *DEG*, 3 April 1917, p. 2.
203. Parliamentary Debates, House of Commons, Fifth Series, Vol. 85, 18 April 1917, column 1662.
204. *The Times*, 4 May 1917, p. 10.
205. *The Catholic Bulletin*, 2 June 1917, p. 1; *The Catholic Advance*, 16 June 1917, p. 13; *The Catholic Weekly*, 26 July 1917, p. 4.
206. TNA: HO 45/23540, part 49, ALIENS (See separate headings for NATIONALITY and NATURALISATION): monks of German origin at Buckfast Abbey: restriction measures, Home Office file, 17 November 1919, p. 2
207. *WT*, 9 March 1917, p. 2; *WT*, 3 April 1917, p. 5.
208. Graf, *Anscar Vonier*, p. 62n.
209. DHC: 5182A/0/PX/1, Minute book of Dunkeswell Parish Council, 1894–1967, 30 September 1918, p. 68.
210. *WT*, 7 May 1918, p. 2.
211. *WMN*, 12 November 1918, pp. 1, 5.
212. DHC: 3830/F14, Diary, February 1918 - May 1919, 11 November 1918.
213. *The Diaries of Sir Ernest Satow, 1912–1920: Volume 2 (1917–1920)*, 11 November 1918.
214. *WMN*, 12 November 1918, p. 5.
215. *DEG*, 12 November 1918, p. 3.
216. *DEG*, 12 November 1918, p. 5.
217. *DEG*, 12 November 1918, p. 3; *WMN*, 12 November 1918, p. 5.
218. Devon Federation of Women's Institutes, *Devon within Living Memory* (Newbury, 1993) p.184
219. *Letters of Stephen Reynolds*, p. 333.

Conclusion

1. *DEG*, 20 July 1915, p. 5.
2. *DEG*, 20 July 1915, p. 5.
3. *DEG*, 20 July 1915, p. 5.
4. *DEG*, 20 July 1915, p. 5.

5. *Letters of Stephen Reynolds*, p. 291.
6. *CCNDG*, 29 April 1916, p. 6.
7. *The Cornishman and Cornish Telegraph*, 10 January 1918, p. 3.
8. *WMN*, 10 July 1939, p. 4
9. *WT*, 19 October 1915, p. 7.
10. Reynolds, Woolley and Woolley, *Seems So!*, p. 27
11. DHC: 1262M/0/O/LD/153/53, Letter from Apsley Petre Peter, 1915.
12. DHC: 1262M/0/O/LD/155/45, Typed notes, p. 4.
13. *WT*, 23 October 1915, p. 3.
14. DHC: 1262M/0/O/LD/155/45, Typed notes, p. 4.
15. DHC: 1262M/0/O/LD/153/23, Letter from Editor, *Daily Chronicle*, to Lord Fortescue, 31 August 1915.
16. *WMN*, 12 December 1918, p. 8.
17. DHC: 1262M/0/O/LD/155/45, Typed notes, p. 1.
18. *DEG*, 28 May 1915, p. 10.
19. DHC: 1262M/0/FH/42, Typescript of Work of Lord Fortescue during First World War, p. 40.

Bibliography

Devon Heritage Centre (DHC)

DHC: 1037M/LG4/5/6, Printed circular letter from Lord Fortescue about recruitment for the Navy and Army, 1914.

DHC: 1037M/LG4/5/13, Letter to Mr Ford from Mr Steele King of Branscombe Vicarage regarding 'Lord Derby's Scheme' and a meeting for the Honiton division to select canvassers', c1915.

DHC: 1122A/PP1, Minute book of West Alvington Parish Council, 1901–1940.

DHC: 1262M/0/FD/46, Personal Diary of the 3rd Lord Ebrington, 1914–1916.

DHC: 1262M/0/FD/47, Personal Diary of the 3rd Lord Ebrington, 1916–1918.

DHC: 1262M/0/FH/42, Typescript of work of Lord Fortescue during 1st World War, post 1919.

DHC: 1262M/0/O/LD/114/5, Letter to Fortescue from Gretton, 15 July 1915.

DHC: 1262M/0/O/LD/116/24, Letter to Fortescue from Hugh Breton, 20 November 1915.

DHC: 1262M/0/O/LD/116/25, Typed Letter from Fortescue to Derby containing some handwritten notes, 20 November 1915.

DHC: 1262M/0/O/LD/116/27, Letter to Fortescue from Rowell, 22 November 1915.

DHC: 1262M/0/O/LD/116/31, Letter from Fortescue to Carnegie, 23 November 1915.

DHC: 1262M/0/O/LD/116/35, Letter to Fortescue from Powell-Williams, 10 December 1915.

DHC: 1262M/0/O/LD/120/21, Notes of Recruiting meetings and marches, n.d. (c March 1915).

DHC: 1262M/0/O/LD/120/30, The War: An Appeal to Devon Men and Women issued by the Devon Parliamentary Recruiting Committee, 1 February 1915.

DHC: 1262M/0/O/LD/129/81, Letter to Lord Fortescue from WH Bolt, 5 September 1914.

DHC: 1262M/0/O/LD/129/116, Letter from Lord Fortescue to Asquith & Lloyd George, 14 September 1914.

DHC: 1262M/0/O/LD/129/227, Letter from Lord Fortescue to Sir W. Acland, 28 October 1914.

DHC: 1262M/0/O/LD/143/37, Draft letter from Chairman of Devon Agricultural Executive Committee discussing threat by disgruntled farmers to put cattle in fields laid up for hay. Table of police numbers and stations on the back of sheet, 30 May 1918.

DHC: 1262M/0/O/LD/151/33, Letter to Lord Fortescue from Mr Ian Amory, 16 June 1918.

DHC: 1262M/0/O/LD/151/38, Letter to Lord Fortescue from Mr R. F. Woodcock and schedule, 20 June 1918

DHC: 1262M/0/O/LD/153/2, Letter (fragment) about reluctance to enlist, 9 November 1914.

DHC: 1262M/0/O/LD/153/3, Table 1: Analysis of recruiting by War Office up to 10/10/1914, 10 October 1914.

DHC: 1262M/0/O/LD/153/5, Speech (incomplete), December 1914.

DHC: 1262M/0/O/LD/153/13, Newspaper cutting, 1914.

DHC: 1262M/0/O/LD/153/21, Letter from C. Fursdon to Lord Fortescue, January 1915.

DHC: 1262M/0/O/LD/153/23, Letter from Editor, *Daily Chronicle*, to Lord Fortescue, 31 August 1915.
DHC: 1262M/0/O/LD/153/24, Letter from Lord Fortescue to Deputy Lieutenants, 1915.
DHC: 1262M/0/O/LD/153/25, Recruitment of non conformists, Letter from Gulland to Steel Maitland, 13 May 1915.
DHC: 1262M/0/O/LD/153/38, Letter from the Admiralty to Lord Fortescue, 26 March 1915.
DHC: 1262M/0/O/LD/153/39, Letter from the Admiralty to Lord Fortescue, 30 March 1915.
DHC: 1262M/0/O/LD/153/41, Letter from Lord Fortescue to Colonel Western, 31 March 1915.
DHC: 1262M/0/O/LD/153/42, Memorandum re route march, 1915.
DHC: 1262M/0/O/LD/153/44, Itinerary and table for route march, 1915.
DHC: 1262M/0/O/LD/153/53, Letter from Apsley Petre Peter, 1915.
DHC: 1262M/0/O/LD/153/54, Letter from Apsley Petre Peter, 1915.
DHC: 1262M/0/O/LD/153/57, Letter from T.E. Hopewell and W.S. Wade to Devon Parliamentary Recruiting Committee, 1915.
DHC: 1262M/0/O/LD/153/67, Anonymous letter to Lord Fortescue, c. 1915.
DHC: 1262M/0/O/LD/153/74, Acknowledgement of role as Canvasser of Recruits, 2 November 1915.
DHC: 1262M/0/O/LD/153/84, Letter from James Bucknell to Lord Fortescue, 1915.
DHC: 1262M/0/O/LD/153/85, Letter from King's Nympton Rectory to Lord Fortescue, 1915.
DHC: 1262M/0/O/LD/153/128, Recruiting Statistics, 1915.
DHC: 1262M/0/O/LD/155/20, Typed report, Feb 1918.
DHC: 1262M/0/O/LD/155/45, Typed notes, entitled – as to the Clean Cut in Devonshire and additional hand written notes, June 1918.
DHC: 1857Aadd5/PI8, Diary of Arthur Thompson, vicar, 1908–1996.
DHC: 3248A/13/9, Letter book, Okehampton Borough Council, 18 August 1914 – 22 May 1917.
DHC: 3248A/13/76, Okehampton Borough Correspondence File, November 1914 – December 1915.
DHC: 3830/F14, Diary, February 1918- May 1919.
DHC: 3601A/8/PZ/2, Notice of recruiting route march by detachment of 3rd Battalion of the Devonshire Regiment, 20 April 1915.
DHC: 4478M/F1, Letter to Dollie Hammond from Mabel Hammond, 27 February 1917.
DHC: 5182A/0/PX/1, Minute book of Dunkeswell Parish Council, 1894–1967.
DHC: Exeter City Council Minutes, Volume 2, 1914.
DHC: Exeter City Archive, Town Clerk's Files, Box 3557 (Miscellaneous Papers), Town Clerk's Notes, 1919.
DHC: R237A/C11, Minutes of Buckfastleigh Urban District Council, 1914–1915
DHC: R2372A/C12, Minutes of Buckfastleigh Urban District Council, 1915–1916.
DHC: R4582A/2/BZ/2, Local Military Tribunal Minute book, 1915–1916.
DHC: R7/9/0/C/7, Rural District Council Minutes, 22 May 1915 – 10 December 1921.

Dorset History Centre

Dorset History Centre: RON/2/2/Charmouth/4, '*A few Notes on the Eastern Portion of Charmouth Street including The Lower Sea Lane, The Higher Sea Lane and Some of the People who lived there* by R W J Pavey', 1 March 1969.

Dorset History Centre: D1576/2/8/3/1, Letter to Charles Barnes from his fiancée Frances Ched of Prime Farm, Marshwood, 5 October 1916.

Hansard

'Agriculturalists in Navy and Army (Hansard, 21 February 1917)', 2005, < https://hansard.parliament.uk/commons/1917-02-21/debates/a452dfe6-676e-46f2-ac41-83caf8f00329/AgriculturistsInNavyAndArmy>, 15 October 2021.

'Buckfast Abbey (Hansard, 27 February 1917)', 2005, < https://hansard.parliament.uk/commons/1917-02-27/debates/a477e6c4-fee3-40c4-b541-5cc5767b083c/BuckfastAbbey>, 15 October 2021.

'Devonshire Recruits (Hansard, 16 November 1916)', 2005, < https://hansard.parliament.uk/Commons/1916-11-16/debates/76a45954-a333-4911-9a56-d59462a50ee5/DevonshireRecruits>, 12 March 2013.

'Enemy Aliens (Buckfastleigh Abbey) (Hansard, 18 April 1917)', 2005, < https://hansard.parliament.uk/Commons/1917-04-18/debates/db9d30bf-74f6-4816-8003-e7a7f2607112/OralAnswersToQuestions>, 14 April 2011.

'Government of Ireland (Hansard, 5 November 1918)', 2005, < https://hansard.parliament.uk/commons/1918-11-05/debates/78d57912-4f15-4c9e-8b75-27301e430381/GovernmentOfIreland>, 12 March 2013.

'National Food Supply' (Hansard, 22 May 1916)', 2005, <http://hansard.millbanksystems.com>, 14 April 2011.

Imperial War Museum (IWM)

IWM: 506, Lees, Mary (Oral History), Transcript, 1974.

IWM: 3078, Down on the Farm, Transcript, 1977

Museum of English Rural Life, University of Reading Special Collections

University of Reading Special Collections: National Farmers Union Archive, AD1/2, Minutes of the Executive Committee, December 1916–February 1920.

Plymouth Archives, The Box (PA, TB)

PA, TB: 261/4, Robert Alfred John Walling, Notes, 1913–1920.

PA, TB: 1305/10, Newspaper cuttings, 'Local Patriotism and Organisation in 1803 (By Dr. Trelawny-Ross)', 1914.

PA, TB: 1306/22, Miss Edrica de la Pole, of Tremar, Kingston, Diary, 1914.

PA, TB: 1306/23, Miss Edrica de la Pole, of Tremar, Kingston, Diary, 1915.

PA, TB: 1306/24, Miss Edrica de la Pole, of Tremar, Kingston, Diary, 1916.

PA, TB: 1306/25, Miss Edrica de la Pole, of Tremar, Kingston, Diary, 1917.

PA, TB: 1306/26, Miss Edrica de la Pole, of Tremar, Kingston, Diary, 1918.

PA, TB: 2173/1, J S Wellington of Plymouth, 1913–1957.

PA, TB: 3010/1, Journal of James Thomas Rogers of Plymouth, 1884–1927.

Tiverton Museum of Mid Devon Life

Tiverton Museum of Mid Devon Life: 88/1158/1, J. Heathcoat-Amory factory Logbook, 1900–1929.

The National Archives (TNA)

TNA: HO 45/23540, part 49, ALIENS (See separate headings for NATIONALITY and NATURALISATION): monks of German origin at Buckfast Abbey: restriction measures, Aliens at Buckfast Abbey (Devon), 17 November 1919.

TNA: MAF 59/1, Women's County Committees - organisation of labour, September 1916.
TNA: MAF 80/4998, Devon War Agricultural Committee, 1915–1918.

University of Leeds

University of Leeds: Liddle Collection, DF 148, Recollections relating to the Domestic Front: Lincoln, F. A., 15 July 1993.

Contemporary Journals and Newspapers

Bolton Journal & Guardian
Brixham Western Guardian
The Bystander
The Catholic Advance
The Catholic Bulletin
Catholic Times and Catholic Opinion
The Catholic Weekly
The Cornishman and Cornish Telegraph
The Courier-Journal
Crediton Chronicle and North Devon Gazette
Daily Mail
Daily Telegraph
Devon and Exeter Gazette
Derbyshire Times
East London Observer
Evening Sun
Farnworth Chronicle
Globe
Hartland and Westcountry Chronicle
Hudson Observer, New Jersey
Hull Daily Mail
Illustrated Police News
John Bull
Kentish Express
Maoriland Worker
Middlesex Chronicle
New York Times
North Devon Herald
North Devon Journal
North Wales Weekly News
Northwest Worker
Nuneaton Observer
Pall Mall Gazette
Philadelphia Inquirer
Pioneer
Republican-Gazette
South Devon Weekly Express
Taunton Courier and Western Advertiser
Teignmouth Post and Gazette
The Sphere

The Sun
The Tablet
The Times
Tiverton Gazette & East Devon Herald
West Sussex Gazette
Western Evening Herald
Western Gazette
Western Morning News
Western Times

Articles and Books

'"Sociamur amore Devoniæ."' in R. Pearse Chope (ed), *The London Devonian Year Book for the Year 1910* (London, 1910) p. 20.
'A Devonshire Garland' in R. Pearse Chope (ed), *The London Devonian Year Book for the Year 1910* (London, 1910) pp. 91–108.
'A Song of Devon', *Devonia: The Official Organ of the United Devon Association*, Vol. 6, 4 (June 1907) p. 88
'Annual Dinner' in R. Pearse Chope (ed), *The Devonian Year Book for the Year 1913* (London, 1913) pp. 13–23.
'Armada Day' in R. Pearse Chope (ed), *The Devonian Year Book for the Year 1913* (London, 1913) pp. 24–30.
'Devon to Me!' in R. Pearse Chope (ed), *The Devonian Year Book for the Year 1911* (London, 1911) p. 41.
'Devonshire and the War' in R. Pearse Chope (ed), *The Devonian Year Book for the Year 1915* (London, 1915) (London, 1915) pp. 38–54.
'Devonshire Patriotic Fund' in R. Pearse Chope (ed), *The Devonian Year Book for the Year 1915* (London, 1915) pp. 17–20.
'O Devon! Fair Devon', *Devonia: The Official Organ of the United Devon Association*, Vol. 6, 4 (June 1907) p. 90.
'The Family of Fortescue' in R. Pearse Chope (ed), *The London Devonian Year Book for the year 1910* (London, 1910) pp. 36–38.
'The Years Work' in R. Pearse Chope (ed), *The Devonian Year Book for the Year 1912* (London, 1912) pp. 9–12.
Allen, W. Gore, *John Heathcoat and His Heritage* (London, 1958)
Applegate, Celia, *A Nation of Provincials: The German Idea of Heimat* (Berkeley, CA, 1990)
Armstrong, W. A., 'Kentish Rural Society during the First World War' in B. A. Holdness and M. Turner (eds.), *Land, Labour and Agriculture, 1790–1920: Essays for Gordon Mingray* (London, 1991) pp. 109–131.
Atkinson, C. T., *The Devonshire Regiment, 1914–1918* (Exeter, 1926)
Barlow, Robin, 'Military Tribunals in Carmarthenshire, 1916–1917' in N. Mansfield and C. Horner eds, *The Great War: Localities and Regional Identities* (Newcastle Upon Tyne, 2014) pp. 7–25
Batten, Richard ed., *A Lord Lieutenant in Wartime: The Experiences of the Fourth Earl Fortescue during the First World War* (Woodbridge, 2018)
Becker, Jean-Jacques, *The Great War and the French People*, trans. by Arnold Pomerans (Providence, 1985)
Bessel, Richard, 'Mobilization and demobilization in Germany, 1916–1919' in J. Horne (ed), *State, Society and Mobilization in Europe during the First World War* (Cambridge, 1997) pp. 212–222.

Best, Alan ed., *The Diaries of Albert Best: A resident of Teignmouth: Part 3, 1st January 1914 to 9th September 1920* (Torquay, 2009)

Bettez, David J., *Kentucky and the Great War: World War I on the Home Front* (Lexington, KY, 2016)

Bibbings, Lois S., *Telling Tales about Men: Conceptions of Conscientious Objectors to Military Service during the First World War* (Manchester, 2009)

Bird, J. C., *Control of Enemy Alien Civilians in Great Britain, 1914–1918* (New York, 1986)

Blanchard, Jim, *Winnipeg's Great War: A City Comes of Age* (Winnipeg, 2010)

Boggis, R. J. E., *I Remember* (Exeter, 1947)

Bonzon, Thierry and Belinda Davis, 'Feeding the cities' in J. Winter and J-L. Robert (eds), *Capital Cities at War: Paris, London, Berlin, 1914–1919* (Cambridge, 1999) pp. 305–341.

Brace, Catherine, 'Finding England Everywhere: Regional Identity and the Construction of National Identity, 1890–1940', *Cultural Geographies*, Vol. 6, No. 1 (January 1999), pp. 90–109.

Brown, Cynthia Gaskell, *The Battle's Sound: Drake's Drum and the Drake Flags* (Tiverton, 1996)

Brown, Jonathan, 'Agricultural Policy and the National Farmers' Union, 1908–1939', in J. R. Wordie (ed), *Agriculture and Politics in England, 1815–1939* (Basingstoke, 2000) pp. 178–198.

Bullock, Roy, *Salford, 1914–1920: The County Borough and the First World War* (Manchester, 2001)

Butler, Lewis, *Sir Redvers Buller* (London, 1909)

Cabanes, Bruno, *August 1914: France, the Great War, and a Month that Changed the World Forever*, trans. by Stephanie O'Hara (New Haven, 2016)

Capozzola, Christopher, *Uncle Sam Wants You: World War I and the Making of the Modern American Citizen* (New York, 2008)

Cawood, Ian, *The Liberal Unionist Party: A History* (London, 2012)

Census of England and Wales, 1911: Vol. X (London, 1911)

Chickering, Roger, *The Great War and Urban Life in Germany: Freiburg, 1914–1918* (Cambridge, 2007)

Chope, R. Pearse, 'The Folklore of Devon' in R. Pearse Chope (ed), *The London Devonian Year Book for the Year 1910* (London, 1910) pp. 109–133.

Christie, Peter, 'We bain't Going Till We be Fetched – Military Tribunals in North Devon during the First World War', *Reports and Transactions of the Devonshire Association for the Advancement of Science, Literature and Art*, Vol. 146 (June 2014) pp. 145–172.

Churchill, Winston, *The World Crisis, 1911–1918*, Vol 1. (London, 1938)

Clapp, Cecil R. M., 'The Rivers of the Moor' in R. Pearse Chope (ed), *The Devonian Year Book for the Year 1911* (London, 1911) p. 75.

Clarke, Peter, *Hope and Glory: Britain, 1900–2000*, 2nd edn (London, 2004)

Cliff, Norman D., *To Hell and Back with the Guards* (Braunton, 1988)

Clinton-Baddeley, V. C., *Devon*, 2nd edn (London, 1928)

Coleman, Bruce, 'The Nineteenth Century: Nonconformity' in N. Orme (ed), *Unity and Variety: A History of the Church in Devon and Cornwall* (Exeter, 1991) pp. 129–155.

Collins, William, *Herefordshire and the Great War, with the City and County's Roll of Honour* (Hereford, 1919)

Connelly, Mark, *Steady the Buffs! A Regiment, a Region, and the Great War* (Oxford, 2006)

Cooksley, Peter, *The Home Front: Civilian Life in World War One* (Stroud, 2007)

Craig, F. W. S. (ed), *British Parliamentary Election Results, 1885–1918* (London, 1974)

Dakers, Caroline, *Forever England: The Countryside at War, 1914–1918*, (London, 2016)

Dalley, Stuart 'The response in Cornwall to the outbreak of the First World War', *Cornish Studies*, Vol. 11 (2003) pp. 85–109.
Darrow, Margaret H., *French Women and the First World War: War Stories of the Home Front* (Oxford, 2000)
Daw, Walter George, *Exeter Citizen* (Exeter, 1994)
Dawson, Michael, 'Liberalism in Devon and Cornwall, 1910–1931: "The Old-Time Religion"', *The Historical Journal*, Vol. 38, No. 2 (June 1995) pp. 425–437.
Dawson, Michael, 'Party Politics and the Provincial Press in Early Twentieth Century England: The Case of the South West', *Twentieth Century British History*, Vol. 9, No. 2 (1998) pp. 201–218.
DeGroot, Gerard, *Back in Blighty: The British at Home in World War I* (London, 2014)
Delderfield, Eric R., *Exmouth Milestones: A History* (Exmouth, 1946)
Dennehy, John, *In a Time of War: Tipperary, 1914–1918* (Kildare, 2013)
Devon Federation of Women's Institutes, *Devon within Living Memory* (Newbury, 1993)
Dewey, Peter, *British Agriculture in the First World War* (London, 1989)
Duffett, Rachel, 'A War Unimagined: Food and the rank and file soldier of the First World War' in J. Meyer (ed), *British Popular Culture and the First World War* (Leiden, 2008) pp. 47–70.
Fortescue, Hugh, *A Chronicle of Castle Hill: 1454–1919* (London, 1929)
Fortescue, John W., *My Native Devon* (London, 1925)
French, David, 'Spy Fever in Britain, 1900–1915', *The Historical Journal*, Vol. 12, No. 2 (Jun 1978) pp. 355–370.
French, Henry, 'Introduction' in *Food, Farming and Fishing in Devon during the First World War* (Exeter, 2017) pp. vii-xiv.
French, Henry, 'Introduction', *The Devon Historian*, Vol. 86, (2017) pp. 1–11.
Friend, Hilderic, *Bygone Devonshire* (London, 1898)
Gallagher, Niamh, *Ireland and the Great War: A Social and Political History* (London, 2020)
Gatrell, Peter, *Russia's First World War: A Social and Economic History* (Harlow, 2005)
Gibbs, Ken, *The Steam Workshops of the Great Western Railway* (Stroud, 2014)
Graf, Dom Ernest, *Anscar Vonier, Abbot of Buckfast: with some account of the restoration of the Abbey and its Church* (London, 1957)
Grant, Peter, *Philanthropy and Voluntary Action in the First World War: Mobilizing Charity* (New York, 2014)
Gray, Todd, *Elizabethan Devon* (Exeter, 2001)
Gray, Todd, *Uncle Tom Cobley and All: The history of 'Widdicombe Fair'* (Exeter, 2019)
Grayzel, Susan R., *At Home and Under Fire: Air Raids and Culture in Britain from the Great War to the Blitz* (Cambridge, 2012)
Grayzel, Susan R., *Women's Identities at War: Gender, Motherhood, and Politics in Britain and France during the First World War* (Chapel Hill, 1999)
Great Western Railway Company, *Devon: The Shire of the Sea Kings*, (London, 1906)
Gregory, Adrian, 'Military Service Tribunals: Civic Society in Action, 1916–1918' in J. Harris (ed), *Civil Society in British History: Ideas, Identities, Institutions* (Oxford, 2005) pp. 177–190.
Gregory, Adrian, 'Railway stations: gateways and termini' in J. Winter and J-L. Robert (eds), *Capital Cities at War: Paris, London, Berlin, 1914–1919, Volume 2: A Cultural History* (Cambridge, 2007) pp. 23–56.
Gregory, Adrian, *The Last Great War: British Society and the First World War* (Cambridge, 2008)
Gregory, Alfred T., *Recollections of a Country Editor* (London, 1932)
Grieves, Keith ed., *Sussex in the First World War* (Lewes, 2004)

Grieves, Keith, '"Lowther's Lambs": Rural Paternalism and Voluntary Recruitment in the First World War', *Rural History*, Vol. 4, No. 1 (1993) pp. 55–75.

Grieves, Keith, 'Military Tribunal Papers: The Case of Leek Tribunal in the First World War', *Archives* Vol. 16, No. 70 (October 1983) pp. 145–150

Grieves, Keith, 'The quiet of the country and the restless excitement of the towns: rural perspectives on the home front, 1914–1918' in M. Tebbutt (ed), *Rural and Urban Encounters in the Nineteenth and Twentieth Centuries: Regional Perspectives* (Manchester, 2004) pp. 79–97.

Grieves, Keith, 'War Comes to the Fields: Sacrifice, Localism and Ploughing up the English Countryside in 1917' in I. F. W. Beckett (ed), *1917: Beyond the Western Front* (Leiden, 2009) pp. 159–176.

Gullace, Nicoletta F., 'White Feathers and Wounded Men: Female Patriotism and the Memory of the Great War', *Journal of British Studies*, Vol. 36, No. 2 (April 1997) pp. 178–206.

Gullace, Nicoletta F., *'The Blood of Our Sons': Men, Women and the Renegotiation of British Citizenship during the Great War* (New York, 2002)

Haggard, H. Rider, *Rural England: Being an Account of Agricultural and Social Researches carried out in the years 1901 & 1902*, Vol. 1 (London, 1906)

Harris, J. Henry, *My Devonshire Book: 'In the Land of Junket and Cream'* (Plymouth, 1907)

Healy, Maureen, *Vienna and the Fall of the Habsburg Empire: Total War and Everyday Life in World War I* (Cambridge, 2004)

Heathcoat-Amory, Roderick, *Reminiscences* (Chippenham, 1989)

Hilditch, Peter, 'Devon and Naval Strategy since 1815', in M. Duffy, S. Fisher, D. Greenhill, D. J. Starkey and J. Youings (eds), *The New Maritime History of Devon, Volume II: From the Late Eighteenth Century to the Present Day* (London, 1994) pp. 155–166.

Hilditch, Peter, 'The Dockyard in the Local Economy' in M. Duffy, S. Fisher, D. Greenhill, D. J. Starkey and J. Youings (eds), *The New Maritime History of Devon, Volume II: From the Late Eighteenth Century to the Present Day* (London, 1994) pp. 215–225.

Hockin, Olive, *Two Girls on the Land: Wartime on a Dartmoor Farm* (London, 1918)

Hodges, Adam J., *World War I and Urban Order: The Local Class Politics of National Mobilization* (Basingstoke, 2016)

Horn, Pamela, *Rural Life in England in the First World War* (Dublin, 1984)

Horne, John, 'Introduction: mobilizing for "total war", 1914–1918' in J. Horne (ed), *State, Society and Mobilization in Europe during the First World War* (Cambridge, 1997) pp. 1–17.

Horne, John, 'Patriotism and the Enemy: Political Identity as a Weapon' in N. Wouters and L. van Ypersele eds., *Nations, Identities and the First World War: Shifting Loyalties to the Fatherland* (London, 2018) pp. 17–37.

Horne, John, 'Remobilizing for "total war": France and Britain, 1917–1918' in J. Horne (ed), *State, Society and Mobilization in Europe during the First World War* (Cambridge, 1997) pp. 195–211.

Horne, John, 'Social Identity in War: France, 1914–1918' in T. G. Fraser and K. Jeffrey (eds), *Men, Women and War* (Dublin, 1993) pp. 119–135.

Horne, John, 'Soldiers, Civilians and the Warfare of Attrition: Representations of Combat in France, 1914–1918' in F. Coetzee and M. Shevin-Coetzee (eds), *Authority, Identity and the Social History of the Great War* (Providence, 1995) pp. 223–249.

Hoskins, W. G., *Devon* (Chichester, 2003)

Hoskins, W. G., *Devon and its people* (Exeter, 1959)

Hough, Emerson, *The Web: A Revelation of Patriotism* (Chicago, 1919)

Howkins, Alun, *The Death of Rural England: A Social History of the Countryside Since 1900* (London, 2003)

Howkins, Alun, 'The discovery of rural England' in R. Colls & P. Dodd (eds), *Englishness, Politics and Culture, 1880–1920* 2nd ed (London, 2014) pp. 85–11.

Hutchinson, Robert, *The Spanish Armada* (London, 2014)

Hyman, Nigel, 'Inshore Fisheries in Wartime Devon' in *Food, Farming and Fishing in Devon during the First World War* (Exeter, 2017) pp. 75–80.

Jackson, Alexander *Football's Great War: Association Football on the English Home Front, 1914–1918* (Barnsley, 2022)

Jackson, Daniel M., *Popular Opposition to Irish Home Rule in Edwardian Britain* (Liverpool, 2009)

James, Melanie, 'Indifferent or Just Different? The Cornish Response to the Declaration of War in August 1914' in G. Tregidga and T. Fidler eds., *Cornwall and the Great War: Perspectives on Conflict and Peace* (Penryn, 2018) pp. 7–31.

Jones, Elizabeth B., *Gender and Rural Modernity: Farm Women and the Politics of Labor in Germany, 1871–1933* (Farnham, 2009)

Judson, Pieter M., *The Habsburg Empire: A New History* (Cambridge, MA, 2016)

Keith, Jeanette, *Rich Man's War, Poor Man's Fight: Race, Class, and Power in the Rural South during the First World War* (Chapel Hill, 2004)

Kelly's Directory of Devon, 1902 (London, 1902)

Kinnear, Michael, *The British Voter: An Atlas and Survey since 1885*, 2nd edn (London, 1981)

Kirkby, Andrew, *In the cause of Liberty: Exeter Trades Council, 1890–1990* (Exeter, 1990)

Knight, Francis A. and Louie M. (Knight) Dutton, *Devonshire* (Cambridge, 1910)

Kornweibel Jr, Theodore, *"Investigate Everything": Federal Efforts to Compel Black Loyalty during World War I* (Bloomington, IN, 2002)

Lambe, Paul, 'The Politics of Place: Three Devon Constituencies and the 1900 General Election', *Southern History: A Review of the History of Southern England*, Vol. 23 (2001) pp. 148–168.

Lambert, Sophia, 'A Devon By-Election: South Molton, 1891', *Reports and Transactions of the Devonshire Association for the Advancement of Science, Literature and Art*, Vol. 142 (June 2010) pp. 237–260.

Littlewood, David, *Military Service Tribunals and Boards in the Great War* (Abingdon, 2018)

Lord Bishop of Exeter, 'Address of the President', *Reports and Transactions of the Devonshire Association for the Advancement of Science, Literature and Art*, Vol. 39 (July 1907) pp. 44–55.

Lunn, Joe Harris, 'Kande Kamara Speaks: An Oral History of the West African Experience in France, 1914–18' in M. E. Page ed., *Africa and the First World War* (Basingstoke, 1987) pp. 28–53.

Mansfield, Nicholas, 'Farmworkers, the Marches and the impact of the Great War' in M. Tebbutt (ed), *Rural and Urban Encounters in the Nineteenth and Twentieth Centuries: Regional Perspectives* (Manchester, 2004) pp. 99–113.

Mansfield, Nicholas, 'Volunteers and Recruiting' in G. Gliddon (ed), *Norfolk & Suffolk in the Great War* (Norwich, 1988) pp. 18–32.

Mansfield, Nicholas, *English Farmworkers and Local Patriotism, 1900–1930* (Aldershot, 2001)

Marti, Steve, *For Home and Empire: Voluntary Mobilization in Australia, Canada, and New Zealand during the First World War* (Vancouver, 2019)

Martin, Colin and Geoffrey Parker, *Armada: The Spanish Enterprise and England's Deliverance in 1588* (New Haven, 2022)

Martin, Peter, '*Dulce et Decorum*: Irish Nobles and the Great War, 1914–19' in A. Gregory and S. Pašeta (eds), *Ireland and the Great War: 'A war to unite us all'?* (Manchester, 2002) pp. 28–48.

Marwick, Arthur, *The Deluge: British Society and the First World War*, 2nd edn (Basingstoke, 2006)

May, F. B., 'Victorian and Edwardian Ilfracombe' in J. K. Walton and J. Walvin (eds), *Leisure in Britain, 1780–1939* (Manchester, 1983) pp. 187–202.

McCartney, Helen B., *Citizen Soldiers: The Liverpool Territorials in the First World War* (Cambridge, 2005)

McDermott, James, *British Military Service Tribunals, 1916–1918: 'A very much abused body of men'* (Manchester, 2011)

McQuilton, John, *Rural Australia and the Great War: From Tarrawingee to Tangambalanga* (Victoria, 2001)

Meeres, Frank, *Norfolk in the First World War* (Chichester, 2004)

Miller, Stephen M., 'Redvers Buller' in S. J. Corvi & I. F. W. Beckett (eds), *Victoria's Generals* (Barnsley, 2009) pp. 51–73.

Millgate, Michael ed., *Letters of Emma and Florence Hardy* (Oxford, 1996)

Millman, Brock, *Polarity, Patriotism, and Dissent in Great War Canada, 1914–1919* (Toronto, 2016)

Mitchinson, K. W., *England's Last Hope: The Territorial Force, 1908–1914* (Basingstoke, 2008)

Moncrieff, A. R. Hope, *Black's Guide to Devonshire*, 17th edn (London, 1902)

Monger, David, *Patriotism and Propaganda in First World War Britain: The National War Aims Committee and Civilian Morale* (Liverpool, 2012)

Moore, Julie, 'Feeding the city' in J. Mein, A. Wares & S. Mann (eds), *St Albans: Life on the Home Front, 1914–1918* (Hatfield, 2016) pp. 163–199.

Morelon, Claire, 'A Threat to National Unity? The urban-rural antagonism in Prague during the First World War in a comparative perspective' in W. Dornik, J. Walleczek-Fritz and S. Wedrac (eds) *Frontwechsel: Österreich-Ungarns "Großer Krieg"* (Vienna, 2014) pp. 325–342.

Morgan, Nigel J. and Annette Pritchard, *Power and Politics at the Seaside: The Development of Devon's Resorts in the Twentieth Century* (Exeter, 1999)

Munson, James ed., *Echoes of the Great War: The Diary of the Reverend Andrew Clark, 1914–1919* (Oxford, 1985)

Neville, Julia, 'Devon County Council and First World War Food Production Policy: A Challenge to Landlordism and Squirearchy?', *The Devon Historian* Vol. 86, 2017, pp. 63–75.

Neville, Julia, 'Mary Sylvia Calmady-Hamlyn (1881–1962)' in J. Neville, M. Auchterlonie, P. Auchterlonie & A. Roberts (eds), *Devon Women in Public and Professional Life, 1900–1950: Votes, Voices and Vocations* (Exeter, 2021) pp. 203–225.

Newton, Robert, *Victorian Exeter, 1837–1914* (Leicester, 1968)

North, Diane M. T., *California at War: The State and the People during World War I* (Kansas, 2018)

Offer, Avner, *The First World War: An Agrarian Interpretation* (Oxford, 1989)

Orme, Nicholas, 'The Twentieth Century, Part 2: Devon and General' in N. Orme (ed), *Unity and Variety: A History of the Church in Devon and Cornwall* (Exeter, 1991) pp. 175–197.

Osborne, John Morton, 'Defining Their Own Patriotism: British Volunteer Training Corps in the First World War', *Journal of Contemporary History*, Vol. 23, No. 1 (January 1988) pp. 59–75.

Osborne, John Morton, *The Voluntary Recruiting Movement in Britain, 1914–1916* (New York, 1982)

Otte, T. G., *July Crisis: The World's Descent into War, Summer 1914* (Cambridge, 2014)

Packer, Ian, *Lloyd George, Liberalism and the Land: The Land Issue and Party Politics in England, 1906–1914* (Woodbridge, 2001)

Panayi, Panikos, *Prisoners of Britain: German civilian and combatant internees during the First World War* (Manchester, 2012)

Panayi, Panikos, *The Enemy in our Midst: Germans in Britain during the First World War* (Oxford, 1991)

Parker, David, *Edwardian Devon: Before the Lights Went Out* (Stroud, 2016)
Parker, David, *Hertfordshire Children in War and Peace, 1914–1939* (Hatfield, 2007)
Parker, David, *The People of Devon in the First World War* (Stroud, 2013)
Pelling, Henry, *Social Geography of British Elections: 1885–1910* (London, 1967)
Pennell, Catriona, *A Kingdom United: Popular Responses to the Outbreak of the First World War in Britain and Ireland* (Oxford, 2012)
Pennell, Catriona, 'Believing the Unbelievable: The Myth of the Russians with "Snow on their Boots" in the United Kingdom, 1914', *Cultural and Social History*, Vol. 11, 1 (2014) pp. 69–88.
Penwill, F. Ralph, *Paignton in Six Reigns: Being the History of Local Government in Paignton* (Paignton, 1953)
Perren, Richard, 'Farmers and consumers under strain: allied meat supplies in the First World War', *The Agricultural History Review*, Vol. 53, No. 2 (2005) pp. 212–228.
Phipps, W. J. H., *Devon Worthies: Biographies arranged as a Reader for Secondary Schools and the Upper Standards of Elementary Schools* (Exeter, 1903)
Playne, Caroline E., *Society at War: 1914–1916* (Boston, MA, 1931)
Pope, William, *Glimpses of the Past* (Tiverton, 1927)
Porter, Mark, 'Devon's Fishing Industry, 1880–1990' in M. Duffy, S. Fisher, B. Greenhill, D. J. Starkey and J. Youings (eds), *The New Maritime History of Devon, Volume II: From the Late Eighteenth Century to the Present Day* (London, 1994) pp. 243–249.
Powell, Geoffrey, *Buller: A Scapegoat? A Life of General Sir Redvers Buller VC* (London, 1994)
Proctor, Tammy M., *Civilians in a World at War, 1914–1918* (New York, 2010)
Purseigle, Pierre, '"Wither the Local?" Nationalization, Modernization, and the Mobilization of Urban Communities in England and France, c. 1900–18' in W. Whyte and O. Zimmer (eds), *Nationalism and the reshaping of Urban Communities in Europe, 1848–1914* (Basingstoke, 2011) pp. 182–203.
Purseigle, Pierre, 'An Urban Geography of the World at War, 1911–1923' in N. Wouters and L. van Ypersele eds., *Nations, Identities and the First World War: Shifting Loyalties to the Fatherland* (London, 2018) pp. 235–253.
Purseigle, Pierre, 'Between Participation and Victimization: World War I Urban Mobilization in Comparative Perspective' in F. Lenger ed., *Kollektive Gewalt in der Stadt: Europa 1890–1939* (Munich, 2013) pp. 51–68.
Purseigle, Pierre, 'Beyond and Below the Nations: Towards a Comparative History of Local Communities at War' in J. Macleod and P. Purseigle (eds), *Uncovered Fields: Perspectives in First World War Studies* (Leiden, 2004) pp. 95–123.
Purseigle, Pierre, 'Introduction: Warfare and Belligerence: Approaches to the First World War' in P. Purseigle ed., *Warfare and Belligerence: Perspectives in First World War Studies* (Leiden, 2005) pp. 1–37.
Readman, Paul, 'The Place of the Past in English Culture, c. 1890–1914', *Past and Present*, No. 186 (February 2005) pp. 147–199.
Readman, Paul, 'Commemorating the past in Edwardian Hampshire: King Alfred, Pageantry and Empire' in M. Taylor (eds) *Southampton: Gateway to the British Empire* (London, 2007) pp. 95–113.
Rendel, Margherita, 'The Campaign in Devon for Women's Suffrage, 1866–1908', *Report and Transactions of the Devonshire Association for the Advancement of Science, Literature and Art*, Vol. 140, (2008) pp. 111–151.
Retter, Frank, *An Exeter Boyhood* (Exeter, 1984)
Reynolds, Stephen, Bob Woolley and Tom Woolley, *Seems So! A Working Class View of Politics*, Shilling edn (London, 1913)

Richards, R. G., *Through the Mists of Memory* (Bideford, 1995)

Richardson, Ralph, *Through war to peace, 1914–1918: Being a short account of the part played by Tavistock and Neighbourhood in the Great War* (Tavistock, 1919)

Riddell, Linda K., *Shetland and the Great War* (Lerwick, 2015)

Robb, George, *British Culture and the First World War*, 2nd edn (Basingstoke, 2015)

Robert, Jean-Louis, 'The image of the profiteer' in J. Winter and J-L Robert (eds), *Capital Cities at War: Paris, London, Berlin, 1914–1919* (Cambridge, 1999) pp. 104–132.

Rousham, A.H., *Exwick during the Great War, 1914–1919* (Exeter, 1920)

Rusiecki, Paul, *The Impact of Catastrophe: The people of Essex and the First World War (1914–1918)* (Chelmsford, 2008)

Ruxton, Ian ed., *The Diaries of Sir Ernest Satow, 1912–1920: Volume 1 (1912–1916)* (Morrisville, NC, 2018)

Ruxton, Ian ed., *The Diaries of Sir Ernest Satow, 1912–1920: Volume 2 (1917–1920)* (Morrisville, NC, 2018)

Sampson, Edward J., 'Thomas Hardy - Justice of the Peace', *Colby Library Quarterly*, Vol. 13, 4 (December 1977) pp. 263–274.

Scheer, Tamara, 'Denunciation and the Decline of the Habsburg Home Front (1914–1918)', *European Review of History: Revue Europeene d'Histoire*, Vol. 24, 2 (2017) pp. 214–228.

Scoble, Christopher, *Fisherman's Friend: A Life of Stephen Reynolds* (Tiverton, 2000)

Silbey, David, *The British Working Class and Enthusiasm for War, 1914–1916*, (London, 2005)

Simkins, Peter, *Kitchener's Army: The raising of the new armies, 1914–1916* (Barnsley, 2007)

Slocombe, Ivor, 'Recruitment into the Armed Forces during the First World War. The work of the Military Tribunals in Wiltshire, 1915–1918', *The Local Historian* Vol. 30, 2 (May 2000) pp. 105–123.

Snell, F. J., *North Devon* (London, 1906)

Snell, K. D. M., *Parish and Belonging: Community, Identity and Welfare in England and Wales, 1700–1950* (Cambridge, 2009)

Sokolov, Emil, 'The Many Faces of the Great War: Local Patriotism and Recruitment in Ilfracombe, 1914–1918', *Devon during the First World War* (Exeter, 2018) pp. 119–121.

Sprinks, Philip and Julie eds., *First World War Military Service Tribunals: Warwick District Appeal Tribunal, 1916–1918* (Stratford Upon Avon, 2017)

Stanes, Robin, *A History of Devon* (Chichester, 1986)

Stanyer, Jeffrey, *A History of Devon County Council, 1889–1989* (Exeter, 1989)

Stéphan, Dom John, *A History of Buckfast Abbey* (Bristol, 1970)

Stevenson, David, *1914–1918: The History of the First World War* (London, 2005)

Stevenson, David, *With Our Backs to the Wall: Victory and Defeat in 1918* (London, 2012)

Stevenson, David, *1917: War, Peace and Revolution* (Oxford, 2017)

Stone, William, *Hero of the Fleet: Two World Wars, One extraordinary life – The Memoirs of Centenarian* (Edinburgh, 2009)

Strachan, Hew, *The First World War, Volume I: To Arms* (Oxford, 2001)

Susser, Bernard, *The Jews of South-West England: The Rise and Decline of their Medieval and Modern Communities* (Exeter, 1993)

Taylor, Matthew, 'The 1914–15 Season', *The Greater Game: A History of Football in World War I* (Oxford, 2014) pp. 7–11.

The Times History of the War, Vol. VI (London, 1916)

Thoday, Francis and Tom Anstey, *The 4th Devons: A History of the 4th (Territorial) Battalion, The Devonshire Regiment, 1852–1952* (Exeter, 1952)

Thorpe, Andrew and Richard Toye eds., *Parliament and Politics in the Age of Asquith and Lloyd George: The Diaries of Cecil Harmsworth, MP, 1909–1922* (Cambridge, 2016)

Tindall, John, *The Sidmouth Volunteers: No. 9 Platoon, C Company, 1st Vol. Battalion, Devon Regiment, 1914–1918* (Sidmouth, 1920)
Torr, Cecil, *Small talk at Wreyland* (Cambridge, 1918)
Toye, Richard, *Lloyd George & Churchill: Rivals for Greatness* (London, 2007)
Travis, John F., *The Rise of Devon Seaside Resorts, 1750–1900* (Exeter, 1993)
Tucker ,G. M., *Ottery St. Mary Congregational Church: A Short History* (Exeter, 1962)
Turner, John, *British Politics and the Great War* (New Haven, 1992)
Ugolini, Laura, *Civvies: Middle-class men on the English Home Front, 1914–18* (Manchester, 2013)
United Devon Association, *The Book of Fair Devon* (Exeter, 1899–1900)
Vella, Stephen, 'Newspapers' in M. Dobson and B. Ziemann eds., *Reading Primary Sources: The Interpretation of Texts from Nineteenth- and Twentieth-Century History*, 2nd edn (Abingdon, 2020) pp. 217–237.
Verdon, Nicola, *Working the Land: A History of the Farmworker in England from 1850 to the Present Day* (London, 2017)
Walsh, Fionnuala, *Irish Women and the Great War* (Cambridge, 2020)
Walton, John K., *The British Seaside: Holidays and resorts in the twentieth century* (Manchester, 2000)
Ward, Paul, '"Women of Britain Say Go": Women's Patriotism in the First World War', *Twentieth Century British History*, Vol. 13, No. 1 (2001) pp. 23–45.
Wasley, Gerard, *Devon in the Great War,1914–1918*, (Tiverton, 2000)
Wathen, Bruce, *Sir Francis Drake: The Construction of a Hero* (Woodbridge, 2009)
Watson, James, 'Patriotism, Profits and Problems: New Zealand Farming during the Great War' in J. Crawford and I. McGibbon eds., *New Zealand's Great War: New Zealand, the Allies & the First World War* (Auckland, 2007) pp. 534–549.
Westcote, Thomas, *A View of Devonshire in MDCXXX, with a Pedigree of Most of its Gentry* (Exeter, 1845)
Whetham, C. D., 'The Tractor' in C. D. Whetham (ed), *An Exeter Book of Verse* (Exeter, 1919) pp. 37–39.
Whitaker's Peerage, Baronetage, Knightage and Companionage for the year 1909 (London, 1909)
White, Bonnie J., 'Feeding the war effort: agricultural experiences in First World War Devon, 1914–1917', *Agricultural History Review*, Vol. 58, Part 1 (2010) pp. 95–112.
White, Bonnie J., 'Food protests and the (in)equality of sacrifice in First World War Devon', *The Local Historian*, Vol. 45, No. 1 (January 2015) pp. 19–32.
White, Bonnie J., 'Sowing the seeds of patriotism? The Women's Land Army in Devon, 1916–1918', *The Local Historian*, Vol. 41, No. 1 (February 2011) pp. 13–27.
White, Bonnie J., 'Volunteerism and Early Recruitment Efforts in Devonshire, August 1914 - December 1915', *The Historical Journal*, Vol. 52, No. 3 (2009) pp. 641–666.
White, Bonnie, *The Women's Land Army in First World War Britain* (Basingstoke, 2014)
Who's who in Devonshire (Hereford, 1934)
Williams, John, *The Home Fronts: Britain, France and Germany, 1914–1918* (London, 1972)
Wilmot, Sarah, 'The South-West: Wiltshire, Dorset, Somerset, Devon, and Cornwall' in E. J. T. Collins (ed), *The Agrarian History of England and Wales, Volume VII, 1850–1914, Part I* (Cambridge, 2000) pp. 411–426.
Wilson, Trevor, *The Myriad Faces of War: Britain and the Great War, 1914–1918* (Cambridge, 1986)
Winegard, Timothy C., *Indigenous Peoples of the British Dominions and the First World War* (Cambridge, 2012)

Winter, J. M., 'Propaganda and the Mobilization of Consent' in H. Strachan (ed), *The Oxford Illustrated History of the First World War* 2nd ed (Oxford, 2014) pp. 216–225.
Winter, Jay, 'Paris, London, Berlin, 1914–1919: capital cities at war', in J. Winter and J-L. Robert (eds), *Capital Cities at War: Paris, London, Berlin, 1914–1919* (Cambridge, 1999) pp. 3–24.
Winter, Jay, 'War and Anxiety in 1917' in M. Abbenhuis, N. Atkinson, K. Baird and G. Romano (eds), *The Myriad Legacies of 1917: A Year of War and Revolution* (Basingstoke, 2018) pp. 13–33.
Winter, Jay, and Antoine Prost, *The Great War in History: Debates and Controversies, 1914 to the Present*, 2nd edn (Cambridge, 2020)
Woollacott, Angela, '"Khaki Fever" and Its Control: Gender, Class, Age and Sexual Morality on the British Homefront in the First World War', *Journal of Contemporary History*, Vol. 29, No. 2 (April 1994) pp. 325–347.
Wright, Harold, ed., *Letters of Stephen Reynolds* (Richmond, 1923)
Yallop, H. J., *The History of the Honiton Lace Industry* (Exeter, 1999)
Ziemann, Benjamin, *War Experiences in Rural Germany, 1914–1923*, trans. by Alex Skinner (Oxford, 2007)

Websites

Argue, Val, 'Heath Farm Dairy and the St Albans Military Tribunal', 24 April 2019, St Albans & Hertfordshire Architectural & Archaeological Society, <https://www.stalbanshistory.org/social-history/war-and-its-impact-on-st-albans/the-home-front-in-st-albans-during-the-first-world-war/heath-farm-dairy-and-the-st-albans-military-tribunal>, [Accessed 5 May 2022]
Clark, Augustine, 'Vonier, Martin [*name in religion* Anscar] (1875–1938)', Oxford University Press, 2004; online edition, September 2004, <https://doi.org/10.1093/ref:odnb/65088>, [Accessed 9 November 2020]
Ermarcora, Matteo, 'Civilian Morale', *International Encyclopaedia of the First World War*, August 2015, <https://encyclopedia.1914-1918-online.net/article/civilian_morale> [Accessed 19 February 2020]
Ermarcora, Matteo, 'Rural Society' *International Encyclopaedia of the First World War*, January 2015, <https://encyclopedia.1914-1918-online.net/article/rural_society> [Accessed 19 February 2020]
Fortescue, Denzil, 'Denzil Fortescue b. 1893 Recollections 1974', <http://fortescue.org/site/wp-content/uploads/2012/11/DGFRecollections2.pdf>, [Accessed 20 February 2020]
Mombauer, Annika, 'July Crisis 1914', *International Encyclopaedia of the First World War*, September 2018, < https://encyclopedia.1914-1918-online.net/article/july_crisis_1914>, [Accessed 14 March 2021].
Scoble, Christopher, 'Reynolds, Stephen Sydney (1881–1919)', *Oxford Dictionary of National Biography*, Oxford University Press, 2004; online edition, Jan 2008, <https://doi.org/10.1093/ref:odnb/47513>, [Accessed 20 February 2020].
Simkins, Peter, 'Pals Battalions', *International Encyclopaedia of the First World War*, March 2018, <https://encyclopedia.1914-1918-online.net/article/pals_battalions>, [Accessed 20 February 2020].
Strachan, Hew, 'Pre-war Military Planning (Great Britain)', *International Encyclopaedia of the First World War*, February 2018, <https://encyclopedia.1914-1918-online.net/article/pre-war_military_planning_great_britain>, [Accessed 14 March 2021].

Unpublished Theses

Dawson, Anthony Michael, 'Politics in Devon and Cornwall, 1900–1931', London School of Economics, PhD thesis, 1991.

Gale, Andy, 'The Westcountry and the First World War: Recruits & Identities', Lancaster University, PhD Thesis, 2010.

Gill, Rebecca, 'Calculating Compassion in War: The "New Humanitarian" Ethos in Britain, 1870–1918', University of Manchester, PhD Thesis, 2005.

Osborne, John Dalton, 'Stephen Reynolds, a biographical and critical study', University of London, PhD Thesis, 1978.

Townsley, Helen, 'The First World War and Voluntary Recruitment: A forum for regional identity? An analysis of the nature, expression and significance of regional identity in Hull, 1900 -1916', University of Sussex, PhD Thesis, 2008.

White, Bonnie, 'War and the Home Front: Devon in the First World War', McMaster University, PhD Thesis, 2008.

Young, Derek Rutherford, 'Voluntary Recruitment in Scotland, 1914–1916', University of Glasgow, PhD Thesis, 2001.

Index